Pirkei

A Jewish Mystical View on The Book of James

Bruno Summa

2019

Pirkei Yaakov
A Jewish Mystical View on The Book of James

Other books from the same author:

The Knowledge of Good and Evil
Summa, B. 2018 All rights reserved

The Torah to the Galatians
Summa, B. 2019 All rights reserved

Torat Yehoshua: According to the Hebrew book of Matthew.
Summa, B. 2019 All rights reserved

First publication july 2019

CONTENTS

PIRKEI YAAKOV

Happy are those whose way is blameless, who follow the Torah of Adonai.

Psalm 119:1

The book of Yaakov, also known as the Book of James, is a clear example of how strong is the connections that the New Testament has with Judaism, with the Jewish people and with the rabbinic mentality of the first century. Among all the books of the bible, there is no other book presented in the way the book of James was composed.

It is not a prophetic or historical book, much less follows the form of Paul's letters. The methodology used by the author of this book is a methodology normally found in the Jewish Mishnah, in Jewish Talmudic teachings, thus making the book of James unique. I believe if this letter had not been adopted by Christianity, it would have been, at least in part, included in a famous Mishnah book called Pirkei Avot.

The Pirkei Avot is one of the oldest and most important books in Judaism. The term PIRKEI () can be translated as "chapters", but when used in reference to the teachings of the Torah, this term can be understood as ETHICS, the term AVOT () refers to fathers.

The Pirkei Avot, or Ethics of the Fathers, is a wonderful compendium of rabbinic teachings on ethics, love of neighbor, love of God, character, study of the Torah, good behavior, society and so on. Such teachings are presented in the form of brief personal comments from each rabbi who have had their teachings eternalized there, these commentaries are presented alongside with biblical quotations and with examples from the secular life.

Throughout the Gospel of Matthew, the letters of Paul and other books in the new testament, it is possible to find several quotations or mentions from the teachings found in the Pirkei Avot. The book of James goes beyond simple mentions, it is written in the same way as the Pirkei Avot is and this caught my attention when I decided to study the teachings of James.

Throughout the book of James, one can find clear teachings on Ethics, moral values and love of neighbor, using only and exclusively the Torah as the base, I found no other way to name this book other than PIRKEI YAAKOV, to make an allusion to this famous part of Mishnah.

Shimon, his son, used to say: all my days I grew up among the sages, and I have found nothing better for a person than silence. Study is not the most important thing, but actions; whoever indulges in too many words brings about sin.

Pirkei Avot 1:17

YAAKOV

James was the chief rabbi of the first messianic community within Jerusalem, his was a Torah teacher par excellence, leader of the *halakhah* (the person who defines the way the law should be observed), judge and teacher of his entire community, as reported by the book of Acts.

James was probable the half-brother of Yeshua, the son of Miriam and a man from the tribe of Levi, by which James received his priestly authority. If we see who James really was, a Jew, a rabbi, a Torah commentator and especially as one who received the Torah teaching from Yeshua, the intention for which his book was composed will become much clearer.

THE BOOK OF JAMES

It is commonly agreed that this book was written in Greek. However, by the grace of HaKadosh, Baruch Hu, I had access to the original books of Matthew, Luke and John, which were also believed to have been written in Greek, in fact, they were composed in the Hebrew language. For this reason I am particularly doubtful whether the original language of the book of James really was Greek.

But whatever the fact is, this book clearly deals with Jewish matters, matters only understood through the Jewish mentality and a Kabbalistic mystique known by few in the Western world, thus making the book of James with a supposedly "obvious" look.

Another point to consider is the way it was composed, it was certainly not written by James, but rather by some student or scribe who frequented his community and listened to his Torah lessons. By the way the lessons are presented, I believe they are teachings about some *parashot* taught on Shabbatot, after the reading of the Torah in the messianic synagogue that James led.

By the topics dealt by James, it is possible to see some characteristics of how this book was composed, since the book does not follow a progressive form of teaching, but rather a compendium of several studies that were passed on depending on the weekly parashah, we see the repetition of some themes in different parts of the book, such as the "tongue" for example, which James addresses in the second chapter and then again in the third one.

By the teachings of James it is possible to know the time that this book was written or taught. By the subjects discussed by James, it is very probable that its composition occurred during the 49 days of Omer, time between the celebration of Pessach and Shavuot. Within these 7 weeks we find the parashat K'doshim (Lev 20: 1 - Lev. 20:27) which has several teachings that are clearly addressed and discussed by James.

PIRKEI YAAKOV

This book presents a mystical Jewish approach on the book of James, the methods of interpretation that will be presented in the following chapters are not the way Christian theology interprets this books. For this purpose some cabbalistic tools and Jewish literatures will be used.

One of them is a book called Zohar HaKadosh, also called by some as the central book of the Kabbalah. The Zohar is a book written in Aramaic and never been translated in completeness into any other language, not even Hebrew. Through allegorical languages, this book approaches the Torah to teach what is hidden from the eyes and what is incomprehensible to the common mind. The Zohar was composed a few years before the Christian book Revelation and the most interesting thing is that they both have the same essence, the same form of teaching and the same mysticism, thus showing that the last book of the Christian bible will never be understood by minds that do not know the essence of the Zohar and the Jewish mystique.

Other tools that will be widely used and which were part of James's mentality are the Gematria and the analysis of terms in the Hebrew language, by seeking words roots and the connection they have with other terms, as well as the grammatical form that these terms are presented in the verses of the Torah quoted by James.

This might be a difficult book for those who are not accustomed to Jewish mystical language or to those who do not know some basic concepts of the mindset that forms the Torah "between the lines" analysis. Like every book that deals with a mystical analysis of the bible, this book should be read more than once, perhaps two or even three, so that a better understanding can be obtained.

Such teachings have been kept hidden for many years, but through the compassion of The One who IS, I will publish some of them, for the time to gather the lost tribes of Israel has come and they are the targets of this book.

Hillel and Shammai received [the oral tradition] from them. Hillel

used to say: be of the disciples of Aaron, loving peace and pursuing peace, loving mankind and drawing them close to the Torah.
He [also] used to say: one who makes his name great causes his name to be destroyed; one who does not add [to his knowledge] causes [it] to cease; one who does not study [the Torah] deserves death; on who makes [unworthy] use of the crown [of learning] shall pass away.
He [also] used to say: If I am not for myself, who is for me? But if I am for my own self [only], what am I? And if not now, when?
Shammai used to say: make your [study of the] Torah a fixed practice; speak little, but do much; and receive all men with a pleasant countenance.

Pirkei Avot 1:12-15

GEMATRIA

Gematria is a numerological system by which the Hebrew letters has a correspondence to certain numerical values. This system is part of the Kabbalah and is a very powerful tool for interpreting biblical texts.

Each letter of the Hebrew alphabet is represented by a number. One can then calculate the numerical value of the Hebrew words of the Bible for a more mystical understanding and a do hidden exegesis of what the Word of God is teaching. In the world of biblical exegesis, many commentators and sages of the Torah base their arguments on the numerical equivalence of words. When a word has a numerical value equal to that of another word, there is a mystical connection between the two words. This shows that both words can be used in both contexts, that is, one can take the place of the other and vice versa, revealing a unique understanding of biblical passages.

Many sages believe that Adonai created the universe through the letters of the Hebrew alphabet and therefore, there is a hidden power behind each one of them. The numbers that each represents, serves to hide the secrets of the Creator from the sight of the common man.

On the other hand, we must be very careful with the Gematria, because it is a tool for exclusively Biblical use. To make use of it in a secular way as means of divination or prediction of the future is something vehemently forbidden by the Torah and by God several times. This method has so much power that many pseudo-cabalists now a day, offer this teaching to lay people for secular use. Many occult sects also know this tool and use it to strengthen their spells and witchcraft. Therefore, I emphasize, Gematria should not be used outside a biblical context and should not be learned by secular ways, such as books of unknown authors and people without direct connection with the divine Torah, it can only be taught and learned by rabbis who use it as a tool for biblical interpretation.

Gematria is a tool that I use a lot throughout this book. There are numerous ways to use it, in this book I will use some forms that will follow the tables presented below:

GEMATRIA'S CHART

80	פ/ף	9	ט	1	א
90	צ/ץ	10	י	2	ב
100	ק	20	כ/ך	3	ג
200	ר	30	ל	4	ד
300	ש	40	מ/ם	5	ה
400	ת	50	נ/ן	6	ו
		60	ס	7	ז
		70	ע	8	ח

Absolute Value

17	פ/ף	9	ט	1	א
18	צ/ץ	10	י	2	ב
19	ק	11	כ/ך	3	ג
20	ר	12	ל	4	ד
21	ש	13	מ/ם	5	ה
22	ת	14	נ/ן	6	ו
		15	ס	7	ז
		16	ע	8	ח

Mispar Siduri

8	פ/ף	9	ט	1	א
9	צ/ץ	1	י	2	ב
1	ק	2	כ/ך	3	ג
2	ר	3	ל	4	ד
3	ש	4	מ/ם	5	ה
4	ת	5	נ/ן	6	ו
		6	ס	7	ז
		7	ע	8	ח

Mispar Katan

6	פ/ף	50	ט	400	א
5	צ/ץ	40	י	300	ב
4	ק	30	כ/ך	200	ג
3	ר	20	ל	100	ד
2	ש	10	מ/ם	90	ה
1	ת	9	נ/ן	80	ו
		8	ס	70	ז
		7	ע	60	ח

EtBash

100	ק	10	י	1	א
200	ר	20	כ	2	ב
300	ש	30	ל	3	ג
400	ת	40	מ	4	ד
500	ך	50	נ	5	ה
600	ם	60	ס	6	ו
700	ן	70	ע	7	ז
800	ף	80	פ	8	ח
900	ץ	90	צ	9	ט

Absolute Value with Sofit

TERMINOLOGY

For those who do not know the Hebrew language or are

not accustomed to rabbinical terminology, it is vitally important that the following terms be studied and understood before reading this book, because they are terms used a lot by the Book of Matthew and I so also use them in my studies, because it is a terminology that loses its essence when translated:

Written Torah - The first five books of the Bible - Genesis, Exodus, Leviticus, Numbers, Deuteronomy - also known as the Law of Moses. The Torah is the holiest of all books, for it is the only one that reveals the true "self" of the Creator of all things.

Mishnah - It is another for the Oral Torah, it addresses all the commandments from the Torah.

Gemarah - These are rabbinical commentaries on the Mishnah. It is also known as the Talmud, and it has numerous laws created by the sages and imposed upon the Jewish people over the years.

Midrash - Sages' commentaries on the biblical passages, the Midrashim were composed in Aramaic and possess an unique wisdom.

Talmud - Mishnah + Gemarah + some external teachings.

Tzadik (tzadikim, plural) - This is a vital term for understanding the words of Yeshua. A TZADIK is a person who observes and obeys the Laws of the Torah. This term was translated as "righteous" and thereby lost all its essence. Being a Tzadik, is the life's goal of any Jew who loves God.

Kasher - Although this term is associated with nourishment, the word kasher is an adjective given to anything that is in conformity with the Torah. A person who follows the Laws of God faithfully is a kasher person.

Tshuvah - Another very important term vastly used in the New Testament. Tshuvah in a direct translation means "answer", but it is a rabbinic term to refer to repentance. Unlike Christian repentance that is nothing but something inner oneself, Tshuvah is more like an action, whoever does Tshuvah is the person who decides to adopt a lifestyle according to the Torah.

Mitzvah (Mitzvot, plural) - Torah's Commandment.

Mashiach - Messiah, the anointed one.

Tanakh – Torah + Prophets + Writing = The Hebrew bible or old testament.

Parashah – The Torah is divided into 54 portions, know as parashah, they are read every Saturday during the 54 Saturdays of the year.

EVERY PASSAGE FROM THE TANAKH, FROM THE MIDRASHIM, FROM THE TALMUD, FROM THE ZOHAR AND FROM THE RABBINICAL COMMENTARIES USED IN THIS BOOK, HAVE BEEN TRANSLATED FROM ITS ORIGINAL LANGUAGE (HEBREW OR ARAMAIC) BY THE AUTHOR HIMSELF, LEST IT IS MENTIONED WHERE THE TRANSLATIONS IS FROM. FOR THIS REASON, THOSE PASSAGES MIGHT PRESENT SOME DIFFERENCES WHEN COMPARED TO THE MOST USUAL WESTERN LANGUAGE'S TRANSLATIONS.

THIS BOOK MAY BE OFFENSIVE TO SOME PEOPLE DUE TO THEIR CREED AND FAITH. IF THE READER DEEPLY BELIEVES IN THE CHURCH, IN THEIR DOGMAS, THEOLOGIES AND TEACHINGS, AND SEE THEM AS AN ABSOLUTE AND IRREVOCABLE TRUTH. PELASE DO NOT READ THIS BOOK.

I - THE SCATTERED TRIBES

James, a servant of God and of the Lord Yeshua HaMashiach to the twelve tribes which are scattered abroad, greeting.

James 1:1

It's common sense among some scholars that the book of James was written around the year 66 CE, a little before the destruction of the second Temple, which occurred around 70 CE. Along with this fact, the Roman Empire exiled all the inhabitants of Judah and dispersed them all over the world, such exile endures until the present day.

When I first read the first verse of James, this historical fact came to my mind, for how could he refer to the twelve scattered tribes if at the time of the compositions of his book, two of these twelve tribes, Judah and Benjamin, were still in the land of Israel, that is, two were not yet scattered?

That made me wonder and I began to do a research what the Christian understanding about this was. I found only a few comments that specifically address this verse, but those I found were somehow very similar and not so insightful. In general, they claim that these dispersed "tribes" are the churches that were found in the diaspora.

This Christian theology's interpretation is flawed in many ways. First, because there were no churches. Second, because James was not an apostle to the Gentile world, but Paul, so he is talking to his own kin. Third, there was, and there is still, a reality among the Jews about these tribes and such reality is not an effective part of the Christian faith. Therefore, such church teaching, in this case, is not coherent.

However, after much researching, I was able to find in an age-old version of a German-language bible, dated back to 1763 and compiled by Johann Rudolf, with a very interesting translation of this verse:

Jakobus, ein Knecht Gottes und des Herrn Yesu Christvs, den ***zehn*** *Geschlechtern, die da sind hin und her: Freude zuvor!*
Jakobus 1:1

James, a servant of God and of the Lord Yesu Christvs, to the ***TEN*** *tribes which are there and here, happiness.*
James 1:1

I really do not know what happened to those many years of translations, retranslations and revisions after revisions, what I do know is that we have lost what was actually written and certainly this is not the only case that it happens. I believe we can now begin more coherently about this scattered tribes quotation, a quotation that is presented alongside with the name Yeshua HaMashiach, and this is where James's intentions lies.

If there is one thing I have never correctly heard from any Christian, at least among those I know, is a compelling definition of what it is to be MASHIACH. Whenever I ask a Christian in this regard, I do normally get half-truths or non-coherent theological definitions as answer.

Some people simply define him as the anointed one, some others define Mashiach merely as the savior, others say that Mashiach is to be the son of God and there are some that claim that Mashiach is some sort of god. From what I understand, to fully know the conception of what it is to be Mashiach, to the Christian faith in general, is not relevant, for that faith defines him as a member of the trinity, making the title of Mashiach something secondary and of no real importance.

The non-understanding of this has generated enormous

dogmas within the Christian faith since its inception, the lack of understanding of what Yeshua declared to be, ended up making him many things, a god, a hippie, an elevated soul, a savior, a revolutionary, among many other titles. In order for us to remove these teachings made by the ancient church from our minds, let us enter into what he himself declared to be, The Mashiach.

MASHIACH

Many people who follow jesus consider him the Messiah and believe that the mission of messiah on this earth is to bring salvation to mankind. But this does not define exactly what it is to be Mashiach. As many know, the Hebrew word Mashiach means "anointed", for he was chosen and anointed by God to lead and perform His work on this reality. The word "Mashiach" appears 39 times throughout the Tanakh and the belief in his coming is part of the 13 foundations of the Jewish faith, as described by Maimonides.

Mashiach will have authority given by the Creator to rule over all the nations of the world, to impose the Laws of God, to teach the true will of the One who IS, to end iniquity and to bring the true meaning to man's creation. Therefore, a faith in a messiah who abolished the Torah is to believe in a mythical being created by human minds, which is nothing different from the paganism of ancient times. That is why it is vitally important to understand what it is to be Mashiach.

Two Mashiachim

Our sages teach that there will be two Mashiachim, one named Mashiach Ben Yosef and the second Mashiach Ben David. In fact, Ben Yosef and Ben David do not represent two people, but two distinct missions that will be performed by a single Mashiach in different eras.

The oral Torah has several tractates that deal with this belief, let's look at some:

Rabbi Ben Dosa says: the earth will lament over the

Mashiach that will be murdered... ...This explains that the cause is the murder of Mashiach Ben Yosef.

Talmud of Babylon, Tractate Sukkah 52a

The beginning of the war of Gog and Magog will begin with the coming of Mashiach Ben David.

Kol HaTor 1:14

Mashiach Ben Yosef will be the first representation of Mashiach and as reported by the sages, he will be murdered. According to an archaeological finding called "*stone manuscript of the dead sea*", dated around 110 years before Yeshua, Mashiach Ben Yosef, after his death, would resuscitate, so, what happened to Yeshua wasn't something unexpected by the jews.

On the other side, Mashiach Ben David will have the mission to rule over the whole world, to defeat God's enemies, to restore the Temple and to reign for a thousand years.

Mashiach's Mission

For a better understanding about Mashiach, knowing his mission is essential.

The earthly mission of Mashiach Ben Yosef has three fronts: revelation of the mysteries of the Torah, returning the exiled and removing the unclean spirit from the earth.

Kol HaTor 1:11

The mission of Mashiach Ben Yosef, the one Yeshua declared to be, has three folds, to teach the Torah, to return the exiled from the TEN lost tribes of Israel and to remove the unclean spirit.

For this reason, let's take a short look at the history of Israel.

THE KINGDOM OF ISRAEL

After the death of King Solomon around 922 BCE, Israel was divided into two realms, the northern kingdom known as the Kingdom of Israel, which included the tribes of Reuven, Shimeon, Dan, Naphtali, Gad, Asher, Issachar, Zevulum, Ephraim and Menasseh, and the southern kingdom, called Yehudah, formed by the tribes of Judah and Benjamin and the Levites circulating between both kingdoms.

In 722 BCE, after many warnings from God, the Assyrian empire invaded Israel and the northern kingdom was conquered due to the evil ways of its kings. The great majority of the people of Israel were exiled, the Assyrian empire displaced almost all the inhabitants of the northern kingdom and dispersed them throughout the world, most of them were taken to Media and Aram-Naharaim and, in their places, several people from other regions of the empire were brought to inhabit these lands.

The lost tribes of the Kingdom of Israel is one of the greatest mysteries in the Jewish history. Multiple theories have been created on top of that, there are those who say that some are in India, others in Nigeria and there are some others who dare to say that the descendants of these tribes are the native Indians of North America.

Numerous archaeological evidences prove that these people of the Kingdom of Israel were eventually absorbed and assimilated into gentile societies and therefore, the people of these tribes were lost and disappeared completely. Today nobody knows what really happened to them, the only thing left was a prophecy about the descendants of these tribes:

And you, mortal, take a rod and write on it: Of Yehudah and the Israelites associated with him. And take another rod and write therein: Of Yoseph, the rod of Ephraim, and all the house of Israel associated with him.
Draw them near to one another, that they may become a single rod, and put them together by your hands... ...Thus said Adonai, I will take the rod of Joseph, which is in the hands of Ephraim, and the tribes of Israel associated with him and I will place it on the rod of Yehudah and so I will make them a single rod, joined by my hands.

Ezekiel 37:16-19

Many rabbis teach that in the era of Mashiach, the descendants of these tribes will be reunited in the land of Israel by the hands of the Creator Himself. They also teach that there is something hidden within each descendant of the People of Israel that sets them apart from all other nations, even if they are now absorbed. All the descendants of Yaakov have a divine spark within their souls, a spark that is passed down from generation to generation. The descendants of these tribes, now scattered throughout the four corners of the world, even if they do not know that they are part of God's chosen people, there is something inside of them that will start shining as a beacon when time comes. Many people around the world, among various nationalities and creeds, will be called back through this divine spark that they have inside of them, in their souls. They will be people who, even without knowing or understanding the reasons, will quickly accept God's call that will be made through Mashiach and the Torah.

Rabbi Eliezer says: Just as the day is followed by darkness and then the light returns, then also, even if it becomes darkness for the lost tribes, God will definitely take them out of the darkness.
Talmud of Babylon, Tractate Sanhedrin 110b

The redemptive work of Mashiach is precisely to gather his people, he will bring back all the descendants of Yaakov to serve him. Rabbi Eliezer's statement is a slight allusion about the Talmud's quotation concerning Isaiah's prophecy seen above; this rabbinic understanding is the probable reason why Matthew makes a point of quoting Isaiah in his book. The fact that Yeshua had a connection with regions outside the land of Judah and with some of the people who lived there, makes a lot of sense about his claim to be Mashiach, for this attitude demonstrates, even for a moment and only in a symbolic way, his connection with the Northern Kingdom. When Yeshua went out to these regions outside the land of Judah, he did not go after the Samaritans or Gentiles, nor did he do "evangelism". He went after the remnants of these tribes, showing by this one of his purposes. In one of these trips he states:

And Yeshua said to him, I was not sent ***except*** *to the lost sheep of the* ***house of Israel.***

Matthew 15:24

Many Christians believe that these "lost sheep of Israel" are the Jews who are under the curse of the law, some also teach that "the sheep" represent the Gentiles who will eventually accept jesus and there are some that say that these sheep is the representation of how the Jewish people are a lost people.

But leaving all these vicious Christian interpretations aside, this claim actually shows that he came after the lost sheep of the House of Israel, these sheep which he refers to are not the Jews, nor the inhabitants of Judah, but the lost descendants of the Kingdom of Israel, the God's chosen people who are scattered, lost and who belonged to the other tribes of Israel.

THE LOST TRIBES AND MASHIACH BEN YOSEF

והיה כל אשר יקרא בשם יהוה ימלט כי בהר **ציון** ובירושלים תהיה
פליטה כאשר אמר יהוה ו**בשרידים** אשר יהוה קרא

But everyone who calls on the name of Adonai shall escape, for there shall be remnants in ***Tzion*** *and in Jerusalem, as Adonai hath promised. Anyone who calls on Adonai will be the one who will be among the* ***survivors.***

Joel 3:5

This is a very strong passage, a prophecy given by the prophet Joel regarding the end of times. Through the mouth of the prophet, God affirms that ONLY those who invoke His Name will be among the survivors.

To understand the secrets of these words, we must ask two questions. For whom this prophecy was made and who, exactly, would this "survivors" be.

Before we continue, let's first look at whom this prophecy was made. According to the text, the prophecy is meant to the people of Zion, as much as for the people of Jerusalem. Jerusalem, the capital of the Kingdom of Judah, represents the Jews, so this is clear. But now, why does the prophet also say Zion? Who are the ones in Zion, since the Jews are represented by Jerusalem?

Let's make some comparisons before we draw any conclusions:

צִיון (TZION)

50ן + 6ו + 10י + 90צ

= **156**

The numerical value of the word Zion led me to make an association with another name, which revealed to me who this prophecy is referring to:

יוסף (YOSEF)

80ף + 60ס + 6ו + 10י

= **156**

Behold, both YOSEF and ZION have a connection, both kinda represent each other. Yosef is also a term that represents Mashiach, in this case, Mashiach Ben Yosef, just as David represents Mashiach Ben David.

This answers one of the questions, just as Jerusalem represents the Jews, the people of the Southern Kingdom. Zion represents the Northern Kingdom, the lost tribes of Israel, the people scattered throughout the Gentile world, for this people is Ben Yosef's target. Hence the prophecy quotes two different places, Zion and Jerusalem, for it speaks to the two peoples who form the twelve tribes of Israel, the true Chosen People.

Now we can continue, let's look at the Gematria of Mashiach Ben Yosef, since he represents Zion:

משיח בן יוסף (MASHIACH BEN YOSEF)
80ף + 60ס + 6ו + 10י + 50ן + 2ב + 8ח + 10י + 300ש + 40מ
= **566**

The term for "survivors" that appears in this passage, in Hebrew, is BASRIDIM (בשרידים), which may also mean "the rest". This is a curious term, for it reveals something that goes far beyond what we can read:

בשרידים (BASRIDIM - SURVIVORS)
40ם + 10י + 4ד + 10י + 200ר + 300ש + 2ב
= **566**

Look at that! Now the passage is clear, let's try a re-reading it:

But everyone who calls on the name of Adonai shall escape, for there will be remnants of the lost tribes of Israel and of the Jews, as Adonai has promised. Anyone who calls on Adonai will be the one who will be brought back by Mashiach Ben Yosef.

And to confirm the association of Zion with the Northern Kingdom, a Psalm:

*Joy of all the earth is Mount **Zion**, in the lands of the **north**, the city of **the** great King.*

Psalm 48:3

The mission of Mashiach Ben David will be to reign over the world based in the city of Jerusalem, in Judah. Mashiach Ben Yosef's mission will be to reign over Zion in Israel, as Ben David and Ben Yosef are the same person with different facets, he is **the** "great King", in the singular form, of that verse. Mashiach will rule over the House of Israel and over the House of Judah.

THIS THEME IS FURTHER DETAILED IN THE BOOK **TORAT YEHOSHUA:

***ACCORDING TO THE HEBREW BOOK OF MATTHEW**, FROM THIS SAME AUTHOR.*

JAMES' INTENTION

According to my understanding, James continues the work of the one who he calls lord and master, Mashiach Ben Yosef, who came to teach Torah and to gather the exiled tribes. At the very beginning of his book he is quite categorical at this point, he is not speaking to the Jews, he is not speaking to the church, he is not speaking to ordinary Gentiles, but rather he is sending a message to those who are part of those tribes and are scattered all over the world.

Through the wisdom of God, James is able to approach both kind of Gentiles. At the same time he sends some direct and superficial teachings to those who, for some reason, became Christians but are not descendants of these dispersed tribes, he is also able to reach those who are the descendants of those tribes with a more hidden and mystical message. Even if they are now mixed with the gentile world, they still have a divine spark within them and it is precisely due to that, they will be able to understand the hidden messages found on James teachings, as we shall see in this book.

II - TEMPTATION

But every man is tempted, when he is drawn away of his own lust, and enticed.
Then when lust has conceived, it brings forth sin: and sin, when it is finished, brings forth death.

James 1:14-15

Sometimes, to make a precise approach is somewhat complex, specially when it concerns a concept that is already very well defined within one's faith. In spite that the Christian definition of "temptation" came from interpretations of New Testament's teachings, when we compare it with the Jewish idea of "temptation", we see that it is actually not the same thing. By the fact that james was no Christian but a rabbi, we should look at the Jewish definition of what "temptation" is.

Temptation is a complex concept, in order for us to fully comprehend the way James used the idea of "temptation", we should bring up some concepts from the Jewish faith.

YETZER HARAH

וייצר יהוה אלהים את האדם עפר מן האדמה ויפח
באפיו נשמת חיים ויהי האדם לנפש חיה

*And Adonai Elohim **formed** the man of the dust of the ground, and breathed into his nostrils the breath of life; and the man became a living soul.*

Genesis 2:7

Our sages teach that the human being was created with two intrinsic Instincts within. The Good Instinct (Yetzer

HaTov) and the evil instinct (Yetzer Harah). Everything in human's life, while in this earthly realm, is defined and controlled by one of these two sides of the same coin.

The proof that we have in this respect is found in the Torah itself, in the above mentioned verse, is where it is revealed to us the creation of these two instincts within every human being. The term "formed" in Hebrew is Yitzar (יצר) and it is used when God formed the animals and the humanity on the sixth day, in Adam's creation the same term is also used, but its spelling comes in a different and unique way throughout the Hebrew literature; In this case, we have the same word Yitzar (ייצר) but with an abnormal repetition of the initial letter YUD (י); This hidden fact reveals that the Torah is showing us that Adam already knew very well what was good and what was bad.

This is because there is another word that is written in the exactly same way as the word Yitzar (יצר), which is the word Yetzer (יצר). This already changes everything, for Yetzer is the name of man's intrinsic inclination. Within each human being the Yetzer HaTov (good inclination) and the Yetzer HaRah (evil inclination) are found, and everything one does and decides regarding his own life is influenced by one of these two inclinations.

Rav Nahman bar Rav Hisda interprets: what does it mean from what is written: "Then Adonai Elohim formed (vayyiter) the man" with two Yud? These two Yud allude to the fact that the Holy One, blessed be He, has created two inclinations, one good and one evil.

Talmud of Babylon, Tractate Brakhot 61a

A deeper understanding of Yetzer Harah is not only necessary in order to comprehend this book, but also he who knows how to deal with it, improves his relationship with God.

Let the one who is wise hear and increase his understanding.

Proverbs 1:5

Many believe that satan is the great men's enemy, which is partly true as we will see later in this book, nevertheless man's arch enemy, the "king of the hill" is the Yetzer Harah itself. His power over man's life, man's decisions and its consequences are far greater than those that satan himself performs. The Yetzer Harah is mixed within the soul of the human being like a soluble coffee that mixes with water, being associated with one's physical and spiritual sensibility.

The Yetzer Harah dominates the secrets of the soul, it becomes the counselor in all that one decides to do. Like a snake waiting to take the bite, the Yetzer Harah lurks in wait for an opportunity to promote the wrong path of the flesh. The Yetzer Harah is a false friend who never sleeps, never rests and never loses a war, only a few battles. As much as one overcomes it, the definitive victory will only come with death, for as long as man lives, man will fight the Yetzer Harah.

By such definitions many will say that this is satan, the devil, but I can assure that not in this case, for the things I described above is not from a spiritual being that exists in the outside, for those things are the definition of you, me, our neighbor, our families and every soul that is incarnated on this earth. The enemy defined above is ourselves, our flesh, our natural tendency of living a life in a natural way, far from the ways of God.

The church has the bad habit on blaming satan for all the bad things that happen and this idea diverges the one who believes in it from the path of truth. For innumerable and countless times I have seen many devout Christians blaming satan for misfortunes that occur in their lives, while in other areas they are people of extreme evil character. The satan within the Christian faith is the perfect scapegoat, because everything that goes wrong is always his fault and not ours. The alcoholic only drinks because satan puts the drink in his glass, drug users do only consume it because satan brings the drug to him, the one who practices sexual immorality only practices it because satan takes the temptation right on his doorstep. Impressive how the Western world has lost the habit of looking at one's own belly and understand that the true culprit of the misfortunes that happen in each one's life is the person who goes through it.

Please do understand, I do not apologize to the figure of satan, nor am I saying that he does not exist and has no influence, what I say here is that we must know this side of ourselves so we can learn how to deal with our Yetzer Harah and stop thinking that everything bad that happens comes from an outside source. That we may live a life in conformity with the will of the Creator and so we may overcome the temptations as James says and in order to do so, one must first remove some Christian theological lies from our minds.

According to the great sage, Rabbi Bachya Ibn Pekuda, in his book *Chovot Levavot,* the temptations of the Yetzer Harah can be basically defined in ten types of temptations, as detailed below:

1 - THERE IS NO LIFE AFTER DEATH

The first temptation the Yetzer Harah brings is doubt about the afterlife, it tries to convince man that the soul cannot exist without a physical body to sustain it. This kind of temptation removes all the fear from the human being, causing him to give himself completely to the pleasures of the flesh, such as sexual immorality, corruption, attachment to material goods, and abusive use of harmful substances in search of momentary pleasures.

2 - THERE IS NO GOD

The Yetzer Harah's second temptation will be to cast doubt on the existence of God. It will try to convince man that the world was an accident and the human being is a result of evolution. The result of this is similar to that mentioned in the previous temptation, but people who doubt the existence of God are extremely aggressive when any idea about God is brought up. These are empty, critical, and depressive people.

3- FALSE GODS

When it cannot overcome man with the two temptations above, it will then try to divert that belief to some lie, bringing confusion about things concerning God. Perhaps among all temptations, this is the most common, for it is easy for the Yetzer Harah of many people to convince them about the existence of various gods, as in the case of the pagan idea of the Christian trinity or of a naturalistic god. When a person understands the true oneness of the Creator, the Yetzer Harah is overcome.

4- TO SERVE GOD IS USELESS

At that moment the Yetzer Harah tells us, "God without you stills God, He does not need you, for He is the almighty and He does not lack anything, He does not need you to get what He wants". Everyone should understand that if that were the case, God would never have created man. The human being is the high point among all of Adonai's creation, He created us, because He seeks a relationship with us, He seeks us so that we can serve Him and relate with Him. Whatever a person lives in the name of the Creator, that person will never be without purpose. If God chooses someone to do something specific, even if He can do it by Himself, it shows the importance one has for Him. One should never doubt the importance one has to Adonai, never, for you are work of His own hand.

5- TORAH'S VALIDITY

This is also very common, the abolition of the Torah and the authenticity of the bible is something much debated in the Western world. Those who believe in those things are people dominated by the Yetzer Harah and their only purpose is to spread this evil belief. This can lead the person to a faith connected with a spiritualism without any basis, where everything is allowed.

6- THERE ARE NO REWARDS AND PUNISHMENTS IN THIS WORLD

If nothing befell then, the Yetzer Harah will try to convince that the events that take place in this world are not according to the justice operated by the Creator. Everything that occurs in our surroundings, both in private life and on earth, is the direct fault of man's bad behavior, as if it were in our own hands the "tools" that caused all disgrace and not as a result of a divine punishment for our behavioral failures. The opposite also applies to blessings.

7- THERE ARE NO REWARDS AND PUNISHMENTS IN THE WORLD TO COME

Even though the person has a belief in "heaven" and "hell", the Yetzer Harah will try to bring confusion in this respect so that it can turn that person's faith into pagan religions.

8- CONCERN WITH THE SECULAR WORLD

Yeshua deals with this theme in several teachings throughout the Gospels. When the Yetzer Harah brings the temptation concerning the secular life, it is when things get complicated. When a concern for money comes, a life devoted to work, to the profession, to the obtaining of goods, fame, power, etc., is when the person, however faithful he may be, deviates and departs from the divine will. The Yetzer Harah tempts man to serve his own self and as Yeshua said, no one can serve two masters, no one can serve God and serve his own self, this is why one must be like the birds, despite having nothing, birds do not lack anything.

9- TO OVERCOME THE MAN

This is when the Yetzer Harah brings up thoughts that make us think and believe that we are nothing and not capable. This is the door to depression.

10- TO DIMINISH THE SAGES

This temptation falls on those who seek God and study His word. The Yetzer Harah will bring doubts by trying to seek logically explanations concerning the confused actions of God. Then comes the true Faith that the New Testament talks so much about, in this case simply believing in a fact is not enough, rather believing in what is held as true and remaining faithful to it, even if all human's logic proves the contrary.

Through TEN temptations, Abraham, our father,
was tested and overcame them all.

Pirkei Avot 5:3

...And they tried me ten times and they did not hear my voice.

Numbers 14:22b

These temptations do not come from God, they do not come from satan, but they come from ourselves, they are things that are part of every human being, regardless of nationality, race, creed and religion. The role of satan is to accuse us when we lose to the Yetzer Harah in any of these areas, he stands before God and will say, "See, he has fallen into the corruption of the flesh!" and so God will give him authority to destroy.

To overcome temptation is not to overcome satan, it is to defeat ourselves.

There is a very interesting midrash about the Yetzer Harah, which may seem contradictory, but mystically this midrash brings an incredible revelation of why every human being needs the Word of the Creator:

Rabbi Nahman said in the name of Rabbi Shmuel: "saw that it was good" refers to Yetzer HaTov (good instinct) and "saw that it was very good" refers to Yezter HaRah (evil instinct). How can Yezter Harah be better than the Yetzer Hatov? That is because without the Yetzer Harah the man would not be able to build a house, to take a wife, to have a child.

Bereshit Rabbah 9:7

How can God have called the Yetzer Harah something "very good"? According to our sages, if it were not for the Yetzer Harah, who is nothing more than our carnal and worldly instincts, we would not have the interest of building a house, for we would only worry about the afterlife, we would not marry and we would not make a child, for we would have no sexual interests. The Yetzer Harah also brings a balance so that we can enjoy God's best on this Earth.

That is, the Yezter Harah only becomes very good when we know how to overcome it and this is only possible through the Torah and the Word of God, faith alone does not solve, for faith, without works, is dead.

THE TEMPTATION

But each is tempted, when attracted and enticed
by his own Yetzer Harah.
Then, having conceived Yezter Harah, gives birth to
sin; and sin, being consummated, begets death.

James 1:14-15

Now James' words become clearer, James does not speak of satan, rather he speaks of ourselves, as well as every new testament's passage that deals with temptation.

James makes this way of thinking very clear in these two verses, the temptation is our own attraction for our own lust, for the Yetzer Harah leads us to sin and then we will be accused by satan and the wage will be death.

A well-known case about temptations and being tempted happened to Yeshua himself as reported in the book of Matthew. From this occurrence in his life many interesting lessons can be observed, lessons that theology and Christian mysticism cannot explain.

YESHUA'S TEMPTATION

Then Yeshua was led by the Holy Spirit into the wilderness

to be tempted by satan.
And Yeshua fasted for forty days and forty
nights, and after that he was hungry.
The tempter came and said to him, "If you are the son
of Elohim, tell this stone to become bread.
And Yeshua answered and said unto him: It is written,
that not by bread alone, and so forth.
Then satan took him to the holy city and stood on
the highest place, above all the Temple.
And he said unto him, If thou be Elohim, jump
down, for it is written, He commanded his angels
to keep thee in all his ways, and so forth.
And Yeshua answered him the second time: you
shall not tempt Adonai your Elohim.
And satan carried him to a very high mountain and showed
him all the kingdoms of the earth and their glories.
And he said unto him, All this I will give thee,
if thou surrender unto me.
Then Yeshua answered him: Go satan, that is satanas, for it is
written that only to Hashem will I pray and only Him will I serve.
Then satan left him and behold, angels approached
him and served him (ministered him).

Matthew 4:1-11

Here we have the golden Christian account of temptation, which is nothing Christian. It is interesting to see how Yeshua fights temptation by using the Torah, not only by quoting it, but by teaching that by living the lifestyle determined by the Law of God is what removes the opponent from the life of man. He did not have to expel him, nor pray, nor do exorcism or whatever, all he did was to show that by his lifestyle, Torah-like lifestyle, was enough to keep the adversary and his tricks away; no matter how much he tries, this overcomes any temptation

In the three encounters that Yeshua had with satan, he uses four simple yet profound passages from the Torah to get rid of the opponent's presence and to show how his temptations are overcome.

... But man shall not live by bread (לחם) alone, but
of all things found in the mouth of Adonai.
Deuteronomy 8:3b

Do not tempt (תנסו) Adonai, your Elohim, as you did in Massah.
Deuteronomy 6:16

I will pray (אתפלל) to Hashem ...
Deuteronomy 9:26a

Only Adonai you shall fear (תירא), your Elohim
and only to Him you shall worship (תעבד) and only
in His name you shall swear (תשבע).
Deuteronomy 6:13

Yeshua was well didactic here, he overcame temptation and kept satan away in a very simple way only by using the Torah. There is something very interesting in this account, the fact that the temptation in this case came from satan, from something external and not internal, shows that Yeshua had his Yetzer Harah totally under control and he could not be tempted by it. In rabbinical terms, to affirm that Yeshua was tempted by satan and not by the Yetzer Harah shows that he had a life without sin, a real tzadik.

If the account only had said that he was tempted, without citing the source, then yes, he was being tempted by the Yetzer Harah and if this was the case, it was because he did not follow Torah in a sinless way, which would make him unfit to be Mashiach.

There are a few things we must keep in mind here, satan provokes only the tzadikim, those who love, believe and live Torah, because concerning the man who doesn't believe in the Word of God, satan doesn't even have to worry about him, for this man will be tempted and beaten by himself. Let's see each of the cases:

LENASOT

In Hebrew, the verbs "to try" or "to tempt" is LENASOT (לנסות) and it is a verb used several times throughout the Torah, both referring to the temptation by which man is proved, as well as to tempt God Himself.

בני ישראל ועל **נסתם** את יהוה
.... and the children of Israel ***tempted*** *Adonai ...*
Exodus 17:7

The *shoresh* (root) of this verb is (נ-ס-ה), from these three letters other words can be formed and in this case, there are two very interesting words that fit perfectly here, the verb LENUS (לנוס) – *to escape* – and the word NES (נס) which means "miracle" or "sign".

The first lesson we can draw from this is how we should face the temptations, because it is a word that has the same *shoresh* as LENUS (to run away, escape), this teaches us that we must run away from temptation and NEVER face it, that is, if a person is faced with something that tempts the flesh, something in which his eyes covet, that he may not think that if he faces it, he will overcome it, for he will not. Everything the flesh covets becomes stronger than anyone who is exposed to it. If anything should tempt you, run!

The second lesson is to understand temptation as a NES (נס), a sign, about something that is happening or will happen in our lives. If we look at both sides of temptation, the one we have learned how to overcome and the other one who still surpass us, we shall see two ways that God communicates with us. If a certain temptation uses to overcome a man, this is a NES (נס) – *a sign* - of what that person should improve in order to walk in perfection before the Creator. On the other hand, when one is able to overcome and master his own Yetzer Harah, it is also a NES (נס) - *a sign* - as James himself teaches us:

Blessed is the man that endures temptation: for when

he is tried, he shall receive the crown of life, which the Lord has promised to them that love him.

James 1:12

This sign is just the sign of the blessing, but in this case, according to the words of James, this blessing is something very specific, the "crown of life" which for James is the NES of being able to overcome the Yetzer Harah. Another term we can form with the *shoresh* of LENASOT (לנסות) is NES NESTAR (נס נסתר), which is a rabbinical term for "a hidden miracle".

Years of life will be added in the life of the one who is tzadikim in the form of a hidden miracle (nes nestar) and this proves the intervention of the hand of God that works miracles in what is hidden within each one of us.

Rabbeinu Bahya, Shemot 30:12

We have a deep secret here and everything is making sense now. Let's see, the word Temptation has the same root as NES NESTAR (נס נסתר), which means a "hidden miracle". We have seen above that temptation is not something external to man, but rather from within, man himself tempts himself, something internal, hidden from the eyes. Then comes James and says that whoever overcomes his temptation will receive from God the miracle of the "crown of life", but he does not say what would that be. Then finally, Rabbi Bahya reveals to us something very interesting, he says that a "hidden miracle" is precisely the addition of years of life on this earth.

That is, "the crown of life" of James is precisely the NES NESTAR, it is the extension of life on earth and this is through a miracle that is hidden, as temptation is something hidden that happens inside, in the occult of man's soul. When this hidden, internal temptation is overcome, God also, in the hidden, brings forth the miracle, He brings the life.

Then when the Yetzer Harah has been conceived, it brings forth sin: and sin, when it is finished, brings forth death.

James 1:15

For this reason James also says that sin brings forth death, because sin begins with temptation and the prize of overcoming temptation is to gain NES NESTAR. By the other hand, the opposite is also true, so to fall into temptation is to lose NES NESTAR, it is to diminish one's days on this earth, i.e. death.

He clearly uses this concept of temptation to make a point about how can one's behavior be improved. The Jewish concept of temptation is very different from the Christian one, which normally casts out Satan and blames him, instead of looking at oneself. For James, temptation is something intrinsic to the human being, man tries to sabotage himself all the time and this is what needs to be overcome in order to overcome temptation. It is enough to look at Yeshua, what did he do? TORAH, for satan did not tempted him, satan only tried to provoke the Yetzer Harah within Yeshua and failed.

III - LIGHT

Every good gift and every perfect gift is from above, and comes down from the ***Father of lights****, who does not change like shifting shadows.*

James 1:17

"Light" is a very difficult concept to define, the propensity that we have to understand "light" as a visual light, the one that enables us to see, is imperative when we read about it.

The simple understanding that this passage brings us, is as if James was calling God as the Father of what gives us clarity in this life, father of something that helps us to see. But this interpretation does not live up to what the Torah teaches us and, indeed, it was in it that James' faith was based on and for this reason, in a totally mystical way, he addresses God as the *"Father of lights"*.

Mystical terms must be analyzed through biblical mysticism and the best way to do that is seeking some clarification in a book called Zohar HaKadosh. This is a book of very difficult comprehension, besides it has never been translated into any other language, it uses an allegoric language to teach very deep biblical insights. We have as follows:

Rabbi Yitzhak said: the moment that HaKadosh, Baruch Hu, created the world, He wanted to reveal from the deepest depths the most hidden secrets. HaKadosh, Baruch Hu, wanted to remove the light particles from within the KLIPAH (darkness), and what was the result of this? He revealed the light from within the darkness. What happens is that the Light of HaKadosh, Baruch Hu, was hidden in the Klipah (darkness), and because of this,

from the darkness, HaKadosh, Baruch Hu, took the Light.
Sefer HaZohar, Parashat K'doshim, 80b

This passage from the Zohar is difficult to understand to those who are not accustomed to its language; because it was written in Aramaic and never been translated, the access to the Zohar by lay people is very restricted. In order for us to understand what the Rabbis are dealing with in this passage, we must raise some millennial concepts of Kabbalah and how these concepts address the actions of Adonai.

TZIMTZUM (צימצום)

Tzimtzum, "shrinking", is the way God created the universe and all things therein. Adonai is not a being found somewhere in the universe, as in a determined place, but the whole universe is found within Him, He is the space for everything that was created, everything was created within Him.

In order for His holiness not to destroy everything, He, Adonai, "shrunk" part of His holiness, His presence and in that space that was unoccupied by His holiness became an empty space, a space without the presence of Adonai, and such a space is called "klipah", or darkness.

Klipah, in a direct translation is VASE, but it is a kabbalistic term used for a type of energy, an energy generated by the absence of Adonai, that is, before creating the heavens, the earth, the light and everything that exists, God created the darkness, the emptiness. This is confirmed in the book of Genesis itself:

Elohim said: let there be light, and there was light.
Elohim saw that the light was good and Elohim separated the light from the darkness.
Genesis 1:3-4

If we pay close attention, Elohim invokes the light and then separates it from the darkness, but He does not call to existence the darkness, He only separates the light from it, which shows us that this "darkness" already existed.

Darkness, despite being a creation of Adonai, was not a direct creation, but a creation that was a result of the "shrinking" of His holiness, and such action would allow all creation to be realized in that space.

THE HIDDEN LIGHT

Elohim said, Let there be light and there was light.

Genesis 1:3

God knew that just as the world could not exist if He did not shrink His holiness, He also knew that the world could not exist without it. Therefore, He removes a particle from His holiness and places it in that "space" He has created for the creation of the world, that is, He places a "piece" of His holiness on Klipah, the darkness.

Rabbi Bar Shmon said: on the first day of creation Hashem said let there be light and then there was light. Before that a very great light came from the sphere of mercy and it struck the surface of the darkness of the abyss, striking all the spirits that came from the absence of holiness. In this way, He removed these spirits from the surface of the abyss.

Sefer HaZohar, Parashat Bo 34b

The Zohar is really not an easy book. In this part we have the account of something that occurred before the moment of the creation of heavens and earth, the moment when God gives off a great chunk of His holiness, treated with the term "light", and brings it into the darkness that He has created before. The moment this particle enters the darkness, as the Zohar tells us, it strikes the spirits that inhabited the places where the presence of Adonai is not.

These spirits were right in the center of that darkness, in a part known as the "surface of the abyss", and when that particle strikes in that place, it disperses, as if the great light became millions of small fragments of light, just like the sand on a beach.

The Torah tells us about this moment when the light comes and strikes the darkness and the Torah also presents us with another "name" for this light:

> *The earth was formless and empty and the darkness over the surface of the abyss and the Ruach of Elohim hovering over the face of the water.*
>
> Genesis 1:2

The book of Genesis tells us about the shape of the earth and relates an abyss, which many interpret as the oceans. In fact, this abyss is the essence of Adonai's absence, it is the center of darkness and this is the moment when the light enters earthly reality.

The interesting thing is how the Torah calls this light, as Ruach. Ruach in a literal translation means wind, but it is also the name given to the Holy Spirit, Ruach HaKadosh. That is, it was when God brought to reality what we have today as the Holy Spirit, although many believe it to be the third member of the trinity, the Holy Spirit is not a living being *per se*, much less a god.

The Holy Spirit is God's manifestation on this earthly realm, it is the name of this light that has entered into our reality so that the human being can have a contact with the Creator, it is a tool created by God and given to men so that men can establish a connection with Him, even being the men in the middle of darkness.

Many believe that God is light, or that the light is God, but this is a flawed claim from pagan religions. Believing that God is light is the same as believing that the sun is a god. The Bible itself shows that light and God are not the same:

> *... and the light dwells with Him.*
>
> Daniel 2:22b

If God were the light, then the light could not dwell

with Him.

After the light has entered into this reality and has been scattered in various particles, the Zohar tells us that these particles mingled with the darkness and they ended up being hidden inside the Klipah. This is proven by the Torah itself, for it does not tell that Elohim created the light (BARAH), but He "called" the light (EHIE), that because the light already existed and was hidden in the middle of the darkness. When He calls out the light, He separates the light that was mixed into the darkness, making both distinct things within our reality.

We must always keep in mind that darkness was no accident, just as the spirits that are in it were no accidents. Everything was planned by God and everything contained therein are His servants and not opponents. Adonai created this force to take up the space where His K'dosha is not, these forces have the obligation to represent what is opposed to His presence and when this is manifest in the human reality, it is when the proliferation of demons happens.

OHR

Light in Hebrew is OHR (אור), coming from the word HEARAT (הארת), which can mean "illuminate", "projection" or "clarification". God is not the light, but the "light" was created by Him so that He can manifest in this world, and one of the functions of this light is known as the Holy Spirit. Let's see from the Torah what each of these translations of the word (הארת) means:

<u>TO ILLUMINATE</u> - The light illuminates our lives when we obey and follow the Word of God, the Torah.

His Torah is the lamp to my feet and the light to my path.

Psalms 119:105

For the commandment is a lamp, its teaching a light,
And rebuke that disciplines are the way to life.

Proverbs 6:23

TO PROJECT - When He manifests Himself in this human reality through miracles, healings, prophetic gifts, revelations and so on, those acts are known as Ruach Elohim, or Holy Spirit.

One of the levels of divine revelation is precisely through the Ruach Hakodesh, Holy Spirit.
Rabbeinu Bahya, Shemot 28:30

Then "the Ruach of God", which is the Ruach Hakodesh, hovered (over water) and stretched over it, and He (God) brought life through it (Holy Spirit).
Likutei Moharan 78:3:2

TO CLARIFY - The manifestation of light that brings the understanding, reason, faith and depth of God within each human being is when man creates a connection with the Divine that elevates him above any materiality.

I believe this is the kind of light which James refers to.

*The **understanding** will be radiant as the **light** that came from the Expansion of heaven (creation), and those who are tzadikim will shine the light like the stars forever and ever.*
Daniel 12:3

THE DIVISION OF LIGHT

וירא אלהים את האור כי טוב **ויבדל** אלהים בין האור ובין החשך
*Elohim saw that the light was good and Elohim **separated** the light from the darkness.*

Genesis 1:4

AND GOD CAUSED THE DIVISION - Here we depend on Agadah's statement: He saw that the wicked were unworthy to use the light; He therefore separated it (יבדל), reserving it to the tzadikim. Seeing that the light was good, He decided that light and darkness should not remain together in a confused form. He then determined one sphere as "day" and the other as "night."
Rashi, Genesis 1:4

According to Rashi, God already knowing about the bad people that would come, made a separation and He did it so because "he saw the good light", which is different from the Western translations that say "God saw that the light was good", giving the impression that He was surprised by something He had just created, which is not true.

God, in fact, not only separated the light from the darkness as one who separates the tares from the wheat, but He separated it as if it were stored, a light so that only the tzadikim would enjoyed it. The verb IAVDEL (יבדל) shows that God has separated, removed the light from those of the darkness. That is, God has withdrawn access to everything about Him from those who have no holiness. It was the creation of the separation of the Holy from the profane. It is as if He had kept the Light hidden and He gives it only to those who serve Him.

And Elohim saw - not that He did not know that it would be good before there was light.

Haamek Davar, Genesis 1:4

Let there be light - It is known that this light was not created to shine on all generations. But it was created, from the beginning, to be hidden and revealed only to the Tzadikim.

Haamek Davar, Genesis 1:3

This is a deep understanding concerning the passage about the light, what happens here is the creation of K'DOSHAH in our realities. Although this word is translated into English as "holiness", its real meaning is "separation", for the holies (K'doshim) are in reality those who are "separated" for God. He has generated the concept of everything that is related to Him must be separated from the profane, so the separation of light is a symbolic act that tells us the creation of this idea in our realm.

There was one person with full understanding of it:

At this time Yeshua said to his talmidim, no man can

work (serve) for two masters unless he loves one and hates the other or honors one and dishonors the other. You cannot work (serve) to EL and to the world.

Matthew 6:24

THE TORAH AND THE LIGHT

The Torah has 613 commandments divided between positive (those a man must do) and negative (those a man should not do) and also between those concerning the relationship between man and God (represented by the first tablet of the Law) and those concerning the relationship between man and his neighbor (represented by the second tablet of the Law). The 613 commandments are not for everyone, there are those for men, for women, for kings, for priests, and so on.

The sages say that the pomegranate, a typical fruit in the land of Israel, has 613 seeds inside it and for this reason King Solomon had a pomegranate orchard in the garden of his palace. In order for us to understand the connection of this "light" with the Torah, we must look at it through the Gematria.

בתורה (BATORAH - IN THE TORAH)

ב2 + ת400 + ו6 + ר200 + ה5

= **613**

וירא אלהים **את האור**

And saw Elohim ***the Light...***

Genesis 1:4a

את האור (ET HAOHR - THE LIGHT)

א1 + ת400 + ה5 + א1 + ו6 + ר200

= **613**

Both terms have the same numerical value and not any value, the value of 613, which is the value that represents the Torah and all its commandments.

THE DIFFERENCE BETWEEN THE LIGHT OF THE FIRST DAY AND THE LIGHT OF THE FOURTH DAY

Elohim made two great luminaries, the greater light to dominate the day and the lesser light to rule the night; and the stars.

Genesis 1:16

I have seen much confusion between these two passages, for how can God have created light on the first day and only in the fourth He creates the sun, which is the source of light in the form as we know it?

This misunderstanding generates some problems, many end up interpreting the first light in a very wrong way, calling it jesus, or the gospel or many other things taught by Christian theology. On the other hand, there are those who use these two basic verses to claim that the Torah is confusing and therefore loses its validity and mocks the Creator's Word.

In order for us not to fall into sophism and man made concepts, let's look a little deeper into this subject. First thing is the clear separation between sun and light that the Word of God does, as the psalmist claims:

You created the light and the sun.

Psalms 74:16

From this passage we can see that the sun and the light are two distinct things in their essences. The Hebrew word for light is OHR (אור) and for luminary, as it appears in verse 16, is MEOHR (מאור). The only difference i the addition of the preposition ME (מ).

This preposition is used to refer to the origin of something. This can be better understood through the word FROM. Then the word MEOHR (מאור) can be translated as FROM LIGHT.

This shows us that these "luminaries" (sun and moon) have the power to illuminate, because they came from the light, that is, they are two physical representations of how the spiritual world works. Just as light is the representation of the Creator, who gives life, so does the sun, generating crops, crops generates food and food generates life. On the other hand, science tells us that what brings balance to Earth is the moon, thus showing that darkness, the other side, the yetzer harah, is what brings balance to man, for it is through it that man will be judged.

The proof of this is that the word LIGHT - OHR - appears exact five times and the word LUMINARY - MEOHR – another exact five times, showing that for each time the term MEOHR appears, there is an OHR giving spiritual support to it, since everything that exist in this earthly realm can only exist if it is sustained by its spiritual counterpart.

MASHIACH AND THE LIGHT

This was explained by Rabbi Simeon Bar Yohai, peace be upon him. He said: the mystery of a formless earth is in reference to the destruction of the first Temple, the mystery of an empty earth is in reference to the destruction of the second Temple and then said Adonai: let there be light (Gn1: 3) - in reference to the future redemption of Mashiach.

Or Neerav 1:38

The allusion that Rabbi Simeon Bar Yohai makes is very profound and mystical. He relates the two characteristics that the earth possessed shortly after its creation, formless and empty, with the destruction of the two Temples and the light that Adonai calls out with the era of Mashiach.

The messianic age will be governed by Mashiach Ben David and in order to prove this relation between the light and the age governed by Mashiach that Simeon makes, we will need the Gematria, as follows:

MASHIACH BEN DAVID (משיח בן דוד)

משיח (MASHIACH)
8 ח + 10 י + 300 ש + 40 מ
= 358 = 3 + 5 + 8 = 16 = 1 + 6 = **7**

בן (BEN)
700 ן + 2 ב
= 702 = 7 + 2 = **9**

דוד (DAVID)
4 ד + 6 ו + 4 ד
=14 = 1 + 4 = **5**

TOTAL = 7 + 9 + 5 = 21 = 2 + 1 = **3**

וַיֹּאמֶר אֱלֹהִים יְהִי אוֹר וַיְהִי-אוֹר = **3**
And Elohim said, let it be light and it was light.
Genesis 1:3

Both "Mashiach Ben David" and the entire verse 3 from the first chapter of Genesis, which relates the light, possess the absolute value of 3, thus making a connection of that light with the messianic age.

This allusion makes perfect sense, for among some missions of Mashiach, we shall have the revelation of how the Torah is to be followed and thus bringing us understanding (CLARIFYING). He will rule over the nations according to these Laws (ILLUMINATE) and he will represent the apex of God's plan for humanity (PROJECT). These are the three meanings of the word HEARAT (הארת), from the same root as the word OHR (אור), as already seen.

The understanding of these things is for the few, for it is something that was concealed by God, it is a mystery revealed to the chosen. The light is hidden, it is a mystery, or as in Hebrew, a RAZ (רז) - *mystery*.

רז (RAZ - MYSTERY)
7ז + 400ר
= **407**

אור (OHR - LIGHT)
400ר + 6ו + 1א
= **407**

God, may His name be elevated, decreed that this light of King Mashiach should not be revealed to the world and should be kept in secret with Him. Happy are the eyes that see these things.
Or HaChaim, Bereshit 1

JAMES AND THE LIGHT

After all of the presented above, we still have a question to answer, what is the true and profound meaning of the Light that led James to call God the "Father of Lights"?

את האור כי טוב
...that the light is good...

Genesis 1:4

If we take the last letters of each of these words, we will have the term BRIT (ברית) which means covenant.

James is actually talking about covenant, by bringing up this term he indirectly says that those who are aligned to God must be separated from the profane, just as the light has been separated from the darkness. They must know the Torah as the only truth and in order to have their lives enlightened, they must receive the understanding from God, thus generating faith and finally, these people must project God on earth, doing what we call as *Tikkun Olam*, that is, “to fix” the world by obeying the Word of God and mirroring His being in this reality.

The term "*Father of lights*" when used by Jewish mystical

minds automatically resembles holy attitudes before Adonai and such attitudes are meant to fix the world we live in, in order to hasten the coming of Mashiach.

THE SEFIROT

For an even more mystical understanding of these "lights", let us look at the mystery of the sefirot. The sefirot are emanations from the One God and through them, His actions are accomplished in this realm. They constitute the ten "methods" by which the Creator acts and reveals Himself to men. For a more didactic explanation, they are like ten beams of light used by God to act on the "nothingness" He created by the "removal" of His essence. This "nothingness", which is the opened space within Him for the creation of all things, could not bear His total presence, just as it could not exist without it, by that fact He projects His essence into this reality through these emanations called sefirot (plural of sefirah).

The sefirot are widely used in various means of magic, divinations, and sorceries associated with unclean spirits. Those practices makes use of them with slightly altered definitions from the true ones, for the sefirot are secrets only to be applied in the Torah, so that an understanding about God would be more deeply through His word. Many of these occultism teachings create sefirot and some others eliminate sefirot, that is, some have nine, some others eleven and so on, but what we must always keep in mind is that they are TEN, no more and no less and it should never be used outside the word of God, never should be used for magic, divination, predictions of the future, and manipulations of reality, as many teach and do.

We must also keep in mind that the sefirot are not God, nor God the sefirot and the sefirot are not intrinsic part of God. The sefirot, without God, cannot not exist, however God, without the sefirot, would continue existing without any change. The sefirot are only ways for a better explanation of how the manifestations and the actions of God work in this earthly reality.

The sefirot are named according to their properties of performance and representation in our reality. As follows:

1- KETER (כתר) - CROWN
Associations: origin, holy spirit, root of the roots.

2- CHOKHMAH (חכמה) - WISDOM
Associations: revelations, mastery, Torah secrets, Abba.

3- BINAH (בינה) - KNOWLEDGE
Associations: Torah's deep knowledge, Tshuvah (repentance), freedom.

4- CHESSED (חסד) - MERCY, GOODNESS
Associations: grace, love of God

5- GEVURAH (גבורה) - JUDGMENT
Associations: laws, commandments, strength of God, forgiveness.

6- TIFERET (תפארת) - COMPASSION
Associations: harmony, beauty, God as King, miracles.

7- NETZACH (נצח) - VICTORY
Associations: eternity, prophecy, redemption.

8-HOD (הוד) - GLORY
Associations: majesty, splendor, truth.

9- YESOD (יסוד) - FOUNDATION
Associations: Almighty God, lower heavens, tzadik.

10- MALKHUT (מלכות) - KINGDOM
Associations: earth, Shekhinah, holiness, Shabbat.

Within the ten sefirot we find all the characteristics of the Creator God and whenever one of them is manifest in the life of the human being, this sefirah (light) causes what is associated with it, for example, when a man is worthy of God's mercy, the sefirah of Chessed comes into his life. The way the

Torah presents them is somewhat mystical, in addition to the names of these sefirot appearing several times by the Tanakh, the way their power is manifested is through the names given to God. We will see each one of them:

1- EHYEH (אהיה) - KETER (כתר)

2-YAH (יה) -CHOKHMAH (חכמה)

3- YHWH with nekudot (יְהֹוָה) - BINAH (בינה)

4- EL (אל) - CHESSED (חסד)

5-ELOHEI (אלהי) - GEVURAH (גבורה)

6- YHWH without nekudot (יהוה) -TIFERETE (תפארת)

7- TZEVA'OT (צבאת) - NETZACH (נצח)

8- EL HAI (אל חי) - HOD (הוד)

9- SHADDAI (שדי) - YESOD (יסוד)

10- ADONAI (אדוני) - MALKHUT (מלכות)

The names of God revealed to us by the Torah represent divine appeals of the One God that reveal the form that God is working in this earthly reality. Many believe that the Sefirah Keter is God, but this is not true, even though KETER is the root of all other sefirot, since it was the first and originated all the others, KETER is also a creation.

Within the sefirot, there is an aspect called DA'AT (דעת) - *understanding* - which is not a sefirah. The DA'AT (דעת) refers to human natural intelligence, linked to earthly things and has nothing to do with the lights that emanate from God. Many people rely on the DA'AT (human capacity) to be able to acquire knowledge about God and His word through theological studies in order to try to define Him. Such an attitude is valid in some way, but just as everything in this reality has a beginning, a middle and an end (i.e. death), this kind of biblical interpretation or definition of the Creator, ultimately also ends with death. A very clear example of this is the Christian theology itself, since it is based on the human DA'AT for interpretations of what the human mind is not apt to, its days will come to an end eventually.

The "lights" of the sefirot illuminate one another, and for this reason it is possible to find mercy in judgment, glory in victory, wisdom in the knowledge of the Torah, and so on. These lights, when they touch this reality, they cause the will of the Creator to be realized, they cause the world to act according to His will.

Another important factor about the sefirot is that they are interconnected, that is, if one is "nullified" all the others lose the balance they represent and thus making judgment without mercy, understanding without compassion, earthly realm without wisdom and a foundation without the glory of God. A very common example of this is the annulment of the Torah, which is connected to CHOCKMAH (wisdom) and BINAH (knowledge), claiming that only CHESSED (grace) is enough, when this happens, there is a disorder of the way God manifests in one's life, in other words, understanding and wisdom will not be part of those who believe so, this disconnection can cause the disorder reported above. I believe that the way James calls God, as the "*father of lights*" in the plural, it is in reference to the sefirot, what represent the acts and attributes of God.

This is only a brief account about the sefirot and not a complete study, far from it. We shall see this theme again later.

IV - THE GOD WHO DOES NOT CHANGE

*Every good gift and every perfect gift comes from above, descending from the Father of lights, in whom there is **no change nor shadow of variation**.*

James 1:17

*For I am Adonai and **I DO NOT** change ...*

Malachi 3:6a

When someone changes, this change can basically be seen in two ways, behavioral which is a change of ideas and attitudes, or an existential change, that is, a change of who the person is, of what defines that person as a person.

When James quotes that there is "*no change nor shadow of variation*" in God, I believe he refers to all forms of change, which are defined by the two ways one can change, behavioral or existential. For this reason, I see James's book as something much more concerned with Judaism than with Christianity, for this assertion is not in conformity with some foundations of the Christian faith.

BEHAVIORAL CHANGE

If God were a god who changed his behavior, that is, if he has the habit to say something and then change his mind, he would not be a trustworthy god. Some rabbis, like James, deal extensively with this theme:

CHANGE: He does not have two words, Adonai does not speak without a reason, nor does anything without a reason, for He does not change.

Radak, Malachi 3:6

If God does not change, how can He choose a people to call His own and then, just because these people did not accept jesus, He changes His mind and replace the real Israel with the church? What sense does that make for a God who does not change?

If God does not change, how can He determine how the people who serve Him should live and behave through His Torah and then He changes His mind by replacing His Torah with the famous Christian grace? How can a God who does not change, change his mind so much? And when He declares on several occasions that the Torah is eternal? Did He suddenly changed His mind and decided that it would be no longer valid? I think this is a very weird belief that many people have.

We must be very careful with the theological lies that we hear by many leaders everywhere we go. These topic brings me some verses in mind:

Thus said the LORD, Who established the sun for light by day, The laws of moon and stars for light by night, Who stirs up the sea into roaring waves, Whose name is ADONAI TZ'VAOT: If these laws should ever be annulled by Me — declares the LORD— Only then would the offspring of Israel cease To be a nation before Me for all time.

Jeremiah 31:35-36

His Torah *is true from the beginning and every one of His* ***ordinances*** *lasts* ***forever****.*

Psalm 119:160

But the ***word of the Lord*** *remains* ***forever*** *(at that time there was only the Tanakh).*

1 Peter 1:25

And You have confirmed Your people ***Israel****, as* ***Your people forever****.*

2 Samuel 7:24

You are the same, and Your years will never end.
Psalm 102:8

EXISTENTIAL CHANGE

This is a type of change that Christian theology stumbles upon, here it is not a change of attitude, but a change in what defines God, let us see:

I am Adonai and besides me, there is no other god...
Isaiah 45:5a

Adonai is our Elohim, Adonai is ONE...
Deuteronomy 6:4

The understanding that the Creator is ONE is not for everyone. It is not ONE in the numerical sense, for the concepts of "one" composed, mutable and with manifolds do not apply to Him. The word ONE in reference to Him is only a didactic example in order for the human mind to have a small glimpse about His essence. The number one is a number that is sustained by itself, is the beginning of all and is a number that is potentially within all other numbers.

When God is called ONE, it is in reference to His emanations that are found throughout all that He created, for He is the beginning and the cause of all things that exist. Therefore, He is the cause of everything, just as the number ONE can be found in all others somehow. If the number ONE were to be removed from all numbers, all others would be abolished, except the number ONE itself. This is the power of the divine oneness.

The same is true about God, if His essence were taken from everything that exists, everything would cease to exist except Him. He is the creative agent behind everything and everything is supported by Him, He does not depend on anything that He created, even if everything were destroyed, He would remain the same.

The Trinitarian theology, which claims that God, even

though He is one, he is also three, removes all the essence of that power from God. The belief in a plurality of gods, whatever they may be, is to believe that God changes, for He repeatedly affirms that He is THE ONLY GOD. If God were three, either god changed or god lied. A god who changes or a god who lies, is not God.

Many believe that trinity is a biblical concept, but it is not. Both the Tanakh and the authors of the New Testament make this very clear, besides the passages quoted above, let us look at some others:

Father, the time has come, glorify your son so that your son may glorify you. This is eternal life, absorbing knowledge of you, THE ONLY AND TRUE GOD, and the one you sent, Yeshua HaMashiach.

John 17:1-3

THE ONLY AND TRUE GOD, Yeshua's heavenly father, who raised up his son.

Acts 10:40

For us, however, THERE IS ONE SINGLE GOD, from which everything proceeds...

1 Corinthians 8:6a

It was to You Israel that He showed all of this, so that they would know that Adonai is God, the ONLY ONE and beyond Him there is no other.

Deuteronomy 4:35

...the idol has no meaning in the world and there is ONLY ONE GOD.

1 Corinthians 8:4b

There is ONE GOD and Father of all, who is over all, through all and in all.

Ephesians 4:6

Trinitarianism is a human concept, idolatrous and of pagan origin, which has nothing to do with the ONE TRUE

GOD, with Yeshua, with the new testament, and with the apostles. Believing in this concept is like calling God a liar.

God forbid.

V - EMET

Of his own will begat he us with the ***word of truth****, that we should be a kind of first fruits of his creatures.*

James 1:18

Truth is the essence of Your word, Your just commandments are eternal.

Psalm 119:160

The "word of truth" is the Torah.

Machzor Rosh Hashanah Ashkenaz 46

First of all, it is vital that it is clear that this "*word of truth*" refers to the Torah. Both the psalm and the Machzor, which is a prayer book read during the celebration of Rosh Hashanah, make this very clear. Within the Jewish mentality, the term EMET DABAR (אמת דבר) – *word of truth* - is a direct reference to the Torah. But in order to dive deeper into the words of James, let us conceptualize what this "truth" would be and why that term defines the Torah itself.

TRUTH, in Hebrew, is EMET, one of the few words that does not have a plural form, because TRUTH, in the holy language, there is only one. Therefore, the "*word of truth*" quoted by James can be no other than the Torah. But the best way to conceptualize something is to conceptualize its opposite, the TRUTH is better understood when the LIE also is.

שקר (SHEKER - LIE)

200ר + 100ק + 300ש

= 600 = **6**

If we observe the Hebrew alphabet, we will see that the letters from the word SHEKER (שקר) - *lie* - are adjacent letters, they are side by side right in the middle of the alphabet. This shows that LIES are easily found, for they are always "near". Another thing one must observe concerning this word is its bottom, it gives the impression that SHEKER (שקר) balances on only one leg, which shows how easily a LIE could fall, that is, lies don't travel far, pretty much like someone with only one leg.

אמת (EMET - TRUTH)
400ת + 40מ + 1א
= 801 = 8+1 = **9**

Just as truth and lie are opposite things, their Gematria values prove that, 6 for SHEKER - *lie* - and 9 for EMET - *truth*.

Also in the Hebrew alphabet, the letters that form the word EMET are as far apart as possible, being the letter ALEF (א) the first and TAV (ת) the last, because the truth is something rare to find and something distant in the lives of a lot of people. Also, the bottom of the word EMET (אמת) is straight and unlike the one legged SKEKER (שקר), the EMET (אמת) can sustain itself.

Emet and death

With a more mystical analysis on the Hebrew word EMET, we shall see how harmful EMET can be if its essence is not properly understood.

As already seen before, each letter in the Hebrew alphabet has an equivalent number. Due to those numerical values, certain letters are matched to certain things or certain beings, as we can see in the Hebrew letter ALEF (א), for being the very first letter of the Hebrew alphabet and because it has a numerical value of 1, which represents oneness, the letter ALEF (א) stands for ADONAI.

Therefore, if we take the word EMET (אמת) and if we remove God from that truth, that is, if we remove ALEF (א) letter from the word EMET (אמת), we will have only MET (מת) which means "death". With this we learn that, even though there are a lot of "truth" in every creed and beliefs all over, the "truth" that doesn't have the God Of Israel as its foundation, even if they look like real truths, they will bring only death at the end.

Another revelation that this word brings is its deep connection with the Torah. The first letter of the word TORAH (תורה) is the letter TAV (ת), which is the same letter the word EMET (אמת) ends. If there is a "truth" that is not according to the Torah, it would be like removing the letter TAV (ת) from the word EMET (אמת) and thus we would end up having EME (אמה).

This term can mean something like a "matrix", a non-existent parallel reality, that is, whoever lives any kind of "truth" that is not connected with the Torah somehow, whether it is any kind of religion or concepts created by the minds of men, lives in a false reality, in a false world, a false faith, and such things bring only agony, depression, disgust, disgrace and so on.

To conclude this analysis, it is interesting to look at James, who was a Jew, a rabbi, a Pharisee and a sage, and see how he used to understand this term according to his background:

His justice is eternal and His Torah is THE EMET.

Psalm 119:142

And His Torah is EMET, for all His commandments are EMET and the reason for the existence of the world.

Radak, Psalms 119:142

You are near Adonai, and all Yours mitzvot (commandments) are the EMET.

Psalm 119:151

The individual who is committed to the Torah may be called as Emet, because his reason for existing becomes a truth and not a false reality.

Chomat Anakh, Psalms 119:151

And truth (EMET) refers only to the Torah, as it is written: buy the truth and do not sale it, as well as wisdom, guidance and understanding.

Talmud of Babylon, Tractate Brakhot 5b

Reish Lakish said: The letter TAV (ת) is the last letter of the seal of the Holy One, Blessed Be He, and Rabbi Hanina said: The seal of the Holy One, Blessed Be He, is the TRUTH (EMET - אמת), which ends with the letter TAV (ת). Rabbi Shmuel teaches that the Torah should be followed from ALEF (א) to TAV (ת), from beginning to end.

Talmud of Babylon, Tractate Brakhot 55a

The Beginning of Truth

בראשי**ת** בר**א** אלהי**ם** את השמים ואת הארץ

In the beginning God created the heavens and the earth.

Genesis 1:1

Although everyone understands that everything was a created, many still have a small difficulty in including certain abstract concepts within this "everything", as the concept of goodness for instance. Such concept was "created" within our reality because it is one of the attributes that represents the Creator, on the other hand, He also had to create its opposite, the evil, because without it, how could possibly the human being understand goodness?

The same happens with the TRUTH. Before the creation of all things, and when all was taken by the presence of Adonai, the TRUTH was not a concept, but the only existing reality. When Adonai shrinks His presence, His light, so that in this space all things could be created, He had to include in this reality this TRUTH and the opposite of it. Since TRUTH is the basis of everything and the most important concept of all, Adonai inserted it into the human reality before all the other attributes, that is, in order for His attributes to be Truth in this realm, He had to bring the TRUTH before any other attribute of His that came through the "light" reported at the end of the first verse.

In the first three words of the Torah is where this action occurs, it is when Adonai brings into our reality THE TRUTH and defines it. This is shown to us in the last three letters of each of the first three words:

ALEF (א) - MEM (מ/ם) - TAV (ת) = EMET (אמת)

This teaches us that the only truth is what is linked to Elohim, His Word and His will. All the rest, all the "truths" of men and religions, even if they look like “truth”, they are no more than lies!

VI - BEGOTTEN BY THE WORD

According to his will, ***he begotten us by the word of truth,*** *that we might be the firstfruits among his creatures.*

James 1:18

The most common theological interpretation we have about this verse is referring to the power of the word pronounced by Adonai, who, created everything through spoken words. But the claim that James makes is not quite so, for he actually says that God has begotten us by the "*word of truth*", and that term refers not to the creative power from the mouth of Adonai but to the creative power of the Word of God, i.e. the Torah, as already seen.

BERESHIT

בראשית ברא אלהים את השמים ואת הארץ

In the beginning Elohim created the heavens and the earth.

Genesis 1:1

Right in the very first sentence of the book of Genesis in its original language, we have many hidden secrets. The initial term, BERESHIT (בראשית), customarily translated as "in the beginning", suffers from translations into Western languages.

In order for us to have a defined beginning, as "THE beginning", the term used in Hebrew should have been B**A**RE-SHIT, but the word that appears is B**E**RESHIT, showing us that it is not actually "in the beginning" but rather "in a certain beginning". A non unique beginning.

It may seem irrelevant, but such a statement reveals that the beginning of all things as reported by the bible, was not a single beginning, it was just one beginning among other beginnings. Everything that was created in this "beginning" is very well described in the Torah, the heavens, the earth, the animals, the nature, the human being and so on. However, all over the Tanakh some things are presented to its reader which are not described at the moment of creation, things that simply exist and are not revealed when they were created, which proves that the "in the beginning" of the book of Genesis is not really the beginning of everything, but rather a beginning among other beginnings.

The sages teach that before the creation of the reality where we are inserted in, there were seven other "beginnings", that is, God created seven things before what is reported in the book of Bereshit. These "beginnings" are presented to us out of the blue throughout the Tanakh, which reveals to us that they already existed before all things. Understanding some of them may bring us some revelations. They are as follow:

1- THE THRONE OF GLORY (כסא הכבוד)
2- TORAH (תורה)
3- THE HOLY TEMPLE (בית המקדש)
4- REPENTANCE (תשובה)
5- PARADISE (גן עדן)
6- GAHINAM (גיהנם)
7- NAME OF MASHIACH (שמו של משיח)

The sages say that God is like an engineer, an architect, who developed and created the whole universe. Every project has basically three steps, the first is the idealization, the second is the planning and finally, the realization.

The Torah has three moments in history, the first is precisely the moment we are addressing. Like every good builder, God first idealizes all of his work and then he develops a "plant". He sets up a project whereby all things will work and it is at that moment that he created the Torah, so that through it, He could create all things.

The Torah is not just a book, but it is the will and idealization of God, all creation, like nature, animals and stars, behave according to the will of God. This will was born in that act. When God creates the Torah, He establishes how His whole creation would behave and obey Him. If He had created all things without establishing these rules beforehand, the world would have been a total mess.

Adonai created me (Torah) as the beginning of His course, as the first of His works in antiquity.

Proverbs 8:22

The second moment of the Torah occurs at the end of the creation of all things, as reported in the book of Genesis:

And Adonai blessed the seventh day, and hallowed it, for in it Adonai finished what He had made to do.

Genesis 2:3

This translation is a little different from the ones we have in English, I tried to keep the most of its original form in order to show its strangeness. What does it mean "God finished what He had made to do"? It is a claim that makes no apparent sense, but if we pay attention, what God “made to do” refers to the Torah, the Shabbat was the day that God brought into reality the Torah, it was when He established His Laws all over His creation. This is why it is written "He finished", for it means that He just finished establishing all the Laws of the Torah in the world.

Shabbat is not only the day of rest, but also the day that represents the Torah, because it was on that day that God established the modus operandi of this world, that is why that day was sanctified.

Finally, we have the materialization of the Torah as reported in the book of Exodus. Moses goes up to Mount Sinai and God gives him the Torah. It is interesting to note that it does not say that God created the Torah, but rather that God gave it. If God gave the Torah, it means that it already existed, and since the Torah does not report its own creation, it means that it was created even before the first word of Bereshit has been written.

This is proven in an ancient Midrash, which confirms that the Torah was the "plant" for the creation of the heavens and the earth:

IN THE BEGINNING (Gn1:1) - This is what the scriptures refer to when it says: Adonai, with wisdom (Torah), founded the earth (Proverbs 3:19). That is, when the Holy One, Blessed Be He, resolved to create the earth, He consulted the Torah to draw upon His creation. How was the Torah written? It was written with letters of black fire on white fire surfaces.

Midrash Tanchumah, Bereshit 1

The first word in the Torah, BERESHIT (בראשית), also reveals many other secrets. If we separate this word in two according to its terms, we shall have BE (ב) - *in* - and RESHIT (ראשית) - *beginning.*

BE (ב), does not only mean the preposition IN, but it can also be translated as BY, so we can also translate BERESHIT (בראשית) as "BY THE BEGINNING". In this case we would have something a little strange, but if we look at the word RESHIT (ראשית), we will find other meanings for it, as Rabbi Rashi teaches us:

Rashi understands the word RESHIT (ראשית) in reference to the Torah, for it is called RESHIT (ראשית) elsewhere.

Daat Zkenim, Bereshit 1:2

According to Rabbi Rashi, the term RESHIT (ראשית) refers to the Torah and he makes this claim based on other biblical passages:

ראשית חכמה יראת יהוה שכל טוב לכל עשיהם תהלתו עמדת לעד

The beginning (RESHIT) of wisdom / the fear of Adonai is all good, all who practice it gain understanding. Praised be forever.

Psalms 111:10

יהוה קנני **ראשית** דרכו קדם מפעליו מעז

Adonai created me (Torah) as RESHIT of His course, as the firstfruit of His works in antiquity.

Proverbs 8:22

These two passages poorly translated into English relate the term RESHIT (ראשית) to the Torah. The first one says that RESHIT (ראשית) is wisdom and as everyone knows, wisdom is the Creator's own Word, the Torah. The second claims that God created the Torah as RESHIT (ראשית). This shows us in what Rabbi Rashi relied upon to affirm that RESHIT (ראשית) refers to the Torah.

If we join both terms BE (ב) - *by* - with RESHIT (ראשית) as meaning the Torah, we can read the first verse of Genesis as follows:

***By the Torah** Elohim created the heavens and the earth.*

Genesis 1:1

With an analysis of a verse from the book of Deuteronomy, we will have a confirmation of all that has been addressed thus far:

ויאמר יהוה מסיני בא וזרח משעיר למו הופיע מהר פארן

ואתה מרבבת קדש מימינו אשדת **אש דת** למו

*And he said, Adonai came from Sinai, He shone on them from Seir. He appeared on Mount Paran and approached Ribeboth-Kodesh. In his right hand was a **FIRE LAW** for them.*

Deuteronomy 33:2

In the middle of the word RESHIT (ראשית) we find the word ESH (אש), which means "fire". As seen in this Hebrew verse, the word ESH (אש) comes associated with the word DAT (דת), which can be translated as LAW in this case.

This reveals that the fire that was in God's hand was the Torah which was written in fire and was the basis for all creation, it was revealed to man through the right hand of the Creator in the form of Laws.

When James states "begotten us by the word of truth", he affirms the ancient understanding that everything was created by the Torah, including us, thus emphasizing its importance to his hearers.

VII - FIRSTFRUITS

According to His will, he begotten us by the word of truth,
*that we might be the **firstfruits among his creatures**.*
James 1:18

A simple reading of the story of creation is enough to see that human beings were not the firstfruits among God's creatures, for all animals have come before. In fact, man was the last creature to be created, so how could James claim that we are the "firstfruits among his creatures"?

In order to understand what James stated, we should look at some passages in the Torah and in this case, in Hebrew:

ראשית בכורי אדמתך תביא בית יהוה
*Choose the **firstfruits** (RESHIT) of your land and*
bring them to the House of Adonai...
Exodus 23:19a

והבאתם את עמד **ראשית** קצירכם אל הכהן
*...You must bring the **firstfruits** (RESHIT)*
of your harvest to the priest.
Leviticus 23:10b

Look how interesting, the English word for "firstfruits" appears as RESHIT (ראשית) in the Torah, the exactly same term discussed earlier. If we associate both, the word RESHIT (ראשית) representing Torah (as seen before), we may re-read the words of James as follows:

According to his will, he begotten us by the Torah,

so we be like TORAH among his creatures.

For a real meaning to this new re-reading, which sincerely got a little strange, let's look at a common knowledge among the followers of Yeshua, among whom James was one of them. To do so, I will use passages from the book of one of the most mystical followers of Yeshua, John, and the quotations I will make will be from the original version of his book in Hebrew.

John and the Torah

And the Word (Torah) became ***like*** *flesh, and dwelt among us, and we saw its glory (of the Word), as the glory of the only begotten of the Father, full of grace and truth.*
John 1:14, from the original Hebrew Gospel

The differences that exist between the Western version of the book of John and its original counterpart are absurd and frightening. Such differences have been used as basis to the creation of many dogmas by Christian theology that are not according to the bible.

As we read carefully, we can see that John claims that the Word, in this case the Torah, became LIKE flesh. What he affirms here is that Yeshua lived the Torah in such a profound and a complete way that it was as if he were the Torah incarnate, the living Torah.

The habit of "naming" great men of God in reference to holy things is very common within Judaism. We see students of famous rabbis calling them as "pillars", referring to the columns of the Temple's entrance or sometimes some sages being called "tzitzit" because of the long tzitzit they had in their robes and so on.

This is a habit so customary that Yeshua himself used it to refer to himself:

And I am the way to the truth that gives life. No one comes to the Father except through this.

John 14:6, from the original Hebrew Gospel

He claims to be "the way", that is, such an affirmation within the Jewish mentality shows that his teachings concerning the Torah is what leads to the true interpretation of it and this interpretation gives life.

James, in this verse does the same thing, he states that his hearers should be like Living Torahs, just as Yeshua was, among all creatures. In simpler words, just as Yeshua was the Living Torah, he states that everyone should do the same, all should follow the Torah in the same way as Yeshua followed and by the way he taught that it should be followed.

Then we can understand the verse as follows:

According to His will, He has begotten us through the Torah (as He has begotten all things), so that we may follow Torah (as Yeshua followed and taught) among men (for we must be examples of how to serve God before the nations).

James 1:18

VIII - TO HEAR

Why, my beloved brothers, let every man be swift to hear, slow to speak, slow to wrath:

James 1:19

The act of "hearing" within the Jewish mentality has so many profound meanings that, in order to be properly able to approach all of them, we would require a book with more than a thousand pages.

"Hear", in Hebrew, is SHMA (שמע), and that term represents the maxim of Israel's faith, for in it is condensed the most important principles of what the Creator wants from those who serve Him. To fully understand those words from James, it first requires a deeper insight of how the Jewish people understand the term "hear".

The most famous biblical "hear" is the one found on the book of Deuteronomy and in this "hear", also know as SHMA ISRAEL, is where it is taught how the real faith on the real God must be:

שמע ישראל יהוה אלהינו יהוה אחד ואהבת את יהוה
אלהיך בכל לבבך ובכל נפשך ובכל מאדך

Hear (SHMA) Israel, Adonai is our Elohim, Adonai is ONE. And you shall love Adonai your Elohim with all his heart, with all his soul and with all his lot.

Deuteronomy 6:4-5

This passage is of utmost importance to the People of Israel, within it we can see basic concepts of conduct and a summary of the entire Torah in just two verses. These verses are so powerful that they are recited three times a day by the Jews, they are written inside the tephilim (phylacteries) and inside the mezuzot placed on the doorposts.

The first thing is that Adonai (יהוה) is the God of the People of Israel and He is ONE and that ONE is an absolute ONE, indivisible and not a compound, as many believe. Next we have the command to love Him, not to simply love Him, but to love Him with all our HEART, with all our SOUL and with all our MUCH. These three ways that He desires to be loved are much discussed throughout the Jewish literature:

> *As it is written, "And you shall love Adonai your Elohim with all your heart," it means with your evil inclination and with your good inclination, for both should be subjugated to God. "With all your soul" means that you must love God to the cost of your soul. "with all your much" means with all your money and possessions. "Another understanding:" with all your much" Is to submit to the mitzvot of Adonai.*
>
> Talmud of Babylon, Tractate Brakhot 54a

The Talmud quotes this relationship between "loving God" with the mitzvot (commandments) related to "man x God". To love God above all things must be through one's inclinations, wills, dreams and feelings, for to love God must be greater than self-love and this is only done through the observance of ALL the commandments from the Torah that concerns the relationship "man x God".

The "hear", as used by James, gives us a simple but profound teaching on how we should control ourselves even when we are wronged or verbally attacked, we must have self control so we shall not use offensive words. If we look at the source of this teaching of James, along with the Jewish understanding of "hearing" as seen so far, perhaps we can learn more than meets the eyes.

In Hebrew, an impatient person, someone who is easily angered, is called as someone who does **not** have a CHASH-

MAL LEV. This term is used for a kind of emotional energy, but without a direct translation into English. In the Hebrew language, being called so has a negative connotation, when one is called as someone with no CHASHMAL LEV, it means that this someone has something that needs to be fixed in his behavior.

CHASHMAL LEV matches very well with what James is talking about in this verse, for this term deals with the one who knows how to hear, someone who, instead of getting anger, patient listens and talk few. With that in mind, we can now see the solution that James proposed for this type of behavior, a simple word, HEAR (שמע).

Now we have something difficult to understand, how can "hear" improve the behavior of a person who has a "short temper"?

חשמל לב (CHASHMAL LEV)

2ב + 30ל + 30ל + 40מ + 300ש + 8ח

= **410**

שמע (SHMA)

70ע + 40מ + 300ש

= **410**

We see here that both SHMA and CHASMAL LEV, the one who is patient, have the same numerical value. This leads us to understand that what changes behavior, what makes an aggressive person into a patient and loving one is just the SHMA, hear, as described in Deuteronomy 6:4-5 and this is impressive.

So far we have only half the conclusion, for knowing that SHMA can change a man's behavior for the better is not enough unless we know how to understand these mystical words of the Torah.

To do so, it is vital to detail each of the terms that appear in SHMA:

1- SHMA (שמע)

The Torah does not say SEE ISRAEL, but rather, HEAR ISRAEL. This is because our knowledge of God is based on sensory perceptions. During the time prior to the Torah, little was known about God, this conception of a single God reigning over the whole earth was a very abstract idea and inconsistent with the post-flood common mentality.

For God to make Himself known, He had to seek men, introduced Himself to them, and through these men, He accomplished great deeds. If we make a comparison of the time of Abraham, of Moses and of the prophets with the present day, the impression we will have is that, over time, God hid Himself, His "apparitions" and great miracles were slowly becoming a rare thing. On the other hand, the access that any individual has, whoever he is, poor or rich, white or black, Latin or Asian, to the Word of God and to the knowledge about who He is, is unrestricted. Because of this fact, the Torah commands: HEAR! Hear who God is, hear what He has done, hear His prowess, hear His wonders, for in these days it is through this "hearing" that God becomes known in the life of man.

Of course, God can reveal Himself to whom He wills, in the way He wants and not just by hearing. But this revelation does not come before we "hear" His Word, about who He is and how He works, for if He presents Himself before that, it is very difficult for the person receiving that vision to have the ability to recognize its source.

2-UM (אחד)

This is a statement that created several theories, especially on the part of those who want to create and justify false gods. The word ECHAD (אחד) - ONE - does not only mean that God is one, but also represents His essence, He is an absolute and not a compound ONE. If God were a compound ONE, then within that composition there would be a grouping, if there is a grouping, it means that someone had to group it, that is, if God is a compound ONE, someone had to compose it, which shows us that there is something, or somebody, greater than

God, for he was able to gather three in one. Faith in a triune god and faith in a god that is not absolute is a strange faith, for a composition had to be created. If one creates the other, then this other does not have the same power as the one who created him, thus breaking the equality they should have to be ONE in balance.

If God were to be three in one, the word would not be ECHAD (אחד) in this passage, but rather ACHER (אחר) - the difference between them is a single Hebrew letter, DALET (ד) and REISH (ר).

3- AND YOU SHALL LOVE (אהבת)

The Hebrew word for love shows a much deeper meaning than those we have in Western languages. AHAVAH (אהבה) - *love* - begins with the letter ALEF (א) and every word that its root begins with this letter, deals with an individual conception, an internal feeling, something reflective. The junction of the letters (הב), the remaining letters of the word AHAVAH, means "to donate". Therefore, the word AHAVAH (אהבה) means something like "self-giving".

When the Torah commands us to love God, it does not refer to an inner feeling, but rather that we give ourselves to God, to His will, and to His plans.

4 - YOUR HEART (לבך)

Giving ourselves to God with all our hearts is not something simple, precisely because of the word "all" that comes before it. For this reason, giving oneself to God is only possible through a recognition of the absolute God's oneness, for it is through this recognition that the human being can understand that "loving with all one's heart" is nothing more than giving up both the good inclination and the evil inclination that exist within of every human being in the hands of God.

The true nature of this mitzvah encompasses the idea that we are ready to give our desires, dreams and wills to God and, if they do not match with what God wants from us, we will gladly give those things up. This is what to love God with ALL one's heart, its not a feeling.

Taking this decision of life and being able to fulfill it brings some consequences that Gematria shows:

לבך (YOUR HEART)
ל30 + ב2+ ך20
= **52**

אנא יהוה הושיעה נא **אנא** יהוה הצליחה נא
I ***beg*** *you, Adonai, save us. I* ***beg*** *you, Adonai, prosper us.*
Psalms 118:25

The term used in this passage translated as "beg" is AN'A (אנא), this is a word used in many prayers to show total devotion and dependence on God. Our sages tell us that it is through AN'A (אנא) that Adonai answers our prayers, this is a very profound term.

אנא (AN'A)
א1 + נ50 + א1
= **52**

What we can see here is the connection between the one who loves the God with ALL OF HIS HEART with the word AN'A (אנא). This teaches us that the individual who reaches this point of love to God, his supplications will be heard and answered by HaKadosh, Baruch Hu.

Now I ask, what kind of supplications will God hear? Easy engouh! ALL OF THEM.

בכל (BECOL - ALL OF THEM)
ב2 + כ20 + ל30
= **52**

Abraham for example, what he begged for? What was

the biggest dream of his life? What was the real representation of "everything" to him? Well, Issac, his SON.

בן (BEN - SON)
50ן + 2ב
= **52**

To surrender the IETZER HARA - *bad inclination* - and the YETZER HATOV - *good inclination* – in God's hands and will, is one of the greatest secrets, blessed are those who discover how, just like Abraham did.

5- YOUR SOUL (נפשך)

The soul represents the true essence of the human being, it defines the closeness that one can have with the Creator and His desires. As the "heart" represents one's dreams and desires in this earthly life, the soul represents one's being, thoughts, character, devotion and acceptance of God.

According to our sages, this is where the commandments enter, for it is through them that the person demonstrates true devotion to God, and that's not all, it is only through them that an intimate relationship with God can be established, that is, through the miracles that happen in our life due to our obedience to God that we will be able to recognize God irrevocably.

To surrender the soul to God is to follow His commandments and His Torah. Although it seems very complicated for many people, this is what brings what many people seek from God, which are, promises and freedom.

נפשך (NEPHSHEIKHA - YOUR SOUL)
100ך + 350ש + 81פ + 106נ
637 = 6+3+7 = **7**

*Mispar Shemi

הבטחות (HAVTACHAH - PROMISES)
400ת + 6ו + 8ח + 9ט + 2ב + 5ה

430 = 4+3 = **7**

חופש (CHOFESH - FREEDOM)
300ש + 80פ + 6ו + 8ח
394 = 3+9+4 = 16 = 1+6 = **7**

The question now lies on what those PROMISES (הבטחות) would be.

430 has a very expressive value within the Torah as much as within the Jewish people. After 430 years from the time God gave the promise to Abraham concerning his son and his genealogy, a group of people are set free by leaving the land of Egypt, thus officially establishing themselves as a people, so fulfilling the promise.

There is no way, those who follow the Laws of God are automatically brought into the true People of Israel and then, they become heirs of the promises. The moment that a person places God above all else, then all these promises that God has for this person will become real and palpable.

6- ALL YOUR MUCH (מאדך)

This Hebrew commandment can be interpreted in two ways. The "much", according to the sages, represents the material possessions that an individual possesses. To surrender to God through our material possessions is to use them to serve Him by having the awareness that everything belongs to Him and also, not breaking any of the commandments to obtain those goods.

But in addition, the term MEOD (מאד) - *much* - can go a little further, it may also represent an obedience to the mitzvot (commandments) of the Torah, as our sages teach. To surrender the "much" to God is how He makes us strong, an example of this is money itself, the more a person gives to God, the more he receives, the richer he gets, the stronger he gets.

This is easily explained by a passage from the book of Psalms:

צדיק כתמר יפרח כארז בלבנון ישגה
The Tzadik shall flourish like a palm tree, and he shall be strengthened as the cedar of Lebanon.
Psalms 92:13

If we take the last letters of the term "*strengthened as the cedar of Lebanon*" in Hebrew (יפרח כארז בלבנון), we will have the following letters:

ח8 + ז7 + ן50
= **65**

To make this even more fantastic:

מאדך (MEODEKHA - YOUR MUCH)
מ40 + א1 + ד4 + ך20
= **65**

There is no way to overcome God, the more Torah someone lives and the more Tzedakah one does, the stronger God will make him.

HEAR! ACCORDING TO JAMES

SHMA ISRAEL has a twin passage that is found on Deuteronomy 11:13 and in its original language we will have the source of the words of James:

והיה אם **שמע תשמעו** אל מצותי אשר אנכי מצוה אתכם היום לאהבה את יהוה אלהיכם ולעבדו בכל לבבכם ובכל נפשכם
*If you then **listen listening** to the mitzvot I command you this day, loving the Adonai, your Elohim and serving Him with all your heart and soul.*
Deuteronomy 11:13

Interesting what we have here, something lost by the translations, which is the repetition of the word SHMA. In this passage, this term appears twice in a row and this teaches us that we should listen at least twice in comparison with how much we speak. Maybe that's why we have two ears and just one mouth, the Torah already teaches this.

SHMA, not the term, but the commandments found in this passage, represent the apex, the goal of all of those who want to serve the true God.

James, by bringing the "hear" to his teaching, makes total coherence with the *parashah* he is dealing with, the *Parashat K'doshim*, which means "holies". This *parashah*, which he addresses so much, begins as follows:

> *...be holy, for I am Holy, I am Adonai, Your Elohim.*
>
> Leviticus 19:2

A complete lack of understanding about what it would be to be "holy" is very common nowadays. The vast majority of the definitions and teachings I have seen, especially in the Christian milieu, is that for a person to be holy one must be separated from the world. In this way, this individual is indoctrinated within what the Christian faith determines as right and wrong and through this Christian puritanical behavior he is led to believe that he is "holy", such a belief is extremely harmful and millions of people are carried away by it, believing that holiness is associated with church or Christianity is foolishness.

In order to have a definitive understanding of biblical holiness, it is enough for us to look at SHMA itself and what it teaches, for it is it who teaches how to be KADOSH (קדוש) - *holy*.

שמע (SHMA)

70ע + 40מ + 300ש

= **410**

קדוש (KADOSH)

300ש + 6ו + 4ד + 100ק

= **410**

In short, to become holy we must first recognize that God is ONE, not two, not three. We must surrender ourselves to His will, rendering ourselves to whatever He commands. Then we must have a behavioral character as determined by His Word and ultimately follow His Torah.

All that Adonai said, WE WILL DO and then WE WILL HEAR
Exodus 24:7

- DOING comes before the HEARING, who does not follow the Torah, does not hear it, does not have SHMA and so, one does have nothing of the above reported.

IX - SALVATION

Why lay apart all filthiness and superfluity of naughtiness, and receive with meekness the engrafted word, which is able to save your souls.
But be you doers of the word, and not hearers only, deceiving your own selves.
For if any be a hearer of the word, and not a doer, he is like to a man beholding his natural face in a glass:
For he beholds himself, and goes his way, and straightway forgets what manner of man he was.
But whoever looks into the perfect law of liberty, and continues therein, he being not a forgetful hearer, but a doer of the work, this man shall be blessed in his deed.

James 1:21-25

Salvation could be a complicated matter to address, especially within Christian theology, which sees it as the eternal life and a life in heaven. The poor understanding that many leaders have, led many Christians to place their faith in wrong definitions, causing many people to seek God after salvation, which is, subconsciously, an escape from this earthly reality.

One of the most common maxims of Christianity is the "only jesus saves" and therefore a frantic seek for that jesus, which is presented by the church to its members, ended up becoming the sole and true motive of the Christian's existence.

Whether or not this jesus saves will not be the subject of this book, however I would like to address what the Bible says about salvation as well as what both Yeshua and Paul say about it, so that a parallel can be drawn to what James says in his book.

First of all, let's look at God's own assertion regarding salvation:

> *I alone am ADONAI, the ONLY one who can save you.*
> Isaiah 43:11

By His own words, God affirms that He alone is the ONLY one who can save, no other. If Yeshua or any of his followers affirmed that Yeshua is the one who saves, they would become heretics and blasphemers, which would totally take away their authority to teach something, which certainly was not the case.

In fact, it is not Yeshua who actually saves, but he was the one who brought salvation to the Gentile world, it is different from being the author of the action itself. This does not make him of less importantance, since bringing it to all nations is a merit that no man, in all history of mankind, has. Through his death, whether or not the Jews or the critics accept it, the access to the Word of God and to the knowledge about the God of Israel spread throughout the world and it was precisely in this way that he, Yeshua, brought salvation, which is given by the hands of God, the Creator.

This already shows us what that salvation would be, many confuse salvation with eternal life, but they are not the same thing, otherwise they would have the same name or be defined as synonyms in dictionaries. Eternal life is a self-explanatory term, and salvation is a path, a status, which must be attained and maintained so that at the end of one's life, the individual obtains eternal life. That is, salvation is the path to eternal life.

In order for an understanding of what is to be saved to be clearly and fully connected with the Word of God, we can use the passage quoted above as an example. God says He saves, but in this case, not to anyone, he speaks specifically to His people, to the People of Israel. At the time when this promise was given through the mouth of the prophet Isaiah there was no Judaism, no Jews, no church, no Christians, but a people, a people that He chose for Himself. In this way, we understand that the promise of salvation is given only to those who really are part of this people. Again, I do not mean Judaism.

To be part of this people does not mean to be part of a religion, it is not to accept jesus, to baptize, to convert to Judaism, none of this, God Himself is very clear on how the foreigner enters this people:

As for the foreigners Who attach themselves to the LORD,
To minister to Him, And to love the name of the LORD,
To be His servants—All who keep the sabbath and do not
profane it, And who hold fast to My covenant—
I will bring them to My sacred mount And let them rejoice
in My house of prayer. Their burnt offerings and sacrifices
Shall be welcome on My altar; For My House shall
be called A house of prayer for all peoples."

Isaiah 56:6-7

I think this is very clear, God says that in order for the foreigner to enter this people the foreigner must serve Him, love His name and embrace His Torah, for it is precisely the Torah that differentiates the People of God from the other nations and it is it what sets the human being in conformity with what God has determined.

As many Christians have a habit of just looking at the New Testament, let's look at what some authors of these books say about the relationship between Torah and salvation:

<u>Paul</u>:

And as a boy, you know the Holy Scriptures (Torah),
which can give you wisdom and bring you salvation
through the faithfulness of Yeshua.

2 Timothy 3:15

James:

My brethren, what good is it if someone says he has faith, and he does not have the works (Torah)? Can faith save him?

James 2:14

Yeshua:

At that time Yeshua said to his talmidim, truly I say to you, if you are not tzadikim (Hebrew term for those who observe the Torah) greater than the Pharisees and the sages, will not enter the Kingdom of Heaven.

Matthew 5:20

The one sent to the Gentiles, the leader of the messianic community and Yeshua himself are clear in saying that salvation is strongly associated with the Torah. What many do not understand is when Yeshua is called salvation, this occurs in reference to his teachings on Torah, which were fundamental for he to be able to declare himself as the Mashiach Ben Yosef, the one who will bring the revelation of the Torah. In other words, salvation will be given only by God Himself to those who follow the Torah according to its interpretation given by Mashiach. Finally, let's see what Paul says about the relationship between salvation and being part of the People of Israel:

I say then, Have they stumbled that they should fall? God forbid: but rather through their fall salvation is come to the Gentiles, for to provoke them to jealousy.

And if some of the branches be broken off, and you, being a wild olive tree, were grafted in among them, and with them partake of the root and fatness of the olive tree.

Romans 11:11 and 17

The olive tree is the People of Israel itself, Paul affirms that the saved one is the one who will be grafted onto this people. The grafted ones are those who love, serve, and obey Adonai. And how do we know that the olive tree is Israel?

עץ זית (ETZ ZAIT - OLIVE TREE)
400ת + 10י + 7ז + 90ץ + 70ע
577 = 5+7+7 = 19 = 1+9 = **10**

ישראל (ISRAEL)
30ל + 1א + 200ר + 300ש + 10י
541 = 5+4+1 = **10**

Why did Jeremiah thought it was fitting to compare our ancestors with the olive tree? For all liquids mix together, but the olive oil stands separate even when mixed. So also those who belong to Israel should not mix with idolatry.

Shemot Rabbah 36

We can still have an even deeper analysis on this subject:

תורה (TORAH)
5ה + 200ר + 6ו + 400ת
= **8**

יושע (YOSHIA - SALVATION)
70ע + 300ש + 6ו + 10י
= **8**

משיח בן יוסף (MASHIACH BEN YOSEF)
80ף + 60ס + 6ו + 10י + 50ן + 2ב + 8ח + 10י + 300ש + 40מ
= **8**

יהוה (ADONAI)
5ה + 6ו + 5ה + 10י
= **8**

And to make things even more interesting, the Isaiah verse quoted at the beginning of this chapter also has some secrets in the numerical value of the first letter of each word:

אָנֹכִי **א**ָנֹכִי **י**ְהוָה **ו**ְאֵין **מ**ִבַּלְעָדַי **מ**וֹשִׁיעַ

I alone am ADONAI, the ONLY one who can save.

Isaiah 43:11

40מ + 40מ + 6ו + 10י + 1א + 1א

= **8**

Gematria shows how everything is intertwined between salvation, Adonai, Mashiach and the Torah. The verse where God Himself claims to be the only one who can save, also has the same value, nothing is by chance.

This passage in Isaiah also has something else interesting, it brings the terms anokhi (אנכי) - *I* - twice and this is a "strangeness" that we should pay attention to.

The word "I" in Hebrew is ANI (אני), both in the ancient and in the present Hebrew, both in the Tanakh and in the Talmud. This term has always been the same and has always been used the same way, referring to the first person of the singular form.

But in the Torah, when God speaks "I", He does not only use the word ANI (אני), but also the word ANOKHI (אנכי), especially when He speaks that He is God or when He speaks about some of His attributes. This is a term much used by Adonai when He speaks something in the first person singular. There are some cases where others in the Torah also use *anokhi* to speak something, such as Avraham and Moses for example, but this term is known as something almost exclusive to the Creator, because it is the first word that appears in the ten commandments.

ANOKHI - ***I****ehiva* ***KH****etiva* ***N****e'emamim* ***A****mareha* - "It was written, it was given, Your **statements** are faithful."

These statements refer precisely to the commandments of the Torah and imply that the salvation of God comes through the Torah. This is why the word ANOKHI appears twice, for, as seen above, the acronym of ANOKHI can refer to the faithful statements of God that were written and given, the Torah.

The Torah also has a very strong connection with the Hebrew letter BET (ב), which is represented by the number 2, just like the word ANOKHI appears 2 times. In order to be clearer, I will appeal to a great sage, Rabbi Bahya:

> *You should know that the time that the Torah preceded the creation of the universe until the declaration "let there be light" (Gn1:3) was hidden in the word BE-RESHIT (בראשית). The letter BET (ב) in this word alludes to the two thousand years that the Torah preceded the universe.*
>
> Rabbeinu Bahya, Bereshit 1:3

As seen elsewhere in this book, the Torah served as the basis for the creation of all things, it was the "blueprint" that God created to use in His work. According to Rabbi Bahya, the Torah was created two thousand years before the formation of the light as described in Genesis 1:3 and therefore the Torah also has a mystical connection with the letter BET (ב). This is the reason why God used the term ANOKHI two times in Isaiah 43:11.

But in this case, the letter BET (ב) does not represent a Torah by its commandments, but rather a Torah that represents the will of God and the way He works. As we look at the structure of this letter, we will see that it has only one opening on its left side. If we use the cardinal points, we will see that the only "exit" that exists in this letter is toward the west, the "exits" up (north), down (south) and right (east) are closed.

This reveals to us, not in a clear way, how God operates in this world, a constant and patterned form. For a better comprehension, let us look at some passages in the Tanakh:

> *And they heard the voice of Adonai Elohim moving toward the wind of the day, and they hid themselves, the man and his wife, from before the face of Adonai Elohim in the midst of the trees of the garden.*
>
> Genesis 3:8

This is a verse full of mysteries. If we do a literal translation, it will present us a totally meaningless verse when compared to what we are accustomed to read.

Although it sounds like something foolish, we have great mysteries hidden in this passage, unfortunately due to translations we lost the access to them. If we pay attention, we have a completely new idea of what was happening, Adam and Eve did not simply heard the voice of God echoing through the garden, but they actually felt the voice of God moving out of the garden, as if it were withdrawing from that place. Now I ask, is this what the Torah calls as voice, a voice in the literal meaning of the word?

The verb used for movement in Hebrew is LALECHET (ללכת), but in this passage we have the word MIT'HALEKH (מתהלך) being used as the verb for movement, what is unusual. The difference between one and another is that in the case of *mit'halekh*, the space where the motion takes place is limited within a given area. We can thus understand that the movement made by God's "voice" moves in a way as if it were to withdraw from a certain area where it already "dwelt".

Another interesting term is the LERUACH HAYIOM (לרוח היום) – *to the wind of the day* - this term can only mean two things, "to the direction that the sun rises, East" or "to the direction that the sun sets, West." According to the Aramaic translation of Onkelos, this term refers to the place where the sun sets. Then, God's "voice" that moved out from the predetermined place where it already was, moved towards the West. If we look at the Temple of Solomon, the only thing we have left today is just a wall that was part of the Temple, that wall today is important, because, according to the sages, the presence of God is there, for when it left the Temple, it left it towards that wall and it was the last place of the Temple that the *Shekhinah* touched (because the wall was the "border" of the sacred area of the Temple), because of that the wall kept part of His presence. And this wall is just the WEST WALL. In short, the voice is nothing more than the *Shekhinah* of God, His presence, which came out of the garden towards West, just as it did in the Temple.

And they that shall set their tents before the tabernacle, to the east, before the tabernacle of the congregation, to the east side...

Numbers 3: 38a

Then he led me to the door, to the door that faces the east. And, behold, the glory of the God of Israel came from the way of the east; and his voice was as the voice of many waters, and the earth shone for his glory.

Ezekiel 43:1-2

And after that he brought me back to the entrance of the house, and, behold, there came out waters under the threshold of the house, toward the east; for the face of the house looked toward the east, and the waters came from below, from the right side of the house, from the south side of the altar.

Ezekiel 47:1

The Tabernacle and the Temple were facing the East awaiting the coming of the *Shekhinah*, we also have Ezekiel claiming that the *Shekhinah* of God will come from the East. That is why many sages pray to the East, awaiting the return of the *Shekhinah* of God.

So I understand that the movement established by God is from east to west, as well as the earth's motion around the sun.

Adam was thrown out of the garden toward the East. When the people of Israel were taken into Babylonian exile, they also headed east. That is, when we go in the opposite direction of what God determines, we will always end up in exile, thrown out and separated from the blessing. This was all set by God at that very moment after the sin in the garden of Eden, so his "voice" went west and Adam's expulsion went eastward, opposite directions.

This is the greatest representation of the letter BET (ב) and that is why the Torah begins with this letter, for right away it reveals God's movement pattern, the direction that represents the works of His hands nad will.

שכינה (SHEKHINAH)
5ה + 50נ + 10י + 20כ + 300ש
= **7**

ממזרח (FROM THE EAST)
8ח + 200ר + 7ז + 40מ + 40מ
= **7**

God's *Shekhinah* comes from the East towards the west, it is the *Shekhinah's* intention to find a dwelling place, so the letter BET (ב) also means BEIT (בית) - *home* - for when one follows the will of God, metaphorically walking towards west, thus the *Shekhinah* finds rest in that someone, he becomes its "home".

BET (ב) = **2**

שכינה (SHEKHINAH) = **7**

7 (Shekhinah) + 2 (BET) = 9

למערב (TO THE WEST)

2ב + 200ר + 70ע + 40מ + 30ל

= **9**

When man walks in the will of God and receives His *Shekhinah*, he becomes a dwelling place (בית) of the true presence of God, which is represented by the number 9, for mystically it is as if he "walks westward". Then he will be ready to become one with Adonai, which is represented by the letter ALEF (א) of numerical value 1. When both join together, 1 + 9 = 10 and 10 is the number that represents perfection and completeness.

This clarifies two teachings of Yeshua:

Be perfect as God is perfect.

Matthew 5:48

I and the Father are one.

John 10:30

Many made jesus a god because of this statement, but of course, that was not what Yeshua was saying. By saying that he was one with the Father, he was saying that he walked according to the will of God, that he fulfilled the Torah perfectly as God determined and that he lived a sinless life with the merits of being a dwelling place for the *Shekhinah*, thus making him the number 9 and worthy of God's presence, who is the ALEF (א), The number 1.

When they come together they become 10, perfection, and through that idea he states that his followers should also be perfect. That is, by commanding them to be perfect, it is the same as saying to follow the Torah, to follow what God determines and "to walk westward".

By this we understand some things, the Torah does not save, as Yeshua does not save, for only Adonai saves. This salvation comes through a life according to His will, which is revealed to us by the Torah. Those who learn to follow it with FAITH, will be those who will have the merit of salvation and this opportunity was revealed and delivered to the Gentile world through the death of Yeshua, thus making him the bearer of salvation.

This is why James associates salvation with “doers of the word”, which in this case, is the Torah itself.

X - RELIGION AND DA'AT

Those who consider themselves religious and yet do not keep a tight rein on their tongues deceive themselves, and their religion is worthless.
Religion that God our Father accepts as pure and faultless is this: to look after orphans and widows in their distress and to keep oneself from being polluted by the world.

James 1:26-27

One thing is certain, both Judaism and Christianity, despite being two religions, declare that religion "kills". The members of both religions declare that the way they utter their respective faiths is not in a religious way.

Religion means to seek God by one's own strength, it is a human way of attaining divinity through pre-determined dogmas and concepts, which are often not consistent with what the Word of God determines .

What struck me most in these verses is precisely the term "religion" used by the author. This fact does not only occur in English, but also in the Italian, the German and the Dutch versions. How can the Torah, the basis of everything, declare that God creates for Himself a people and not a religion, and then the leader of the messianic movement of his time declares to his hearers that they should care to be religious by seeking a pure and faultless religion? Actually, the way these verses are presented to us is somewhat shocking.

I see James as a well centered person on his teachings, he

is very attached to the moral character in a very direct way and, if his teachings had not been adopted by the church, they would have ended up in the Pirkei Avot due to the strong similarity that the authors of both books possess in their teachings. But furthermore, because of some of the terms he used at the beginning of this chapter, I believe James had a bit of mysticism about what he was talking about, thus allowing a simple and straightforward message to a general public while he is actually sending hidden messages to whom are able to understand them. In order to find those "hidden messages" we must give a "between the lines" look.

James associates religion with four things: "the tongue", "heart", "the orphan" and "the widow". These apparently disconnected terms have a characteristic in common, and in order to find it out, we must first analyze them in James' original language, in Hebrew:

-The tongue – (הלשון)
-Heart - (לבבך)
-The widow and the orphan - (האלמנה והיתום)

Let us begin by using the Gematria on this three terms:

Halashon (הלשון) – the tongue, as in Sl 34:14
50ן + 6ו + 300ש + 30ל + 5ה
= **4**

Al Levavekha (על לבבך) – on your heart, as in Dt 6:6
500ך + 2ב + 2ב + 30ל + 30ל + 70ע
= **4**

* Mispar Gadol

HaAlmanah VeHaYatom (האלמנה והיתום) – the widow and the orphan, as in Ex 22:21
40ם + 6ו + 400ת + 10י + 5ה + 6ו + 5ה + 50נ + 40מ + 30ל + 1א + 5ה

= 4

Through Gematria, all the terms used by James have a mystical connection among themselves, besides representing this "religion" James is speaking of. But that still does not bring us any conclusion, so let's take a closer look at what the sages teach us about "religion", which in Hebrew is DAT (דת).

*For thus said the king. Tell the judgments before all who know the **religion (DAT)** and the Laws of the Torah, because they have **knowledge (DA'AT)**.*

Midrash Lekach Tov, Esther 1:13

According to our sages, there is an association between the word DAT (דת) - *religion* - and the word DA'AT (דעת) - *knowledge*. If we look at both terms in Hebrew, we will see that the only difference between them is the central letter of the word DAAT (דעת), the letter AYIN (ע).

AYIN (ע), besides being the name of a letter is also the Hebrew word for both EYE and FOUNTAIN. Now we can understand more hidden teachings from some Cabbalistics sages:

From the fountain (AYIN), knowledge (DA'AT) is the approach of the Torah. Through the Torah comes knowledge (DA'AT), for the Torah is the revelation of knowledge (DA'AT) and through it the fountain (AYIN) is made. The fountain's (AYIN) waters in the garden that causes the herbs to grow.

Likutey Moharan, Torah 8:7:5

The book *Likutey Moharan* is an extremely mystical book about the Torah, by its difficult words in this passage we can see that the fountain of knowledge is the Torah itself. It is it what waters the garden (us) and causes the herbs to grow (spiritual development) through the wisdom it teaches.

Now we have an indirect definition for the term AYIN (ע), besides being "eye" and "fountain", we can understand it as the Torah itself. Now it is clear to what turns RELIGION (דת)

into KNOWLEDGE (דעת), and it is precisely the letter AYIN (ע), which in this case we can understand it as the Torah. That is, the knowledge and study of the Torah is what differs a real sage, one who knows how to truly connect himself with the Creator, from a religious person, who relies on dogmas, theories and theologies to try to draw near to God.

The text also states that in order for this "fountain" (Torah) - AYIN (ע) - to become knowledge - DA'AT (דעת) - we must seek it through its approach, its study. When the author makes this word pun using words from the same root, he affirms that religion (דת) will become knowledge (דעת) through the fountain (ע). In simpler words, only through constant study of the Torah, religion will become knowledge.

But that makes James's quote even more hazy, for would he be defending a religious life, a life without the Word of God since His Word is what transforms religion into knowledge? Let's look at this AYIN (ע) that turns religion into knowledge one more time and now by using Gematria:

AYIN (עין)
50ן + 10י + 70ע
= **4**

This fountain that turns religion (דת) into knowledge (דעת) has the same numerical value as the other four terms quoted by James, "the tongue", "heart", "the orphan" and "the widow", as seen above.

*Life and death are in the power of the **tongue**, those who use it in the study of the Torah, will eat the fruits of it in the world to come.*
Proverbs 18:21

*And you shall love Adonai, your Elohim with all your **heart**...*
Deuteronomy 6:5a

*You should not mistreat any **widow or orphan**.*
Exodus 22:21

*Learn to do good. If you devote yourself to justice, Respect the rights of the **orphans** and defend the **widow's** cause*
Isaiah 1:17

Through the Gematria's numerical values we see that James is in fact quoting the Torah. In a mystical way, what James is talking about is NOT to be a religious one, but rather through the Torah [by quoting four examples, tongue (= 4), heart (= 4), orphan (= 4) and widow (= 4)] we should turn this religion into knowledge [AYIN (= 4)], thus forsaking to serve human dogmas in order to follow the true will of the Creator.

This makes total sense with what James has been talking about so far. The statement that the author makes when he says that faith without works is dead, is proved in the versed seen above, for these "works" are in reference to Torah, the fountain that gives life to faith. When one does not study the Torah, one cannot practice it, that is, one cannot do those "works" that he speaks so much about, the lack of this knowledge leads one to place faith in other things, such as religious dogmas for example. If faith is placed in dogmas, which are what define religions, something dead, then consequently faith is also dead. The faith to which James refers in his book is not to believe in the existence of a single God and in Mashiach, but a faith that represents obedience.

He sends two messages in a single message, the first one directly teaches ethical and moral values that enhance society and the person as human being; the second, by the usage of these examples (language, heart, widow and orphan) he reveals in a hidden way that knowledge, the one that differentiates the wise man from the religious man, comes only through the constant and practical study of the Torah. The wise men believe and practice the Torah, which is the truth (as we have seen), the religious one practices what was determined by men as being something godly.

He who seeks the Torah is the one who first studies it

then practices it. This is what turns religion into wisdom and knowledge. In Hebrew, the word for study is LILMOD (ללמוד), but there is another unusual one for when a very dedicated study takes place, something like a total dedication on the subject to be learned, this verb is LEAIEN (לעיין) from the same root of the word AYIN (ע).

This reveals to us the dedication we should have on things that concern Adonai in order to not be religious and to receive knowledge and wisdom.

WORLD'S POLLUTION

Religion that God our Father accepts as pure and faultless is this: to look after orphans and widows in their distress and to keep oneself from the ***world's pollution****.*

James 1:27

To conclude, James quotes that all these things are for his hearers to avoid falling into the world's pollution. I think it is interesting to look at this in two ways, the most direct one through the knowledge from rabbinical teachings and in a more mysterious way. The first place where this term appears in the Torah is early in the book of Genesis:

The earth was filled with corruption (pollution) before the face of God, and the land was filled with violence.

Genesis 6:11

Now, in order for us to understand what this corruption is all about, we must look at what the sages teach:

As it is written, "the earth was full of corruption". The school of Rabbi Yishmael teaches: wherever corruption is found, it is a place where the worship of idols happens.

Talmud of Babylon, Tractate Sanhedrin 57a

According to the Jewish mentality, corruption or pollution, deals with worship of idols.

What strikes me most about this is the way James gives this message. As seen above, he cites four examples in relation to knowledge and religion, they are:

Widow - אלמנה
Heart - לב
Orphan - יתום
Tongue - לשון

If we take the first letters of the four words and join them, we will have (אליל) - ALIL - which means IDOL!

The angels of destruction has dominion over those who practice corruption (ALIL), until they are removed from the world in a terrible way.
Kav HaYashar 77:4

CONCLUSION

In two small passages, James leaves a lot of teachings. First of all, he uses four simple Torah's commandments to implicitly tell his listeners that they should not be religious by avoiding to put their faith in dogmas and theologies, but they rather should study the Torah and practice it to obtain true wisdom.

Then he explains the reason why his listeners need to stop being religious and to become wise, this is so that they do not fall into the pollution of the world, that is, to not fall into idolatry, because all religion is idolatrous, especially Christianity.

By connecting both of them, the Torah is the tool to avoid idolatry and this is confirmed by Rashi:

It follows that whoever denies the Torah admits idolatry.
Rashi, Deuteronomy 11:28

And observe (SHAMRU) all things (DEVARIM)
as I have commanded you, forever.

Matthew 28:20

XI - POOR

My brothers, have not the faith of our Lord Jesus Christ,
the Lord of glory, with respect of persons.
For if there come to your assembly a man with a gold ring, in goodly apparel, and there come in also a poor man in vile raiment;
And you have respect to him that wears the gay clothing, and say to him, Sit you here in a good place; and say to the poor, Stand you there, or sit here under my footstool:
Are you not then partial in yourselves, and are become judges of evil thoughts?
Listen, my beloved brothers, Has not God chosen the poor of this world rich in faith, and heirs of the kingdom which he has promised to them that love him?
But you have despised the poor. Do not rich men oppress you, and draw you before the judgment seats?

James 2:1-6

There are two interconnected themes in those teachings of James, the "poor" and the "judgment". The best way to understand this message from a Jewish perspective is to inquire from whence he drew such teachings.

THE POOR

כי יהיה **בך אביון מאחד אחיך** באחד שעריך בארצך אשר יהוה אלהיך נתן לך לא תאמץ את לבבך ולא תקפץ את ידך מאחיך האביון

If, however, there is a ***poor among you, one of your kinsmen*** *inside your gates and inside the land that the LORD your God is giving you, do not harden your heart*

and shut your hand against your needy kinsman.
Deuteronomy 15:7

I particularly believe that this was one of the passages that were in James' mind when he quoted the "poor". The Torah, throughout many passages, is quite insistent on how the poor should be treated.

Unfortunately, due to the translations we have in Western languages, we have lost much of the "messages" that the Torah wants to pass on. An analysis of this passage in its original language, by the terms that appear in it, may bring up an understanding that goes beyond what meets the eyes, understandings that perfectly fit with the whole teaching of James, thus revealing an interpretation that goes further of what is simply taught in his book.

Beikha Ev'Yon (בך אביון) - poor among you

There is a redundancy in this verse, first it is written "*poor among you*" and then it is written "*the poor inside your gates and inside the land*". If the poor are already inside the land, it means that the poor are already among the people, he is already "among you". This shows us that this supposed redundancy has another message.

The Talmud comments on why there are poor people in our midst:

Turnus Rufus, the pervert, asks Rabbi Akiva: If God loves the poor, why does He not help them? Rabbi Akiva replies: He commands us to support the poor, for it is through them and through the charity that we are to give them that we will be saved from the judgment of the Gehinam.
Talmud of Babylon, Tractate Bava Batra 10a

Rabbi Akiva brings up something very insightful, he explains that the existence of the poor is necessary in order for us to be saved from the judgment of the Gehinam by the help and charity that we should give them. The existence of the poor serves as a scale in God's judgment.

With this in mind, as we look again at the term *Beikha Ev'Yon* (בך אביון), which appears at the beginning of the verse, and if we read it as a single word, the meaning is no longer "*poor among you*", but rather "*poor because of you*", "*poor for your sake*" and that changes everything, for that redundancy is not actually a redundancy .

With that, we can understand from the verse that "for our sake, for our good, there will be poor inside our gates and inside our land" The Torah teaches us that there will always be the poor so that through the charity made to them, we may be saved from unfavorable judgment; the existence of the poor has been given to us so that we may become righteous and receive merit before Adonai, something for our own good .

Helping the poor through charity is called in Hebrew TZEDAKAH (צדקה) and is the subject of many discussions among the sages:

Shimon HaTzadik said: on three things the world stands:
in the Torah, in the service to God and in Tzedakah.

Pirkei Avot 1:2

He who does tzedakah has the merit of eternal life.

Talmud of Babylon, Tractate Rosh Hashanah 4a

And when you do tzedakah, that your left hand
does not know what the right does
So that your offering is a secret offering and your Father,
who secretly sees, completes you (rewards).

Matthew 6:3-4

By Gematria:

Beikha Ev'Yon (בך אביון)

50ן + 6ו + 10י + 2ב + 1א + 20ך + 2ב

91 = 9+1 = **10**

TZDAKAHA (צדקה)

5ה + 100ק + 4ד + 90צ

199 = 1+9+9 = 19 = 1+9 = **10**

MeAchad Acheikha (מאחד אחיך) - one of your brothers

The statement "ONE of your brothers" gives an impression that this ONE is a special person, otherwise the passage would simply quote "among your brothers", which is not the case. This ONE that we have here must be understood as a specific person.

> *MeEchad (מאחד), as we have in Genesis 26:10, can always be understood as an allusion to the one we look forward to and is coming, the Mashiach.*
>
> Or HaChaim, Genesis 26

According to the sages, every time the term MeEchad (מאחד) appears in the Torah, it can be understood as an allusion to Mashiach. In the case of the analyzed verse, we have exactly the same term, which leads us to understand that this specific one is precisely Mashiach.

There is something very interesting here, the term used in this passage for poor is EVYON (אביון), which in fact, is not quite the miserable poor, for to that the used word would be ANI (עני). EVYON (אביון), besides meaning someone who does not have money, also means someone who is not attached to money, someone who is not attached to material goods, a simple person of spirit and who does penance.

When Yeshua came, many believe that he was a poor person, an ANI person (עני), but in fact he was not the kind of poor that people think he was, but rather an EVYON (אביון) person, that is, a person without attachment to money, simple in spirit and in penitence, even if he had all the money.

Yeshua not only declared himself to be Mashiach, but he declared to be the facet of Mashiach Ben Yosef. The sages teach us that if the people are worthy, Mashiach will come with diamonds, silver, power and wealth, but if the people are not worthy, Mashiach will come riding on a she-ass according to

Zechariah 9:9 and in the book of Matthew we have the following story

They brought the she-ass and the colt, and Yeshua rode upon it while the others placed their garments and clothes upon them. Then they made the ascent.

Matthew 21:7

Because the people were not worthy of a glorious coming of Mashiach, he came upon a she-ass, he came as an EVYON, a simple person of spirit, without attachment to wealth and with a humble lifestyle and penance. Now we can understand the term MeEchad Acheikha (מאחד אחיך) from this passage:

EVYON (אביון)

50ן + 6ו + 10י + 2ב + 1א

69 = 6+9 = 15 = 1+5 = **6**

MASHIACH BEN YOSEF (משיח בן יוסף)

80ף + 60ס + 6ו + 10י + 50ן + 2ב + 8ח + 10י + 300ש + 40מ

= **566**

MeEchad Acheikha (מאחד אחיך)

500ך + 10י + 8ח + 1א + 4ד + 8ח + 1א + 40מ

= **572**

*Mispar Gadol

As Mashiach Ben Yosef came as an EVYON (אביון), for the people did not deserve a king at that time, so we have:

566 + 6 = 572

This confirms us what the sages teach, this Me'echad (מאחד) refers precisely to Mashiach. Notice this Cabalistic passage from the Book of Zohar:

*Rabbi Eliezer says: When the whole congregation is penitent within the **gates**, it will immediately bring Mashiach to our **lands**, which Adonai has given us. It will be for*

these lands that Mashiach will come cheerfully.
Zohar HaChadash, Parashat Noach 8

Bringing together everything we have seen so far, we can re-read the verse of Deuteronomy 15:7 as follow:

The Tzedakah that has been given to you for your benefit, is so that you are not of hard hearts and you may financially help the brothers for your own sake. This will bring Mashiach within your gates and within your lands, this is what Adonai gives to you.

I see that this passage fits well with what James is teaching, besides referring to the poor and the charity, he opens the chapter two precisely by quoting Yeshua, his Mashiach and this talks about Mashiach.

Another thing that makes me believe that James had this passage in mind is that it deals with attitudes, which are the focus of the teaching of James, attitudes that hasten the coming of Mashiach to dwell among us, as he states:

Be you also patient; establish your hearts: for the coming of the Lord draws near.
James 5:8

A STRANGE PASSAGE

Listen, my beloved brothers, Has not God chosen the poor of this world rich in faith, and heirs of the kingdom which he has promised to them that love him?
James 2:5

This verse has something very strange. We can see financially poor people every day and everywhere we go, what caught my attention here is that among them there are many who have no faith at all and on the other hand, there are many rich people who have an unshakable faith. An understanding by only what meets the eyes of this verse might lead to errors, for it gives an impression that one who possesses money will never have faith.

This verse in James was much used by Rome to enrich at the expense of its followers, preaching that they should be poor to be exalted. However, in this passage, James does not refer to the poor who does not possess goods and money, he refers to the spirit of EVYON (אביון).

Lest we be victims of religious sophistry, the real reason for Mashiach to be EVYON (אביון) is not because he was bound to some kind of poverty, for he was not. EVYON (אביון) is a term that follows the same form of three other words used both for Mashiach and for those who lead a humble spirit life.

EVYON (אביון) = ELYON (עליון) - CHISAYON (חסיון) - HIGAYON (הגיון);
EVYON (poor) = ELEVATED - REFUGE - LOGICAL UNDERSTANDING OF THE LAW;

Now we know why Yeshua was treated as "poor", not because he was financially unlucky, but because the mystical term referred to three expected characteristics of Mashiach. An elevated soul, a refuge to those who seek him and the true revelation and understanding of the Torah, all this has made him an EVYON (אביון).

Following this line of thought, James says the same thing, that those who seek an elevated soul through the will of the Creator, who become refuges for the brothers by extending their hands to help them and people who know and live the true Torah, will be the true rich in faith and heirs of the kingdom.

This makes the person a true TZADIK. Thus Yeshua's words become clearer:

*Ashrei the **EVYONim**, for they shall **inherit** the earth.*
Matthew 5:5

*Ashrei those persecuted for being **tzadikim**, for theirs is the Kingdom of Heaven.*

Matthew 5:10

XII - JUDGMENT

Do not judge lest you be judged.
With this judgment you will be judged and with
this measure you will be measured.
And why do you see the straw in the eye of your neighbor
and not see the beam that is in your eyes?
And how will you speak to your neighbor: wait a little
and I will cast the straw out of your eyes and behold,
the beam is in your eyes ?!
Hypocrite! cast your beam out first of your eyes, and
afterwards cast the straw out of your neighbor's eyes.

Matthew 7:1-5

I believe that none of the teachings of the Sermon on the Mount has been as misunderstood as the teaching about judgment. Many understand this teaching as a prohibition of judgment, but such an idea is not consistent with what Yeshua taught.

We can observe from other passages that judgment is essential to man and that he must always do it, to judge between right and wrong, between light and darkness are attitudes necessary for any human being 's life who decides to follow God. The interesting thing is that even in this case, which deals with the judgment of the neighbor, Yeshua does bring any prohibition, what he does is to encourage the judgment, but rather a personal judgment, an introspective about one's own attitudes and after that judgment, if one is in accordance with the Word of God, then he will have authority to judge his neighbor.

It may seem strange, but that is precisely what he teaches. However, due to our fallen nature, we have the propensity to make bad judgments, both about to ourselves and about our neighbor, we have a tendency to be very light on us and much heavier on our neighbor. And in that case, we'd better be quiet. We must be very careful when we try to remove something from the eyes of our neighbor when we have something much bigger in our eyes. We should have great discernment if we are to have a life according to the Torah.

If we fall into this error, the same will happen to us, because if we are unfair to our neighbor, they will eventually be unfair to us. The individual who feels always wronged before others judgments, must begin to analyze his own self, because this can be the result of his own bad attitudes towards others.

You shall not falsify measures of length, weight, or capacity.
Leviticus 19:35

The beginning for a man to judge is that he judges through his study of the Torah, what comes next is rest.
Mishneh Torah, Studies of the Torah 3:5

Two very interesting things, the first is the Torah itself talking about judgment, it does not prohibit it as Yeshua did not prohibit it, but both require the same condition of not being dishonest and this can be tricky.

The *Mishneh Torah* states that in order for us to judge a little better, this judgment must be elaborated through the study of the Torah, that is, it is the basis that must be taken into account at the time of judgment.

Finally, let's look from where Yeshua took such teaching and interpretation:

לא תשנא את אחיך בלבבך **הוכח תוכיח**
את עמיתך ולא תשא עליו חטא
You shall not hate your kinsfolk in your heart. Reprove your kinsman but incur no guilt because of him.

Leviticus 19:17

In this passage in Leviticus, in Hebrew, the term “reboke” appears twice in succession. According to Rabbi Baal Shem Tov, this repetition is due to how the person should approach his brother when judging him, the first refers to own self and the second to the neighbor. I believe that is the exactly same interpretation of Yeshua.

CONCLUSION

James teaches behavioral attitudes, but with well-defined intrinsic ideas in his words. First of all, he talks about the judgment, in this case, by using as an example something very common in the whole society, to judge someone by the appearance or by the social position that the person has.

He at no time forbids or condemns the judgment itself, but he reproves when judgment is made through appearance. As we have seen above, judgment can only be done when we must reprove abhorrent acts that one in our midst is practicing and this judgment can only be done through the Torah.

So James brings the "poor" as an example, he uses word puns to show that the disadvantaged one on this earth will be spiritually favored. But this understanding is somewhat prejudiced, for it excludes those who are not poor from being spiritually elevated.

What James presents to us is the "poor in spirit", the EVYON, who regardless of the social position on this earth, everyone can become an EVYON.

The basis of James's teaching is the Torah, and the only way to reach his counsel is through the Torah.

XIII - TO LOVE THE NEIGHBOR

If you fulfill the royal law according to the scripture, You shall love your neighbor as yourself, you do well:

James 2:8

Classical rabbinical affirmation. This is not only quoted by James, but also by Yeshua and Paul. This statement is another thing that served as basis for Christian theology to move Christians even further away from the Bible, let's take a look at the words of Yeshua and Paul to understand James:

For all the law is fulfilled in one word, even in this; You shall love your neighbor as yourself.

Galatians 5:14

The second is this, you shall love your neighbor as yourself.

Matthew 22:39

The Torah has a total of 613 commandments, these commandments are not applicable to every single person. There are commandments only for men, others only for women, others for kings, priests, judges, and so on. With the exception of the commandments concerning ethics, sexual morality and character, all commandments fit into certain groups and are not generally applicable.

The commandments of the Torah can be divided into two parts in two different ways. The first division is between the positive commandments and the negative commandments, i.e. the ones you MUST do and those you SHOULD NOT do.

There are 365 negative commandments, which cannot be practiced, as if we should say a "no" per day for an entire year. The positives has a total of 248 commandments, which require care and attention to their observance. 248 is also the total number of bones and organs that the human body possesses, something like if the whole body were willing to give a "yes" to God.

The second division is made according to the type of commandment, which may be related to a relationship "man x God" or "man x man". In the first group we find the commandments concerning Shabbat, feasts, kashrut and so on. In the second we have the commandments concerning sexual immorality, murder, robbery and so on. This division is represented by the very tablets of the Law given by God to Moses on Mount Sinai, in the first tablet we have the commandments referring to "man x God" and in the second, the commandments referring "man x man".

James does not refer to a feeling here, for to love strangers is an unnatural thing to the human being, but love, in this case, refers to attitudes towards others and such attitudes are defined only by the Torah. Let's see where he got this concept from:

You shall not take vengeance or bear a grudge against your countrymen. Love your fellow as yourself: I am the LORD.

Leviticus 19:18

Rabbi Akiva says: To love one's neighbor is the highest principle of the Torah.

Talmud of Jerusalem, Tractate Nedarim 30b

Every morning, before your prayers, commit yourself to love your neighbor as yourself. Then your prayers will be accepted and bear fruit.

Rabbi Yitzchak Luria

Do you hear what they say in the heavenly academy? That loving your neighbor means loving the wicked as you love the righteous.

Maguid of Mezeritch

The true love of one's neighbor is the summit of the observance of Torah's commandments referring to "man x man", only in this way can one achieve such a feat.

XIV - SNOW BALL

For whoever shall keep the whole law, and yet offend in one point, he is guilty of all. For he that said, Do not commit adultery, said also, Do not kill. Now if you commit no adultery, yet if you kill, you are become a transgressor of the law.

James 2:10-11

These two passages are sources of great Christian dogmas. The misinterpretation of these words led many to think that it is better not to keep the Law at all rather becoming guilty for breaking the whole Law, for many believe that it is impossible to fulfill it in a correct way.

There are many things we should keep in mind regarding this line of thinking. First, I believe that it is a little unfair on the part of a God who declares Himself a good God to deliver a law that is impossible to observe to the people He calls His own, that would give the impression of a sadistic god and who takes pleasure in punishing, which It's not the case.

Second thing to take into consideration refers to the difficulty that the Torah represents for some people. It is well known that the Torah is the perfect will of God and it is that which reveals what is right and what is wrong, so when some law presents a certain difficulty to some person, it reveals that this person has something in his life that must be fixed, that is, a habit or a practice that is not conforming to God's will. The big problem is the difficulty that the human being has when it comes to a change of habit, in this case, the Torah really may be difficult. Serving the true God is not for everyone.

Finally, the idea of *"being guilty for offending in one point"* fits only those who observe the law is a misleading mistake, for everyone who doesn't observe it, is also guilty; otherwise it would be like saying that only those who serve God commit sin and those who do not serve Him, because they do not know what sin is, do not commit it. Such a belief is absurd!

Both the observant and the one who does not know what Torah is, when they do something that is defined as sin, they sin. It may seem unfair, but the wages that sin brings come to those who serve God as well as to those who have never heard of Him. Something to think about.

This is a concept that must be removed from one's minds in order to understand what James is stating in these passages. The first time I read them, although translations make things a bit more hazy, it is possible to see what James is talking about. He uses a typical rabbinical explanation of something typical rabbinic, something known as Mitzvot Kalot (light commandments) and Mitzvot HaMurot (heavy or serious commandments), and this becomes clear when he makes comparisons between commandments.

THE MITZVOT

Among the 613 mitzvot (commandments) in the Torah, there are those that are considered "serious" for they have harmful consequences for the one who breaks it and those that are considered "light", because they deal with sporadic observances that do not inflict any apparent direct loss.

In order for us to have a better idea, let's look at two examples in the Torah, the first a Mitzvah Kalah (light commandment) and the second a Mitzvah Murah (heavy commandment):

If, along the road, you chance upon a bird's nest, in any tree or on the ground, with fledglings or eggs and the mother sitting over the fledglings or on the eggs, do not take the mother together with her young.

Let the mother go, and take only the young, in order that you may fare well and have a long life.
Deuteronomy 22:6-7

Honor your father and your mother, that you may long endure on the land that the LORD your God is assigning to you.
Exodus 20:12

Here we have two examples of what the rabbis classify as "light commandment" and "heavy commandment". The command to not remove the young when the mother is nearby is considered a light commandment, however honoring father and mother is something that demands much more attention from everyone, because everyone has a father and a mother, and many people never in life will have the opportunity to remove some animal from its mother, which makes this command relative or improbable to a certain extent. The interesting thing is that both deal with kinship and prolongation of days on earth.

The problem that can occur here is the contempt of light commandment, which is very common in all the communities that observe the Torah, giving more importance in what they call heavy ones. In fact, this distinction, heavy and light, was made by the rabbis not to disparage the lights but to overrate the heavy ones, requiring special attention to them.

This teaching of James is very common even today in all Yeshivot around the world, there is a great deal of concern on the part of the rabbis, especially with the seemingly light commandments, for it is through them that the heavy ones are broken. If we look at the prohibition of murder, a clearly heavy commandment that must be observed by everyone at all costs, and if we compare it with the one that forbids the hatred of the neighbor, we shall see that they are both the same:

You shall not take vengeance or bear a grudge against your countrymen. Love your fellow as yourself: I am the LORD.

Leviticus 19:18

Although this commandment stress a very common habit among many people, this is a commandment that if not properly observed, it might end up becoming something bigger than one could think, as we can see as follow:

Thou shalt not kill: with the hand; or with the tongue, or falsely testimony is the same as committing murder; or if you gossip; or if you gives a bad advice; or if you discover a secret that can save someone and do not share it, you're like a killer.

Ibn Ezra, Exodus 20:13

This commentary from the great Rabbi Ibn Ezra deals precisely with this, he cites mundane things, such as gossip, or evil-speaking, which are day-to-day things that many people do and then he compares them to the sin of murder itself. For gossip can generate anger, anger can generate hatred and hatred can lead to murder. So what we see here is when a light or a small commandment is broken, it can and it will lead one to break more serious commandments sometime in the future.

He who violates a light commandment will inevitably violate a heavy one; he who violates "love your brother as yourself" (Leviticus 19:18), will surely violate "You must not hate your brother in your heart (Leviticus 19:17)" and "You shall not take vengeance nor bear hatred" (Leviticus 25 : 35) "and also" He shall abide with you (Leviticus 25:35)", and in the end he shall shed blood.

Sifrei Devarim, Shoftim 187

We must be very careful, the bloodshed begins with a simple gossip, adultery begins with a simple look, revenge begins with a simple mockery, robbery begins with a simple bad judgment, disgrace begins with a simple disrespect.

Sexual immorality exists on many levels, from a look of desire to the unlawful relationship with a virgin or a widow.

Rabbi Saadia Gaon, Deuteronomy 23

And he said unto them, you hearken to the words of
the ancients, you shall not commit adultery.
And I say unto you that whosoever looks upon a woman, and
desires her, yet commits adultery with her in the heart.
Matthew 5:27-28

The message of James is not a counsel not to observe the Law, for if it were the case, he would be a heretic. His message is to take care of God's commandments, for what good is not killing when you sleep with your neighbor's wife? Or what's the use of not killing when you talk evil about your neighbor? Or what good is not stealing when you act with greed? Let no one brag about what he has already observed, but let us seek to improve upon the commandments that are difficult for us, for they point out to failures in our behaviors that need to be changed and differently of what many people think about this verse, James is actually warning that one must obey God with care, this is the true message of James.

You shall faithfully observe My laws: I the LORD make you holy.
Leviticus 20:8

Rabbi Said: which is the straight path that a man should choose
for himself? One which is an honor to the person adopting it,
and [on account of which] honor [accrues] to him from others.
And be careful with a light commandment as with a grave
one, for you did know not the reward for the fulfillment of the
commandments. Also, reckon the loss [that may be sustained
through the fulfillment] of a commandment against the reward
[accruing] thereby, and the gain [that may be obtained through
the committing] of a transgression against the loss [entailed]
thereby. Apply your mind to three things and you will not come
into the clutches of sin: Know what there is above you: an eye that
sees, an ear that hears, and all your deeds are written in a book.
Pirkei Avot 2:1

XV - LAW OF LIBERTY?

So speak you, and so do, as they that shall be judged by the law of liberty.

James 2:12

Among various teachings and interpretations I read concerning this passage and concerning this so called "law of liberty", all presented the same conclusions. For many Christian theologians and leaders, the "law of liberty" is the "law of christ", which was given to the Christian in order for them to have a life of freedom.

Such "liberty" is usually presented as a liberty from the law of Moses, thus giving the Christian a false freedom to eat whatever one wants, to celebrate whatever one wants, to observe whatever day one wants and to behave as one wishes, as long as those behaviors are in accordance with the "law of christ" and with the church's rules of puritanism. This "law of christ" are men made rules created from misinterpretations of Paul's teachings. This "liberty" tought by the church is nothing more than debauchery and an excuse for those who have no interest in changing their habits.

In order for us to detach this poor and cheap teaching from the words of James, we must first understand what the term "liberty" represents within the Jewish mentality and so we can comprehend what this "law of liberty" truly is.

When a Jew comes across the word "liberty", the first thing that comes to his mind is PESSACH, the Jewish Passover, which represents the departure of the Hebrew people from Egypt, a departure from the house of slavery. The Passover, although is the celebration of the crossing of the sea of reed toward the promised land, it represents much more than this. The true liberty that Pessach represents goes far beyond physical slavery; and its process begins way before the sea crossing itself. Liberty starts at the moment that Moses goes to Pharaoh, going through the ten plagues that strike Egypt, the people's exit from that land and it ends when they arrive at the foot of Mount Sinai, a time known as the feast of Shavuot. This appointed time celebrates the delivery of the Torah to the People of Israel. All this period can be considered as "the liberty of Pessach".

A true understanding of liberty is not possible without first an analysis of what each of those moments represent. We shall see one by one.

THE TEN PLAGUES (עשר מכות)

"The ten plagues" in Hebrew is ESER MAKOT (עשר מכות) - *lit. The ten strokes* - these events have very deep andmystical meanings behind each one of them and they are earthly representations on how God works for His people.

<u>1- DAM (דם) - BLOOD</u>

The first plague that God sends over Egypt "strikes" what the Egyptians had as their main god, the god that represented life for them, the Nile River.

As we read the book of Genesis, the moment that God appears to Moses in the burning bush, He presents Himself to Moses as follows:

> *...Thus shall you say to the Israelites, EHYE (אהיה) has sent me to you.*
>
> Exodus 3:14b

God presents Himself as EHYE (אהיה), which in a direct

translation means "I WILL BE".

DAM (דם) - BLOOD
40ם + 4ד
= **44**

EHYE (אהיה)
Aleph, alef-hei, alef-hei-yud, alef-hei-yud-hei:
1 + (1 + 5) + (1 + 5 + 10) + (1 + 5 + 10 + 5) = **44.**

The first plague represents the liberty from false gods, idolatry and the recognition of the God of Israel as the one and the true God. The liberty that EHYE (אהיה) represents is that HE WILL BE THE ONLY GOD.

Thou shalt have no other gods besides me.
Exodus 20:3

<u>2- TZFARDEA (צפרדע) - FROG</u>

The second plague strikes the understanding and wisdom of the Egyptian people, that is, it affected their common sense, leaving them with fear, for they lost their voice of reason and their ability to define this earthly reality.

This is shown to us by the word FROG, which in Hebrew is TZFARDEA (צפרדע), this Hebrew word is the junction of two other words, TZIPOR (ציפור) - *bird* - and DEAH (דע) - *understanding* - showing us that the "understanding" of Egyptians left as a bird when it flies away.

Another proof can be seen by Gematria:

TZFARDEA (צפרדע) - FROG
70ע + 4ד + 200ר + 80פ + 90צ
= **444**

Now we compare it to the word "judgment or discernment" which is the ability to judge something by what one sees or hears, that is, one's perception of the world:

HAMISPATEI (המשפטי) – JUDGMENT, DISCERNMENT
10י + 9ט + 80פ + 300ש + 40מ + 5ה
= **444**

This plague represents the liberty that God gives concerning the understanding, that is, through it one does not become slave of dogmas and lies of religions and sects. It is a liberty from destruction.

My people are destroyed due to the lack of understanding...
Hosea 4:6a

3- KINIM (כינים) - PARASITES

According to the sages, the third plague that turned Egypt's dust into parasites reflects the symptoms of insubordination. The ability to surrender one's ego to a greater truth is the foundation for any spiritual growth, as well as the ability to confess sin or a wrong doing.

The insubordination that the Egyptians possessed is self-destructive and reduces the essence of life to zero, for just as the parasite sucks blood, this kind of behavior and thought suck the essence of the soul, making the human being a mere animal and nothing more than that.

The liberty of insubordination comes only from those who have the true understanding given by God.

4- AROV (ערוב) - WILD BEAST

The word for "wild beast" in Hebrew is AROV (ערוב), but in the Torah account of this plague, this word appears in an unusual way as (ערב) without the Hebrew letter VAV (ו).

Thus, the word AROV (ערוב) written as found in the Torah (ערב) can also be read as AREV (ערב), which may mean a kind of a "trap".

A liberty that refers to "traps" is what we call in English "deliverance". Have you ever heard of someone who was going to catch a plane, but for some reason that person misses the flight and then he hears on the news that the plane crashed?

I remember a story of a man who worked at the World Trade Center in New York and on September 11, 2001, that person got stuck in traffic like never before and was late to get to work, when he got there, he saw the tower where his office was, in collapse.

What God did by this plague was to leave the Egyptian people to their own fate, it represented the total removal of divine care. This is a liberty that only those who truly serve the Creator possess, is a peace of mind that comes through the assurance of God's care.

AROV (ערב) - *wild beasts* - are presented to us in the Torah (Ex 8:20) as HAAROV K'VAD (הערב כבד) - *the heavy wild beast* - but as seem before, this can also be read as HAAREV K'VAD (הערב כבד) - *the serious trap* - and a "serious trap" represents the opposite of G'ulah (גאולה) - *deliverance*, just as the number 9 is the opposite of the number 6:

HAAREV K'VAD (הערב כבד)

4ד + 2ב + 20כ + 2ב + 200ר + 70ע + 5ה

= **6**

G'ULAH (גאולה)

5ה + 30ל + 6ו + 1א + 3ג

= **9**

...and I will deliver you from wild beasts
and your land from the sword.

Leviticus 26:6b

<u>5- DEVER (דבר) - PLAGUES</u>

The root of this word already shows its spiritual meaning, the letters (ד-ב-ר) are also used to form words like DABAR (דבר) - *words* - DAVAR (דבר) - *thing* - and DEVARIM (דברים) - *things*. However, DEVARIM, besides meaning "things", is also the name of the last book of the Torah, the book of Deuteronomy.

Instead of explaining the association and meaning of

this term, I will let Yeshua himself do it:

> *Again he told them: Everyone who listens to these things (Devarim Torah) and does them is similar to the man who builds the house on the top of a rock.*
> *The rain falls on it and the wind hits it and it does not fall, because its foundation is the rock.*
> *And all who hear "these things" (Eile HaDevarim) and do not do them is similar to the man who is foolish, who builds a house on the sand.*
> *The rains fall and the flood comes and the house falls apart with a great fall.*
> *While Yeshua was saying these words (Devarim), all the people were impressed with his conduct.*
> *For he was preaching before the people with great power, and not as the sages.*
>
> Matthew 7: 24-29

Although a direct translation of this word is valid, it ends up taking away much of the essence of the meaning behind the word DEVARIM. Yeshua says that he who hears these "things" or "words" and does them, is like the man who builds the house on the rock and he who hears these "things" or "words" and does not do them, is like the man who builds the house on the sand. A very profound, but to a certain extent relative, teaching, for I ask, what are these "things"? What are these "words"? One can answer that these "things" and "words" are the teachings of Yeshua and I can even agree with that, but then I ask again, what teachings? And we would enter into a looping, for each answer would generate a new question, unless we can get to the source of his teaching.

DEVARIM means much more than "things" or "words," DEVARIM is the name of the last book of the Torah, the book of Deuteronomy, the book that is the repetition of all the Laws of God, the "grand summary" of what the Creator wants from His people. Perhaps, the "things" and "words" that Yeshua says that we should hear and do are just those that are found in the book of Deuteronomy.

To sum up, anyone who engages in Torah does not fall into theological fallacies (DABAR). A liberty from human dogmas.

6- SHCHIN (שחין) - SKIN DISEASES

In Exodus 9:9, where the account of the sixth plague begins, we have the term SHCHIN (שחין) and not HASHCHIN (השחין). Since the word appears without the article, this reveals us that despite being skin diseases, they were several types of diseases that affect the skin and not a specific one.

This plague shows that, although affecting only the dermis, there are several different types of disease. This reminded me of a small story that happened in Eastern Europe mid-sixteenth century, where a village was plagued by a disease that ended up causing the death of many people who lived there. The interesting thing about this story is that no one from the large Jewish community who lived in this village was affected by any disease from this plague.

As the story unfolds, a Gentile doctor discovers that the reason the Jews were not affected was because they did not mix wool with flax, a command known as *shaatnez*, as ordained in Leviticus 19:19.

Because of the obedience to God that these people possessed, they were freed from diseases and plagues, even from those that plagued everyone around them. The liberty we have here is that of plagues, diseases, and evils that affect physical bodies.

What happened in that village and how that liberty came, is as follows:

SHCHIN (שחין)
50ן + 10י + 8ח + 300ש
= **368**

One of the common words for the Torah is "the five of

fives (חמישי חמישים)" that is, CHAMISHEI chamishim.

CHAMISHEI (חמישי)
10י + 300ש + 10י + 40מ + 8ח
= **368**

The connection that obedience to Torah and liberty from diseases and plagues possesses is said by God Himself in the books of Leviticus and Deuteronomy:

if you reject My laws and spurn My rules, so that you do not observe all My commandments and you break My covenant, I in turn will do this to you: I will wreak misery upon you—consumption and fever, which cause the eyes to pine and the body to languish; you shall sow your seed to no purpose, for your enemies shall eat it.

Leviticus 26:15-16

7- BARAD (ברד) - HAIL

The way the Torah relates this plague is very interesting, as our sages say, "the way that the hail fell on the land of Egypt was as never seen before and will never be seen again". Let's see:

The hail was very heavy—flaming fire in the midst of the hail—such as had not fallen on the land of Egypt since it had become a nation.

Exodus 9:24

The Torah states that in the midst of thehail rain there there was a flaming fire. Some translations bring this term as "thunder" or "lightning", but the word we have in the Torah is ESH (אש) - *fire* - and not thunder.

This reveals the absolute power the Creator has over His creation, where everything does His will, for how can it be possible for a fire to blaze in the midst of a rain? The *midrash Shemot Rabbah* makes the same comment on this fact:

Fire in the midst of hail - a miracle within the miracle,

for hail is water. But to accomplish the will of the Creator, fire and water made peace.

Shemot Rabbah 12:4

This commentary is fantastic, as well as making a miracle within a miracle, God shows His superiority over the natural elements and this teaches us deep things. God makes two opposite things to coexisting, two things, when in contact, cancel each other, but at that moment both worked together, it is as if God brought peace to the essences of these two elements.

We can imagine water and fire as two enemies, where one is found, the another cannot exist. When Elohim brings both together, it is as if He has pacified both enemies. With this we can understand the liberty that this plague represents, the liberty from enemies, the liberty from the sword to cross our lands, crimes, violence, wars and so on.

HaSHLOMI (השלומי) - PEACEFUL

10י + 40מ + 6ו + 30ל + 300ש + 5ה

= **391**

ESH MAYIM (אש מים) - FIRE WATER

40ם + 10י + 40מ + 300ש + 1א

= **391**

This proves how Elohim, besides being the Creator, is the one who has the supreme will and control. Elohim is the name that represents all God's attributes condensed, power, creation, goodness, justice, mercy and so on. Unlike the Tetragrammatons, which represents the essence of the true God, Elohim shows his absolute power and control, only He is capable of such a feat and we can prove it in a simple way:

BARAD (ברד) - HAIL

ב2 + ר200 + ד4

= **206**

ELOHIM (אלהים) - calculated in progressive form + numbers of letters of His name:

א1 + (א1 + ל30) + (א1 + ל30 + ה5) + (א1 + ל30 +
ה5 + י10) + (א1 + ל30 + ה5 + י10 + ם40)

= **200**

5 letters in the name ELOHIM = 200 + 5 = **205**
More 1 KOLEL (a dot representing the letter O) = 205 + 1

אלהים =206

Adonai will make the enemies who attack you to run...
Deuteronomy 28:8a

<u>8- ARBEH (ארבה) - LOCUST</u>

The locusts that came upon Egypt are of an impure specie, a non-kasher specie, which represents a harsh judgment on God's part.

But we must look at other thing, beginning with the way the Torah relates this plague:

...when morning (בוקר) came, the west wind brought the locusts.
Exodus 10:13

By the rabbinic exegesis of the Torah, one can make a connection between two passages when both have the same term, in this case, "the coming of the morning".

...When the morning (בוקר) comes, the LORD will make known who is His and who is holy, and will grant him access to Him.
Numbers 16:5b

In this passage in Numbers, which uses the term BOKER (בוקר) - *morning* - just as we saw in the passage about the locust plague, we see a warning that Moses is giving to Korach about a disaster that was about to happen to him.

...When morning (בוקר) comes, comes our deliverance from disaster.

Isaiah 33:2

In a second example, we have the same term again being used in reference to disaster, which leads us to understand that the symbolism of this pest is the release of disasters.

How many earthquakes happen in Israel? Or volcanoes erupting? Or hurricanes, tornadoes, cyclones, frosts, floods? There are none, the people of the Torah, the land of the chosen People, live in liberty from these misfortunes that decimate many lives.

9- CHOSHECH (חושך) - DARKNESS

This is the only plague that should not be understood literally, for it affected the minds of the Egyptians, as if they had had a mental "blackout".

Has anyone ever asked how could a nation that has just came out of slavery possess a huge amount of gold, an amount capable of building a massive gold calf and various items of the tabernacle? Where did this gold come from? How can slaves possess such a quantity of riches?

Our sages tell us that this darkness which did not allow the Egyptians to see each other for three days refers to a mental confusion that they had, as if it were a "blackout" in their common sense. The Torah also tells us that this darkness had a unique feature, it was palpable, which makes a visualization of what was happening at that moment even more difficult, because this "palpable darkness" has a mystical meaning behind it.

ויאמר יהוה אל משה נטה ידך על השמים ויהי חשך

על ארץ מצרים **וימש חשך**

Adonai said to Moses, raise your hands toward the

sky so that there is darkness all over the land of Egypt, ***a darkness that can be touched****.*

Exodus 10:21

VeYAMESH CHOSHEKH (וימש חשך) - A DARKNESS THAT CAN BE TOUCHED.

20ך + 300ש + 8ח + 300ש + 40מ + 10י + 6ו

= **9**

ZAHAR VeKESEF (זהב וכסף) - SILVER AND GOLD

80ף + 60ס + 20כ + 6ו + 2ב + 5ה + 7ז

= **9**

If we combine these two ideas, we will see that this darkness caused a mental blackout in the Egyptians, and this made them to give all the gold and silver they possessed for the children of Israel. The gold that the people came out of the Egypt was the gold of the Egyptians, which were given to them at the time of the ninth plague, and this was the "light" that could be seen in each one's house, the gold's glow.

...all the children of Israel had the ***light*** *in their houses.*

Exodus 10:24b

OHR (האור) - THE LIGHT

200ר + 6ו + 1א + 5ה

212 = 2+1+2 = **5**

ZAHAV (זהב) - GOLD

2ב + 5ה + 7ז

14 = 1+4 = **5**

The ninth plague is linked to material goods, this teaches us that God liberates from the yoke of the love of money, He frees those who serve Him from the financial dependence of the wicked; this is a liberty from the concern of "what shall I eat tomorrow?" God, when He brings this liberty, will worry in the place of the one who serves Him.

Look at the birds in the sky, they do not plant, they do not harvest (from the ground) nor gather in barns, but your exalted Father who feeds them. Are not you more important than they?

Matthew 6:26

10- BECHOR (בכור) - FIRSTBORN

The "firstborn" is a symbology for the early instincts and motives of the soul that is "hidden" beneath the surface of human consciousness. This dimension of personality is naturally more complicated to enter, for the person himself does not know that it exists within himself.

Eternal death, which is a death represented in the spiritual spheres, begins within the human unconsciousness, the person who forms himself and acts through his own perception of life or human beliefs, ends up developing a subconscious already connected with the eternal death. This is a very long and complicated subject and will be for an upcoming study.

But what we can see here is the liberty resulting from all the previous ones, the liberty that guarantees the merit to enter into the world to come, the eternal life.

PESSACH (פסח)

The moment that best represents Pessach is the crossing of the sea of reeds by the Hebrew people. This crossing, as reported by the Torah and commonly known by many people, is the greatest representation of liberty in the Jewish mentality.

It is the liberty from the yoke of men, from bondage, from wiping, from sorrow, from physical and emotional pain, from humiliation and from the destruction of dreams. But we must be careful here, for I ask, how could we consider this any kind of liberty if, in fact, the people didn't want to leave Egypt? How could it be considered liberty if the motive that made them leave was because Pharaoh expelled them? How could it be liberty since they still had Egypt in their hearts, for they wanted to go back several times? This is a very strange kind of liberty.

The *Zohar HaKadosh* has a very profound teaching about everything that happened during Pessach. It says that Egypt was a representation of the carnal desire, despite the physical suffering, all the immoralities practiced in those lands was the main reason that led the people to be strongly attached to Egypt.

The Egyptians represent the Satanic forces operating in this world, the influence they exerted on the Hebrew people was strong enough to confuse them of what was right and what was wrong. This liberty represented by Pessach is not a freedom of a slave who becomes a free man, but rather it represents a liberty from the chains that slaves man to the desires of the flesh, that is, Pessach represents the most difficult liberty to obtain, the liberty of denying our selves, our desires and our instincts in the name of Heaven.

What we should pay more attention to is how this liberty reached the Hebrew people. Certainly it was not they who sought it, for as much as they wanted to be free from physical slavery, the pleasures that this place made available to them was enough to settle them down there, quietly. With a careful read, we see throughout the story, that the people wasn't seeking this liberty, we see no Hebrew trying to scape from the bondage he was under. Actually this liberty that God gave to His people, started with Him and by Him. It is He who comes after Moses, it is He who plans all redemption, it is He who makes everything happen. He is the one who came after His people and not the otherwise, and this is the most fantastic thing about Pessach.

To be free from the lust of the flesh is a very complicated matter, the example that Pessach brings us clearly shows that such a feat is impossible for the human being, this is only accomplished by those who had been chosen by God, for He is the only one capable to do so. God Himself comes after the one He choses, He sets free the one He choses, He makes the one He choses a great man to represent His Name and HE IS THE ONE WHO WILL COME AFTER OF HIS PEOPLE, not otherwise.

May it be all of us!

OMER (עומר)

The Omer is the time between the crossing of the sea of reeds on Passover to the delivery of the Torah on Mount Sinai, when the feast of Shavuot is celebrated. This is an interim of 49 days, or 7 weeks, representing 1/7 of the year.

But as we are talking about liberty, we must take a different approach to this time of year. By using another form of Gematria's calculation we shall have a numerical value for the word OMER (עומר) of 359.

This is the same value of a well known name in the Christian milieu:

Hasatan (שטן)
50ן + 9ט + 300ש
= **359**

The Omer is the time when the spark within each one from the House of Israel is strengthened and it helps them to overcome the works of satan. The liberty that the 49 days between the Passover and the delivery of the Torah represents is the freedom from the hands of the enemy and in order to do so, the "journey" MUST end at the foot of Mount Sinai, where the Torah was given, for by the Torah all the above are kept .

THE LIBERTY

The Word of God, the Torah, is the apex of the representation of the liberty that only God can give to someone and such liberty can only be achieved through the Torah. A life according to the Word of God, brings us:

-Liberty from idolatry
-Liberty from ignorance and destruction
-Liberty from insubmission
-Liberty from traps - deliverance
-Liberty from religions and human dogmas
-Liberty from disease
-Liberty from violence and war
-Liberty from disasters
-Liberty from financial problems
-Liberty from eternal death
-Liberty from immorality and lust
-Liberty from satan's hands

The Liberty that comes from God, through His Law, is composed of twelve types of liberties, as explained above. For man to receive LIBERTY (חופש) he must follow these twelve steps (**12 -> 1 + 2 = 3**).

HACHOFESH (החופש) – THE LIBERTY
300ש + 80פ + 6ו + 8ח + 5ה
= **3**

This is the "law of liberty" of James, the Torah and not the Christian "law of christ".

TORAT ELOHIM (תורת אלהים) - Torah of Elohim
40ם + 10י + 5ה + 30ל + 1א + 400ת + 200ר + 6ו + 400ת
1092 = 1+9+2 = **3**

But whoever looks into the perfect ***TORAH*** *and continues therein, he being not a forgetful hearer, but a doer of the work, this man shall be blessed in his deed.*

James 1:25

XVI - MERCY

*For he shall have judgment without **mercy**, that has showed no mercy; and **mercy** rejoices against judgment.*

James 2:13

James now brings a very common term, "mercy", though it is a well-understood term, the way to get it is somewhat confusing, for many believe that it something that simply comes.

And he said, "O LORD, God of my master Abraham, grant me kindness (CHESSED) this day, and deal graciously with my master Abraham.

Genesis 24:12

Make thy face to shine upon thy servant; save me for your mercies (CHESSED).

Psalm 31:16

The Hebrew word for grace is CHESSED (חסד). If we look at these two passages, one from the Torah and another from the Tanakh, we shall see that the term CHESSED appears in both, but with different translations, as kindness and mercy.

James was not a Christian theologian, but rather an orthodox Jew, an extreme connoisseur of the Torah and the Talmud. For that fact, let's look at more sources from James' background.

Rav Ben Yehuda in the name of Rav Pinchas says: it is 613 mitzvot (commandments) of Hashem, His holy commandments are basically two laws. 365 are negative and by performing them, one shall sin before the One Who Is, Blessed Be He, and thus one will need His CHESSED (Mercy). Other 257 mitzvot (commandments) are positive and by performing them, one shall have His CHESSED (goodness), where one shall have the favor of the One Who Is, Blessed Be He, so we may live the glory of Adonai upon the Earth.

Talmud of Babylon, Tractate Brakhot 2b

According to the sages, the Talmud and the Tanakh, grace can be understood as two things, the goodness of God and the mercy of God, both are gratuitous attributes of God and certainly no man deserves them.

At the same time that the word CHESSED in Hebrew is associated with two distinct things, their meaning end up being close, obedience and disobedience. When we perform a positive Torah commandment, those that God commands us to do, then we shall receive the CHESSED (goodness) from God in our lives. If, on the other hand, we carry out a negative commandment, that is, if we do what God tells us not to do and repent of such an act, we shall have the CHESSED (mercy) of God in our lives. This is the real God's grace.

Grace is something totally and exclusively connected with the Word of God and His Laws, true grace does not exist without the Torah. Unlike Christian grace, biblical grace requires obedience to the Creator, to seek Him, to follow His ways and this grace is not something relative, that exists only within the human being, but is something that goes beyond the heart of man, real grace is palpable and visible to everyone around the one who receives it. Many see grace as a new testament's creation, but in truth, grace has existed since the Torah was delivered; any grace that is not tied to the Word of God is a false and manipulative grace.

That is why James first speaks about the Law of liberty, the Torah, and then mentions mercy right in the next verse, for both are directly connected. What James says in this verse is that mercy triumphs over judgment.

In other words, to quote the "law of liberty" in the preceding verse, teaches us that a life according to the will of the Creator will bring CHESSED and CHESSED is required in order for someone to receive a positive judgment from God.

XVII - DEMONS

You believe that there is one God; you do well: the demons also believe, and tremble.

James 2:19

The purpose of this book is not to deal with demons, nor about the "dark forces". But as James brings this theme up, a short mention about it according to the Jewish view on demons may help to clarify some things.

There is a lot of confusion about these beings, some believe they are fallen angels and others believe they are creations of satan himself, who by the way creates nothing, but the truth is that although some people know how to deal with them by using exorcism, little is taught about their origins and functions other than how Giordano Bruno and Dante Alighieri defined them.

The best Jewish way to deal with mystical topics is looking at the *Zohar HaKadosh* in order to see how this book approaches these spiritual beings, what it says about their creation, how they act, and how to avoid their influence on our lives. It is worth remembering that the Zohar is a book that goes a little beyond the common human understanding, for besides using a very symbolic language, this book deals with certain topics in an unusual way when compared to other literatures on this matter.

One of the accounts of demons in the Zohar is found in its analysis about the Parashat Vayikra, the first parashah in the book of Leviticus:

When HaKasosh, Baruch Hu, removed the rib from Adam

Harishon, lilith saw it and was taken by hatred. She went and hid herself in the depths of the ocean, next to her servants known as mermaids... ...On some occasions she gets out of the oceans to cause havoc among men.
Zohar HaKadosh, Parashat Vaiykra 19a

Before we get properly into this matter, we must look at this somewhat enigmatic figure. Lilith, according to our sages, was Adam's first wife, a woman he had before Eve and before entering the Garden of Eden. This being, that was created on the sixth day of creation, way before the sin came into the world, possessed incomprehensible powers to the human's comprehension ability that was lowered after Adam's expulsion from the garden.

She was disqualified by God to become Adam's official wife, for she used her negative side, which was intrinsically placed upon her at the time of her creation, to usurp the holiness that Adam possessed for being a chosen person by the Creator, a holiness that he had for being the first living soul.

In the ancient books, we see that lilith ran away from Adam just before Havah (Eve) was created, but we did not learn so, for the female lilith was with Adam, but before Havah's arrival, lilith was attached to Adam with the intention of absorbing his holiness. When Havah was given to Adam, lilith went to the ocean and now she comes out of the water to wound the humans of this world, with her long black hair and scarlet purple robe.
Zohar HaKadosh, Parashat Vaiykra 19a

These "ancient books" referred by the Zohar are: Sefer Yetzirah, Sefer HaYashar and Sefer HaYuval.

In the continuation of its account, the Zohar states that lilith's intention was to absorb the holiness of Adam for some reason that is not revealed to us. When Eve is created and given to Adam, lilith became infuriated and went to hide in the deep of the oceans, however lilith's deeds in human reality is very vivid and current. We can see it in a variety of ways, beginning with Nimrod's wife, Semiramis and her infamous representation holding her baby in her arms, the true inspiration of the Christian mary with the Christian baby jesus in her arms. This mary, to which many Christians are devout, "coincidentally" also has a purple robe in many of her representations.

All of these versions of mary are no more than lilith herself disguised and seeking the worship of men with the intention of destroying them. Another book, pretty much like the Zohar, makes mention of this being:

And there came one of the seven angels which had the seven vials, and talked with me, saying to me, Come here; I will show you the judgment of the great ***whore*** *that sits on many* ***waters****:*
With whom the kings of the earth have committed fornication, and the inhabitants of the earth have been made drunk with the wine of her fornication.
So he carried me away in the spirit into the wilderness: and I saw a woman sit on a ***scarlet colored*** *beast, full of names of blasphemy, having seven heads and ten horns.*
And the woman was arrayed in ***purple and scarlet color****, and decked with gold and precious stones and pearls, having a golden cup in her hand full of abominations and filthiness of her* ***fornication****:*
And on her forehead was a name written, MYSTERY, BABYLON THE GREAT, THE MOTHER OF ***HARLOTS*** *AND ABOMINATIONS OF THE EARTH.*
And I saw the woman drunken with the blood of the saints, and with the blood of the martyrs: and when I saw her, I wondered with great admiration.

Revelation 17:1-6

The great whore, as reported by John in the book of Revelation, is lilith and her destruction represents the destruction of Christianity's paganism. Such paganism is called by John as "wormwood" and according to his account this "wormwood" is something that will poison and kill one-third of men. The interesting thing is that, according to a sense made in 2017, exactly 33% of the world's population, that is, a third, is somehow adept to any branch from Christianity.

With this in mind, another Kabbalistic book brings to light how these demons are formed and how they have authority over the life of man:

Before a couple engages in an illicit sexual intercourse, lilith approaches and waits to see if the man does practice immoral behavior such as an animal behavior. If this occurs and the drops (sperm) fall on soil, lilith takes them to herself and fecundates herself, prostituting herself, thus becoming pregnant and generating demons. These drops that she takes, which come from a sacred organ and have the power to generate life, she uses them to form evil spirits within her.

Pri Etz Chayym, Arizal

This is all very weird, but according to the sages, the demons are generated by lilith when she steals the sperm that falls on the ground after an interrupted intercourse. Understanding this requires a high spiritual level.

The great sage Arizal also teaches that the demon that is generated in this way will act on the life of this couple, because this newborn demon "aggregates" itself to them as if it were their son. God forbid.

In the Torah, there is a very strange case about the interrupted intercourse that falls on the ground, perhaps this is the reason for God's attitude toward such an act:

But Onan, knowing that the seed would not count as his, let it go to waste in soil whenever he joined with his brother's wife, so as not to provide offspring for his brother. What he did was displeasing to the LORD, and He took his life also.

Genesis 38:9-10

After the death of Judah's firstborn, Er, his other son,

Onan, took his wife according to the law of levirate. As Onan did not want to give descent to his older brother, he "wasted" in the soil and this attitude cost his life.

This is only a brief study about the origin of those beings to which the author of the book of James refers. James informs us that demons fear God and this idea is vastly addressed within Jewish teachings, both the Zohar, Rabbi Arizal and the Siddur (book of Jewish prayers) report what causes such great fear in demons as well as how to protect ourselves from them:

Happy are those who learn these secrets, for they will be those who will be saved from the control of these spirits who come from the other side. We shall know that this is only possible by the power of the Torah. When a person engages in Torah, it is as if he is curled up with the name of YHWH and all unclean spirits will fear him, for the whole Torah is the Name above all names, the YHWH and anyone who learns Torah, it is as if the Torah were written all over his body and he will have nothing to fear. The person who knows the hidden and deep secrets of the Torah will overcome all evil spirits.

Zohar HaKadosh, Parshat Vaiykra 19b

I cover myself with the sanctity of the King and in everything I do, no demon can take me.

Arizal

By wrapping oneself in the Talit, with the name of Hashem upon us by the Tefillim and the sword of Hashem at our waist by the tzitzit, the demons will fear Hashem over us.

Siddur HaShacharit

The first thing that keeps the demons away is holiness and such is only gained through the Torah, so the demons will keep themselves away from all who live Torah and live for the Torah. The second is what the demons fear and it is precisely the deepest Name of God, the tetragrammaton (יהוה) and nome the name jesus as many believe.

Now a days, it is common to do exorcism with the use of the "name of jesus", if anyone believes this is the way to do it, so be it. But what the Torah really teaches is the power of the true Name of The One Who Is. I find rather unlikely that Yeshua expelled demons by the name of jesus or even by his own real name, surely he knew this secret and he pronounced THE NAME to drive out those "beings from the other side."

James, of course, knew that very well.

* *here we are dealing with demons and not satan, they are different beings and with different approaches and missions.*

XVIII - ABRAHAM AND RAHABE

Was not Abraham our father justified by works, when
he had offered Isaac his son on the altar?
See you how faith worked with his works, and
by works was faith made perfect?
And the scripture was fulfilled which said, Abraham
believed God, and it was imputed to him for righteousness:
and he was called the Friend of God.
You see then how that by works a man is justified,
and not by faith only.

James 2:21-24

ABRAHAM'S MIDRASH

James, after teaching about the strong connection that faith has with works, i.e. the commandments, and with the Torah, makes a midrash about how these two things walk together and what faith together with works represented in Abraham's life. James quotes a passage from the Torah in order to strengthen his argument and to justify his teaching on faith and works.

The interesting thing is that this teaching of James, within the New Testament, has a very contradictory appearance when compared to Paul's teachings, especially those found in the book of Galatians. The most striking thing is that Paul also uses Abraham as an example and on top of his story, he also sets a midrash, like James, to strengthen his teaching about grace. In order for us to understand what is happening between Paul and James, let us raise some apparent differences.

Even as Abraham believed God, and it was accounted
to him for righteousness.
Know you therefore that they which are of faith,
the same are the children of Abraham.
And the scripture, foreseeing that God would justify
the heathen through faith, preached before the gospel to
Abraham, saying, In you shall all nations be blessed.
So then they which be of faith are blessed with faithful Abraham.
Galatians 3:6-9

Through a quick reading, the discord between Paul and James is undeniable. Paul states that Abraham had faith and that was enough for him, on the other hand, James, by using the same story, says that besides having faith, Abraham also obeyed and only then Abraham was credited as righteous. Who is right?

A poor understanding of what Paul speaks, especially when he speaks as a rabbi, can lead us to profound errors, that is what formed all Christian theology. The misinterpretation of the Pauline teachings served as the basis for the father of the church to create all the garbage they left to mankind. Even though many Christian denominations claim to have a vision of approaching Israel, they still cling to theologies that increasingly alienate Christians and Jews. Although many people claim that Yeshua is Mashiach, in practice, their Messiah ends up being Paul, for to many christians what the apostle taught has a greater weight than what Yeshua taught.

Paul's letters not only have an apparent contradiction with the teachings of Yeshua, but also appear contrary to the other apostles. Let's imagine a ring, on the one side we have Paul, stating that faith and grace have replaced the law, supporting what is taught by Christian theology and on the other side we have James, Yeshua's brother, claiming that faith without Torah is dead and in order to be justified, faith alone does not resolve. The only way to solve that is looking at the example both used.

And because he put his trust in the LORD, He reckoned it to his merit.

Genesis 15:6

This verse is the cornerstone of all Paul's teaching, the great insight that the apostle uses in this passage is precisely the period that existed between the promise made by God to Abraham and his circumcision, that took place 15 years after the given promise. Abraham was circumcised 15 years after receiving the promise, believing in it, and having been justified by having believed in it. That is, it was not a Jewish Abraham who was justified by God, not even a circumcised Abraham, not an Abraham who followed the rabbinic laws, not even an Abraham who had some religion, but an Abraham who above all of this, believed; and this was enough for him to be justified. On top of that, Paul justified that salvation and justification were not related to being a converted Jew or a member of any religion.

Abraham was justified even before he was circumcised, so he is the father in the faith of both Jews and Christians. The insight in Paul's Midrash solves all doubt for the problem of "Faith x Law" and his apparent contradiction with James. The whole argument about faith being contrary to the law is based on erroneous assumptions. Paul, when referring to the law, does not refer to the Laws of God, the Torah or to obedience to God, but rather to a change of status, from being a Gentile in order to become Jewish through religious laws.

This misunderstanding of what Paul was saying is not unique to the church, but it was already in the apostles' own time. If we read the book of Acts in chapter 21, James tells Paul what the people were saying about him, that he was teaching the Jews and the Gentiles to turn away from the Torah. James knew that this was not the case and also knew that people did not understand what Paul was talking about, as we do not understand until today, Paul's letters are very difficult and may become a trap if we read them without a consistent basis concerning the apostle's reality and education.

For this reason I believe that James used this same passage in order to fix some misunderstanding concerning Paul's teaching, for this, James approached this passage with an interpretation that goes beyond Paul's. James agrees with Paul when Abraham had faith and that was enough for him, but after Abraham had faith, he obeyed, he did all that God commanded. If Abraham was not faithful to the commandments of God, his faith in the promise would not be confirmed, it would not make sense, it would be dead. James must have used the same line of thought as Paul to help him in some way before the eyes of the community.

With this in mind, it is clear that both apostles do not contradict each other, for both are addressing different things. For Paul, "works" means conversion and rabbinic laws, for James, "works" means the commandments of God, the Torah itself. Paul never said that we should not observe the Torah, nor did James ever preach about conversion of the Gentiles.

There are no contradictions or anything unusual, it is all about terminology, because according to both apostles, Abraham first believed, was justified by his faith and then obeyed God so his faith would not be dead. Just believing is not enough, it was not enough for Abraham, it is not enough for us.

ABRAHAM, THE TZADIK

Going back to the verse they both used, it sounds a bit odd, for it does not live up to the life that Abraham has taken up until then. Abraham was the man who brought faith in the One God to mankind, he was a man who grew up in the midst of idolatry, under a strong pagan influence within his own home and yet he had faith in that God, which was a strange thing to the society of his day.

Abraham also believed in God's word in countless moments during his journey, beginning when God sends him out of his land, his kinsfolk, and into a land where He would show him. If Abraham had no faith in God and in what He commands, he would never have left his house.

Could it be that even after believing in the One God, His word, His commands, His promises, Abraham needed to believe in a specific promise to be credited as righteous? Thinking in this way gives an impression of injustice, for where is all the merit that he should have received after all that has occurred previously in his life? These doubts are answered by the verse itself, it shows us that Abraham's "faith", by the first time, was not alone.

והאמן ביהוה ויחשבה לו צתקה

And because he put his trust in ADONAI, He reckoned it to his merit.

Genesis 15:6

Using the first two words of this verse, "*And because he put his trust in Adonai*" (וְהֶאֱמִן בַּיהוָה), we have the name of God that is above all names:

יהוָה

5ה + 6ו + 5ה + 10י

= 26 = **8**

Torah (תורה)

5ה + 200ר + 6ו + 400ת

611 = 6+1+1 = **8**

Abraham's faith can also be understood by replacing both terms, since they both have the same numerical value:

Veheemin BaTorah (וְהֶאֱמִן בַּתורה) = *And because*

he put his trust in Torah.

For the first time in the Torah, we have a report about Abraham's faith connected to obedience. This can also be seen from another analysis, which confirms what has been already seen. If we take the whole verse of Gn 15:6 and calculate its value, it has a total of 696. This number represents one's dedication to the Laws and the will of Adonai:

(חֲנֻכָּה בתורה) - Chanukah baTorah - *dedication to the Torah.*
5ה + 200ר + 6ו + 400ת + 2ב + 5ה + 20כ + 50נ + 8ח
= **696**

Every time God commanded Abraham to do something, he did, he obeyed, when God promised something, he believed, it has also been one or another. However, for the first time, in this verse we are shown the level that Abraham reached, a level where he had faith and obedience altogether. With his dedication to the will of God, that is, his faith and his obedience applied TOGETHER, is what made him a righteous man and a friend of God.

This shows us what makes someone a true Tzadik, first the belief in the One God and in His word, then the dedication to it by its fulfillment. Getting to that level was what made Abraham worthy to have Isaac and to receive the promise that he would be the father of many. It was his obedience and faith finally walking together that made him what he was. But one can think, how did Abraham believe in the Torah if it had not yet been delivered? The Torah precedes the creation of the world and is not only a term that simply represents a book, but it represents the obedience to the true will of the Creator, which we now have access to through the Pentateuch (written Torah).

Paul and James certainly knew this and so there would be no contradiction between the two. On the one hand we have Paul using Abraham's faith against the laws of religion and on the other we have James, who focuses his teaching on the need for a person to become a tzadik, that is, to have faith and to live Torah.

You see then how that by works a man is justified,
and not by faith only.

James 2:24

Contrary to Christian theology and the faith of many, just believing is not enough, one have to follow the Torah, which many believe is abolished, in order to become a friend of God.

Blessed is he who understands these things.

RAHAB'S MIDRASH

Likewise also was not Rahab the harlot justified
by works, when she had received the messengers,
and had sent them out another way?
For as the body without the spirit is dead, so
faith without works is dead also.

James 2:25-26

Among many biblical characters who have had their faith represented through their works, James mentions the little-known Rahab.

After Moses' death, the Hebrew people prepared themselves for the invasion of the land of Canaan, the land that God promised to give to His people. Joshua, the 82-year-old leader, before invading the first city, the famous Jericho, sent two spies, Caleb and Pinchas, in order to spy the situation there before the invasion.

The leaders of Jericho discovered that there were spies in their city and went out looking for them. The two men decided to hide in an inn that was in the city's wall. The owner of this place was a woman named Rahab, who acknowledges the God of Israel and decides to hide these two spies for a few days in her property so that they would not be found by the soldiers.

After a few days, so that the two of them could leave the city safely and return to Joshua with the information obtained, she lowered both of them by the city's wall tied to a rope.

Before the departure, Rahabe asks that they show mercy for her and when they invade the city, they would remember her and her family. Rahab's attitude generated so much merit before Adonai that great men came from her offspring, such as King David and Yeshua.

In one of the last dialogues between Rahab and the spies, she says the following:

Now, since I have shown ***chessed*** *to you, swear to me by the LORD that you in turn will show* ***chessed*** *to my family. Provide me with a reliable sign*

Joshua 2:12

Rabbi Moshe Cordovaro, also known as Radak, says that "doing chessed" is the observance of the commandments concerning one's neighbor, such as charity, caring for children, visiting the sick, offering hospitality to strangers, burying the dead, etc.

One of the ways of dividing the 613 commandments of the Torah is among the commandments relating to the relationship "man x man," such as do not kill, do not steal, charity, hospitality and so on. and those referring to the "man x God" commandments, such as the Shabbat, the Kasher food, the feasts, and so on.

The commandments between man and his neighbor are represented by Chesed, mercy, as stated by Radak. On the other hand, the first of the commandments between man and God is the Brit Milah, that is, circumcision, because it is the first commandment that the human being (as a man) fulfills in life on the eighth day. The greatest symbol of circumcision is precisely Abraham, for he was the first man in history to observe this commandment.

I believe that James used Abraham and Rahab as examples by their representation of the commandments. Abraham represents the commandments that refer to man's relationship with God and Rahab represents the commandments between man and his neighbor, thus totaling all 613 commandments, the full Torah.

With this we have the confirmation of what would be the "work" that James refers to, the "work" that gives life to faith is precisely the Torah, for as it happened with Abraham, who beside having faith, lived the Torah and therefore became a tzadik and a friend of God, so must also the man who wants to serve God do so.

Even so faith, if it has not works, is dead, being alone.

James 2:17

XIX - THE TONGUE

Likewise, the tongue is a small part of the body, but it makes great boasts. Consider what a great forest is set on fire by a small spark. The tongue also is a fire, a world of evil among the parts of the body. It corrupts the whole body, sets the whole course of one's life on fire, and is itself set on fire by hell.
All kinds of animals, birds, reptiles and sea creatures are being tamed and have been tamed by mankind,
but no human being can tame the tongue. It is a restless evil, full of deadly poison.

James 3:5-8

James quotes the "tongue" several times throughout his book, so I will approach it a little deeper in order to try to clarify what was the understanding of James and of his listeners in this regard.

You shall not gossip among your people, lest you cause your neighbor's blood. I am Adonai.

Leviticus 19:16

This passage in the book of Leviticus is one of the most serious passage concerning the tongue in the Torah, for this reason I believe that James alludes to this passage to have support for all his teachings on this regard. There is a very serious allusion in this commandment about speaking evil about someone, according to God Himself, it is like "causing the blood of one's neighbor", and this makes this mitzvah much more heavy than it seems. There are many commentaries from the sages that might bring us a deeper understanding concerning this verse.

He who publicly speaks evil of his neighbor,
acts as if shedding his blood.
Talmud of Babylon, Tractate Bava Metzia 58b

Among the many sins that the Torah reveals, there are those that, despite looking different and having no apparent relation between each other, have the same weight before God's eyes. I can cite a few examples, one who denies the Word of God for example, is like someone who practices idolatry:

It follows that anyone who denies the Torah admits idolatry.
Rashi, Deuteronomy 11:28

We do also have sexual immorality for instance, which in God's eyes is like blasphemy:

Rabbi Shimom says: We can understand this in the very context in which it is found, as it says: "They (who practice incest and immorality) will have their souls cut off", for it is like blasphemy.
Mishnah Makkot 3:15

And lastly, we have the seen above, the sin of evil-speaking, which before God's eyes is as serious as murder itself.

This makes things much more complicated, because who does not have the habit of speaking evil of someone? It is always good to keep this teaching in mind. This makes sense with another misunderstood passage from the book of James:

For whoever shall keep the whole law, and yet
offend in one point, he is guilty of all.
James 2:10

The poor interpretation of this passage has led many Christians to believe that it is better not to keep the Law at all than taking the risk of being guilty for having transgressed it all, for keeping the Law is very difficult and no one can do it according to the weak Christian theology.

Interesting thing, this James' statement in the verse above is not found anywhere else in the Torah, or in the Tanakh, or from Yeshua's words, or from anyone else, this is something that came from James himself, it is a particular point of view of his own, who certainly was a Torah observant and by this fact alone, he could not discourage his listeners from ceasing to follow the Law, if that were the case, he would contradict his own book, where he states that faith without works is dead.

What James says here is that there are various transgressions that are comparable to other transgressions, as in the case above, he who speaks evil about his neighbor also commits the sin of murder and bloodshed. This is what James refers to and this is not a counsel to not follow the Law due to it's "difficulty". In fact, let's see what God says about it:

For these commandments that I am giving you today
are not difficult for you, nor far from you.
Deuteronomy 30:11

Now I ask, who is right, God when He states that the commandments are not difficult or the Christian theology when it states that due to the difficulty to follow the Torah, it is better to leave it aside so that the individual does not become transgressor of all the Law? He who does not know the Torah and does not follow it, automatically is a transgressor. Just think about with a little good sense.

Guard your tongue from evil, your lips from deceitful speech.
Psalm 34:14

The Hebrew term for the person who does not know how to control the tongue, i.e. an evil-speaker, is HALASHON HA'RA

(הלשון הרע), which literally means "the bad tongue". The Gematria of this term is quite interesting:

הלשון הרע (HALASHON HA'RA)

ה5 + ל30 + ש300 + ו6 + ן50 + ה5 + ר200 + ע70

= **666**

Enough said.

XX - THE FIG, THE OLIVE AND THE VINE TREE

Can the fig tree, my brothers, bear olive berries? either a vine tree, figs? so can no fountain both yield salt water and fresh.
James 3:12

Both the fig tree and the olive tree in this passage were not by chance, for both have a very strong representation that can be associated with *tefilah* and *emunah*. In order to understand it, it is necessary to enter again into what formed the basis of James's teachings and faith.

There are some things we must pay attention to, why the fig tree, the olive tree and the fruit of both, are used as an examples by James? Perhaps they have some meaning behind them that is not so clear to us.

Before we begin, I must conceptualize two important things through the Jewish view and understanding, the *tefilah* and the *emunah*.

Tefilah

The translation for tefilah is “prayer”, but this definition is horribly inaccurate. A prayer deals with two distinct entities establishing a communication, one of them inferior, making a request to a superior. If that were the case, the word for that in Hebrew would be *bakashah*, from the verb LEVAKESH (לבקש) – *to ask for*. On the other hand, there is also the term SHEVACH (שבח), which means "worship". The tefilah is precisely the junction of these two concepts, a connection of an inferior being with a higher being through worship. A better word to define tefilah would be "communion".

Tefilah is nothing more than the awakening of a hidden love within the heart of the one who loves the Creator through a "conversation" with him, until a state of union is reached. Tefillah is what makes the commandments in one's life something lively and pleasurable. This differs greatly from the traditional prayer.

Emunah

Emunah, translated as "faith", is something that goes far beyond that. The basic concept of faith is more or less like something one believes even without seeing it. But to understand Emunah as being something that is simply believed, is to devalue its real meaning, for as King Solomon said, "the fools also believe".

The Emunah is a perception of the truth that transcends reason. This is something that only comes through three things, wisdom, understanding and knowledge, for this reason it is said that faith comes by hearing the Word of God, for without these three things that comes through the Torah, the faith is nothing more than a fool's belief. When a person has the true Emunah, he feels that what he believes is an intrinsic part of his own existence, to the point where, if he denies that Emunah, he would be denying his reason for existing. It's much deeper than believing in something one does not see.

THE FIG TREE

Why is the fig tree compared to those who study the Torah? For unlike other trees, in which their fruits must be harvested all at once, the figs must be harvested little by little. Just as one who studies the Torah, today he studies a little and tomorrow

a little bit more, because it is not learned in a year or two.
Midrash Tanchumah, Pinchas 11:1

Personally, I think this teaching from *Midrash Tanchumah* fantastic. It compares a person who studies the Torah with the fig tree itself, for to become a tree that always bears fruit, one must always study the Torah to always bear fruit. Just as the fig tree bears fruit little by little, the one who studies the Torah will also bear fruit gradually, for it is something that transforms one's life and walk, which are things that come one step at a time.

The Talmud confirms this with a rather mystical but impressive passage:

He who dreams with a fig tree receives a sign
that the Torah is within him.
Talmud of Babylon, Tractate Brakhot 57a

When one knows God and His Word, thus becoming a "fig tree" and beginning to bear fruit of Torah, that one will have fellowship with God. His life and behavior will be a true worship to HaKadosh Baruch Hu, thus performing the real *Tefilah*. Then when the ways of the Torah become an essential part of one's life, one will receive the true *Emunah*, reaching the promise where everything one asks for, will be given.

James's teachings on "faith" are fully connected with what happened around him. The fig is the Torah, the fig tree is the one who follows the Torah and the one who reaches both, receives the *Emunah* and the *Tefilah*.

THE FIG

Rabbi Hiyya Bar Abba said that Rabbi Yohanan said: what is the meaning of what is written, "He who keeps the fig tree shall eat of its fruit" (Proverbs 27:18)? Why are the things of the Torah compared to the fig? Just as a person who looks for figs to eat, he finds figs in the fig tree, for the fig tree is not dry, and so it is with the Torah. Every time a person meditates upon it, he will find new secrets in it.

Talmud of Babylon, Tractate Eruvin 54a / 54b

According to the Talmud, the fruit of the fig tree represents the Torah and everything that comes out of it. Just as anyone who seeks fig, finds it in a fig tree, so will the person who seeks secrets about God in the Torah, will always find them.

The Talmud makes another analogy:

So the fruit of the Torah will always be found
by the person who seeks it in it.

Ein Yaakov, Eiruvin 5:9

Ein Yaakov is a compilation of Talmudic materials alongside with its commentaries and it teaches that, just as one who is hunger and seeks the fruit of the fig tree, which can always be found , he who seeks God will always find Him when He seeks Him in the Torah .

THE VINE TREE

Within the rabbinical mentality, the vine tree has some representations, sometimes positive, some others negative. Because the fig tree and the fig have a positive symbology, representing the Torah and who studies it, and because James makes a comparison, it would not make sense to compare two good things. So, in my view, in this case we should look at the vine tree in a more negative way.

A commentary from the Talmud might help us on this "side" of that tree:

We learned in a baraita: the tree of which Adam, the first
man, ate, as Rabbi Meir says: it was from a vine tree.

Talmud of Babylon, Tractate Brakhot 40a

Noach found a vine, which came from the garden of Eden and
was laid there by Adam. Then he took his fruit and consumed
it and became drunk and his nakedness was discovered.

Pirkei DeRabbi Eliezer 23:12

We see from these two commentaries that the vine tree and its fruit have a direct relation to sin, for just as wine can represent blessings, its excessive consumption can lead to error.

By stating that the fig cannot be taken from the vine tree, James places in opposite sides the Torah and sin, which leads us to another passage:

What shall we say then? Is the law sin? Not at all, but
I did not know the sin except by the Law...

Romans 7:7a

Here Paul makes the same statement, that the Law, the Torah, is what teaches what sin is and therefore they are antitheses. Thus we understand that James teaches that the only way one may not be as a "vine tree" is by being a “fig tree”, that is, one who follows and believes in the Torah is the one who will actually turn away from sin.

If the vine tree, in this case, represents sin and the sinner, we can understand "*can the vine tree bear figs*?" as "*can the sinner bear fruit of the Torah*?". And that makes perfect sense, for the sinner and the Torah are antagonistic things.

CHOTE (חוטא) - sinner
1א + 9ט + 6ו + 8ח
24 = 2+4 = **6**

TARSH (תרש) - fig
300ש + 200ר + 400ת
900 = **9**

THE OLIVE

Olive, within the rabbinic context, is an extremely positive symbology in almost every sense, almost. The greatest use of the olive is for the production of oil, which was a much-used item in the services of the tabernacle and the Temple, placing it almost in a holy item position.

This "almost" is due to its oil other functions, such as burning and consumption in food and therefore disqualifies it as holy, because what is holy is separated, i.e. can't have other functions.

At first I was intrigued by the James's mention about the conection between fig tree and olive berry. If we understand some things about olive and olive oil, the words of James will certainly have a deeper meaning.

The fig tree, as seen above, represents the person who studies the Torah and the olive berry, so that we may relate it in some way to the Torah itself, the only way is to see it as a source of light, when the burning of its oil generates the flame.

Concerning that, let's look at the bible:

His Word (Torah) is a lamp to my feet and light to my path.

Psalms 119:105

If the Torah is the "light" and the oil generates the "light", then we could understand that the oil represents the Torah, but the Torah is holy and holiness means separation, exclusiveness and in the case of the olive oil, it is not exclusively for generating light.

There were several types of oils in the first century, the two most important were the olive oil (שמן זית - *shemen zait*), which had several functions not only to light a lamp, and also a cheaper oil, called *shemen* (שמן), which comes from fat. This second one, because it was a cheaper oil, it was only used with the function to light lamps. This is the oil that Yeshua quotes when he tells the parable of the ten virgins.

Oil (shemen), that is, the Torah.

Bamidbar Rabbah 13:16

Oil (shemen) represents the Torah itself, just as oil generates light to light our way, the Torah is the light that illuminates our lives. Unlike the olive oil, which can also illuminate and represent the Word of God, also serves as nourishment. However, shemen have a unique function, thus making it a better representation of the Torah, whose sole purpose is to bring the light of the Creator upon our lives.

What can we understand when James says that the fig tree does not produce olives? It teaches us that those who study the Torah cannot produce unholy things, that is, things that are not exclusive and separated for God only. In other words, one who studies the Torah should study it for the benefit of the kingdom and should not be mixed with other things.

SALT AND FRESH WATER

This comparison is self-explanatory, but I will expose a very interesting midrash:

> *Everything was separated by the Creator and the parts of the world that were separated were placed opposite to each other, like fresh water and salt water.*
>
> The Midrash of Philo, 15:10

In the Jewish mentality, fresh water and salt water do not only represent two different kinds of things, but rather two opposite things, as well as Torah and sin.

Now we can look at James' words again from a different perspective:

> ***My brethren, can he who studies the Torah also not separate himself exclusively for God, or the sinner bear fruit from Torah? So neither can a fountain give salt water and fresh, for they are not just different things, but opposites, just as those who live Torah and the sinners.***
>
> **James 3:12**

XXI - CHOKHMAH, BINAH AND DA'AT

Who is a wise man and endued with ***knowledge*** *among you? let him show out of a good conversation his works with meekness of* ***wisdom.***

James 3:13

Many things in the New Testament have an obvious appearance that presents a seemingly clear understanding. It is quite true that the book of James has many direct teachings of easy understanding, but what binds those teachings and what serves as a basis for them, have a deeper and more hidden meaning than what meets the eyes; a meaning which is only understood within the mentality and the faith of those who wrote those books.

James's book, with a simple reading, deals basically with one thing, moral behavior. It is for this reason that the author repeats on several occasions the care with the tongue, the works, the judgment, the brotherhood and the love for the neighbor. But what it does not make clear is where such attitudes come from and how they can be attained and understood. When the author uses terms such as BINAH (בינה) - *knowledge* - and CHOKHMAH (חכמה) - *wisdom* - he reveals, in a somewhat mystical way, the true concepts and the origin of all that he has been teaching.

In the above verse, James seeks those who have knowledge and use it through wisdom. The Western mentality that was formed from the Greek culture, by understanding both terms as the same, creates a huge confusion among them, for I ask: How, in practice, does one who is knowledgeable show his works by wisdom? Would that be like one who reads the bible, memorizes it, and does exactly what it determines? Or such a teaching has something deeper and more spiritual than acting like a robot before the Creator?

In order for us to come to a conclusion that will help us understand the whole book of James, as well as many of the biblical teachings, we must first conceptualize what these terms represent within the Jewish mysticism. Unfortunately a complete approach on this topic takes a long time and since this is not the intention of this book, we shall briefly see what BINAH and CHOKHMAH represent.

SEFIROT'S MANIFESTATIONS

As seen before, each sefirah is associated with a divine name. However, since the sefirot are representations of the essence of the One Who Is, Blessed Be He, they also associate themselves with the name that is above all names, the Name that represents the very essence of the true God, YHWH.

This name is so powerful that every letter that composes it has an immeasurable power that is manifested through the attributes of the sefirot. Each letter connects with God's action as follows:

י (yud) - KETER
ה (hei) - BINAH, CHOKHMAH (DA'AT)
ו (vav) - CHESSED, NETZACH, YESOD, TIFERET, HOD, GEVURAH
ה (hei) - MALKHUT

The sages say that the world was created through knowledge, understanding and wisdom, for everything we live in this reality works in a logical, coherent, synchronized and cyclical way, that is the manifestation of the sefirot more linked to the rational.

For this reason the Torah does not say that "Adonai created", but rather "**Elohim** created", for in that name are the three attributes with which He created all things. The great

Kabbalistic rabbi Moses Cordovero makes the following connection:

*The creation by **Elohim** occurred through the Binah, Chokhmah and Da'at.*

Or Neerav VI:1

As we look at the name of YHWH (יהוה), we will see that these attributes, CHOKHMAH, BINAH and DA'AT are connected with the first letter HEI (ה) of His most sacred name, the number value of that letter is 5, as well as the name of Elohim:

HEI (ה) = **5**

ELOHIM (אלהים)

40ם + 10י + 5ה + 30ל + 1א

86 = 8+6 = **14** = 1+4 = **5**

DA'AT, veBINAH, veCHOKHMAH (דעת ובינה וחכמה)

5ה + 50נ + 10י + 2ב + 6ו + 200ת + 70ע + 4ד

5ה + 40מ + 20כ + 8ח+ 6ו +

426 = 4+2+6 = **14** = 1+4 = **5**

This serves as a proof that God as Elohim, also represented as the first letter HEI (ה) of His most high name (יהוה) manifested Himself through His knowledge, understanding and wisdom to create all things. The ways God manifests in this world, from the creation of all things to a simple blessing in one's life, are through His emanations. Those emantions are according to the attribute with which each one is associated, as already seen.

These emanations associated with the letters of THE NAME reminded me of a very famous teaching of Yeshua:

*Truly, I say to you that even if the heavens and the earth (depart), a **yud** or a nekudah will not be abolished from the*

Torah or the prophets and everything will be fulfilled.
Matthew 5:18

This example, if analyzed more mystically through the sefirot, reveals much. At first Yeshua states that the Torah will never be abolished, that it is true and something that many should pay attention to, but by the Hebrew letter he cites, the letter YUD (י), which is the first letter of the name YHWH (יהוה), Yeshua makes an association with the root of all sefirot, the Sefirah of KETER (כתר).

If KETER (כתר), in a fictitious reality, ceases to exist, all the emanation of God in this earth would also cease to exist, since all others would lose their root, it is as if the central key were turned off and the sefirot would lose their primary energy. If this were to happen, it would be as if God Himself completely ceased to exist within that reality, it would be like as if He has turned his back and left, leaving man to his own fate.

By this we understand that what sustains this world is the Creator Himself and what keeps Him connected with this reality and with His creation is represented by the letter YUD (י), for it is the KETER (כתר), the root of everything God does in this realm.

By the words of Yeshua, we see that he alludes the Torah as being the root of all God's emanations. To put it simply, no Torah no God.

To continue our study on the words of James, let us take a better look at each term he quotes.

BINAH (בינה) - KNOWLEDGE

BINAH, which in a direct translation means "knowledge", is one of the ten sefirot which symbolically represents the essence of the true God. BINAH represents the soul and the power of analysis and reason, both inductive and deductive.

The "knowledge" that BINAH represents is the ability to examine and discern between the true and the false, the good and the bad, and the ability to elucidate both concepts for oneself as well as for others.

The word BINAH (בינה) has the same root as the word BEIN (בין) - *between* – for it represents the ability to distinguish between opposing objects and ideas. Binah can also be defined as man's good sense. It is the Binah that makes the connection between the DA'AT (דעת) - *understanding* - and the CHOKHMAH (חכמה) - *wisdom*.

CHOKHMAH (חכמה) - WISDOM

CHOKHMAH is associated with the elevate soul that is a result from a knowledge that go beyond BINAH, CHOKHMAH represents an understanding of what is hidden from the eyes, something that transcends human consciousness, reaching the most intimate spiritual secrets of the Creator.

The wisdom CHOKHMAH represents is the ability to, through a deep look at something in our reality, understand the spiritual essence of that thing, thus obtaining its axiomatic truth and its reason for being created by God.

CHOKHMAH do not exist without BINAH and a BINAH that does not result in CHOKHMAH is an illusion. The union of the two represents the true act of God and the purpose for which man was created.

CHOKHMAH (חכמה)
5ה + 40מ + 20כ + 8ח
= **73**

BINAH (בינה)
5ה + 50נ + 10י + 2ב
= **67**

(CHOKHMAH) **73** + (BINAH) **67** = **140**

140 is the sum of all squared numbers from 1 to 7

(1x1) + (2x2) + (3x3) + (4x4) + (5x5) + (6x6) + (7x7) = **140**

Every time God acts, somehow, the number 7 appears in some form, for example, the first manifestation of God in the Torah was the creation of the heavens and the earth, the phrase "*in the beginning created Elohim the heavens and the earth*" in Hebrew, is composed of 7 words.

7 days of creation, 7x7 = 49 days of the Omer, 7th day of the week (Shabbat) is the holy day, among many others.

The manifestation of God in the life of man, represented by the number 7, is when he attains CHOKHMAH and BINAH.

DA'AT (דעת) - UNDERSTANDING

DA'AT is associated with the powers of memory and concentration, it is based on the understanding of ideas generated in consciousness. It operates human reason, earthly good sense and works according to what is grasped by the eyes and ears, an earthly and ordinary form of absorption of knowledge.

The DA'AT is the understanding that operates the heart and the soul's emotions.

**THE DA'AT IS NOT A SEFIRAH, FOR IT IS SOMETHING EARTHLY, SOMETHING THAT HAS A BEGINNING, A MIDDLE AND ALWAYS COMES TO AN END.

CHOKHMAH is the apex, it is the closest one can get to the essence of God (יהוה), is when reason, common sense and understanding reach the spiritual spheres. In that moment what is right and wrong, what is good and what is bad and what is false and what is truth comes through a judgment that goes beyond what the common human mind can define.

At this point, the earthly reality becomes an illusion, this happens when the understanding of everything that happens in the physical world is the result of something that happens in the spiritual world and through these physical events, the person with CHOKHMAH will have the ability to recognize them in the celestial spheres, that is, all human logic and definitions are revelations of the divine. In order to make this clearer, I will use some examples, let's imagine the sunlight, the light that comes from the sun is nothing more than the representation of God's emanation in this reality (as previously dealt); or the human feelings for instance, they were given to men so that they can have a better understanding about the Creator, for such feelings were already a part of Him from before the creation of the world; or the commandments about impurities, that reveal to us the *tzimtzum* of God, which is nothing more than the difference between the absence and the presence of His essence.

These concepts are very deep and complicated to teach them in a few words through a book, but we can define them, in a simple way, as faith. Faith is not believing in what does not exist, for Solomon himself says that even fools believe, but faith is a state where the human being can reach and through it he gains the real perception, understanding and judgment about the world, this reality; the reason of his existence goes beyond what fallen nature defines as good, right and true.

The Sefirah of CHOKHMAH is connected to Sefirah of BINAH, which leads the individual to true wisdom. BINAH, in turn, only takes humans to CHOKHMAH when applied correctly. The knowledge that BINAH represents is obtained only through the Word of God, but not through an excessive reading of it, but rather by a search for its teachings so that by putting them into practice, the person will be able to discern whether his walking is right or wrong, this person will realize if what he defines as "good" is really what God defines as "good", if what he judges to be "true" is in conformity with what God claims to be " truth". When the person, through the knowledge and practice of the Word, manages to transform his concepts about reality and when that walk (commandments) becomes part of his essence, that person is prepared to receive CHOKHMAH.

Finally, the lowest concept of all is the DA'AT, the DA'AT is the reason and the logic that the human being possesses, is to judge what is "good" according to what pleases oneself, to judge what is "true" according to what is embedded in one's habits and to judge what is "right" according to what one's eyes see. This is the lowest and most mundane level, when 2 + 2 = 4 and nothing more. Our sages say that the beginning of DA'AT is death, for it is the first certainty that ALL men have in common, that one day he will die and this shows how strong the connection of DA'AT with earthly things is.

There is a passage that confirms all of this, it follows:

תחלת **חכמה** יראת יהוה ו**דעת** קדשים **בינה**

The beginning of CHOKHMAH is the fear of Adonai,
and the DA'AT of the saints is BINAH.

Proverbs 9:10

THE SEFIROT IN THE NEW TESTAMENT

With this in mind many things in the bible become clear, let's start with the words of Yeshua:

He said to them, because of the limitation of your faith,
truly I say to you if there be in you any faith, as a grain of
mustard, if you believe, you will say to this mountain depart
and it will depart, nothing will be without your reach.

Matthew 17:20

If faith to which he refers here is a simple belief that the mountain could depart, it would be an illogical teaching and out of reality, but if we understand that this faith is the CHOKHMAH and the CHOKHMAH is the understanding of the spiritual world being reflected on this earthly reality, then we would understand what he is talking about.

What Yeshua speaks about in this passage is how CHOKHMAH can change the spiritual decrees, or generate them, to which, even they seem inaccessible (as the mountain to depart), these decrees become a palpable thing to those who have the CHOKHMAH, which in other words, could be understood as the faith Yeshua speaks of. That faith where everything one declares, happens.

So then faith comes by hearing, and hearing by the word of God.
Romans 10:17

Another passage misunderstood is the hearing that brings faith. This hearing is not the simple act of "hearing" but rather of "absorbing". When the Word of God is absorbed, it inevitably begins to take space in the life of the hearer, it is at this stage that DA'AT develops into BINAH; when the commandments and a life according to the will of the Creator become intrinsic in the one who hears it, a phase conceived through the Ruach HaKadosh (Holy Spirit), one receives the real faith, and with that faith, the "power" to generate in the spiritual world is given to this one and this is want can move the mountain.

And I will put My spirit within you, and cause you to walk in My statutes, and ye shall keep Mine ordinances, and do them.
Ezekiel 36:27

When God's Law is written in the heart, it is precisely the stage of BINAH and the beginning of the access to CHOKHMAH.

Today it is very common to see large communities, especially Christian ones, using biblical items such as *mezuzah* or *tzitzit* for the purpose of obtaining blessings or financial gains, even some observances of the Torah are practiced with the intentions mentioned. This is nothing more than DA'AT, for such practices are not followed with the intention of a change of conduct, behavior, character and for this reason, they are followed without the Knowledge of what they represent. This, in essence, represents absolutely nothing, for as

DA'AT is the concept connected to this world, where everything has a beginning, a middle and an end, and the end is death, following these habits, even though they are from the Torah, is also dead, it serves only to easy the soul of those who act this way.

James addresses this as well, when he reports the following:

Even so faith, if it has not works, is dead, being alone.
Yes, a man may say, You have faith, and I have
works: show me your faith without your works,
and I will show you my faith by my works.

James 2:17-18

Let's analyze this verse, but in a more mystical way:

Even so CHOKHMAH, if it has not BINAH, is DA'AT alone
That is, the spiritual level, if it is not reached through the Torah as the essence of life, will be nothing more than something mundane, something from the flesh, in which what is good, right and true will continue to be judged according to the lust of the flesh.

Yes, a man may say: You have CHOKHMAH and I have BINAH, show me your CHOKHMAH without your BINAH and I will show you my CHOKHMAH by my BINAH.
What James exposes here is a challenge, he challenges those who claim to be spiritual without having the essence of God's word to show spirituality, for he will show God's essence in him by his behavior according to the Word of God.

What does it profit, my brothers, though a man say he
has faith, and have not works? can faith save him?

James 2:14

This verse goes against the Christian faith, which proclaims that salvation comes through faith and jesus; James says quite the opposite. He says that CHOKHMAH (faith), if it is not reached by the Binah (Torah), is something dead, which saves no one. Also, BINAH (Torah) is what connects GEVURAH - *judgment* - to the CHESSED - *mercy* - if BINAH is "canceled" by annulling the Torah, then the judgment that will come above one's life, will come without any mercy.

We also understand here that believing in certain facts, such as the existence of Yeshua, of Adonai and the Word of God is the way, is not enough to save anyone.

To conclude, a word from Solomon to those who believe that "faith" is only to believe:

Fools also believe...

Proverbs 14:15

Because

Fools despise BINAH...

Proverbs 1:7

The teachings on these topics address things that are much deeper than what has been set forth here, I have simply brought them in a very simple way in order to be able to better explain some words of James. I emphasize, the definitions of the Sefirot here displayed are shallow and superficial.

** BINAH is KNOWLEDGE and not the Torah, I used it as being the Torah, for through it, BINAH is obtained.

** CHOKHMAH is WISDOM and not faith, I did also use it as faith for clarification purposes.

THE SEFIROT AND THE NAME OF YESHUA

Today I see many Christians declaring that Yeshua, or jesus, is the messiah and following his teachings. However, what strikes me the most is that even his name many do not know.

The one who walked on this earth and died so that the Word of God (read salvation) could reach the Gentile world was not called jesus nor Yeshua, but rather Yehoshua. This is a subject I discuss in more detail in another book: "*TORAT YEHOSHUA: According to the Hebrew Gospel of Matthew*".

I am bringing this subject here, because through his name, among many revelations that it brings us, we can see the reason for his rejection, for having become a god, for existing so many misconceptions about him and the reason that only a few know who he really was. Let's take a brief look at his name in Hebrew.

Yehoshua is a junction of a name and a verb, as well as the name Rafael (Rafa - healed + EL - Deus). His name is the NAME ABOVE ALL NAMES, the Tetragram (יהוה) - *YEHOxxx* - and the verb LEHOSHIA (להושיע) – *to save* - conjugated in the future of the third person singular YOSHIA (יושיע).

YEHOxxx (**יהו**ה) + yoSHIA (יו**שע**)
= YEHOSHUA (**יהו-שע**)

The name Yehoshua is the junction of the true and deepest name of the Creator (יהוה) to the verb "to save", so we have ADONAI SAVES, unlike the word jesus, which means nothing. In the book of Matthew, his name appears in the contracted form of Yeshua, but in other books in its originals, like the book of Luke and the book of Yohanan, his full name appears as Yehoshua Ben Yosef.

With this in mind, I will again place the sefirot linked with each letter of the name YHWH (יהוה):

י (yud) - KETER
ה (hei) - BINAH, CHOKHMAH
ו (vav) - CHESSED, NETZACH, YESOD, TIFERET, HOD, GEVURAH
ה (hei) - MALKHUT

As previously discussed, the Sefirah MALKHUT is the lowest of all, the one that is closer to the earthly reality and to everything that exists in it. It is this sefirah that gives man an understanding about his reality, his existence, about how nature works, laws of gravity, engineering, music, and every creative skill of man.

If we look at the name of YEHO-SHUA (יהו-שע), he has only the first three letters of God's name, leaving the last HEI (ה) aside, that is, in his name is concentrated all sefirot, except the most human one, the MALKHUT and through this we can understand some affirmations from the new testament:

He came to his own and his own did not understand him.

John 1:11

And with many words he spoke to them, for they could not understand him.

Mark 4:34

For neither his brothers understood him.

John 7:5

No one has understood him, just as many churches do not understand him and theology does not understand him. For he does not represent the sefirah MALKHUT, the sefirah most connected to the earthly things. That is, he is not understandable by the common human mind. True understanding of who he really was will be given only to those who receive the other lights of God and as we have seen before, the Torah is necessary for this.

I have heard many saying that satan's greatest weapon is to keep people from believing in him, but I think he cares little whether one believes in him or not, for the thing that brings him the most advantage is precisely the lies about the Torah's abolition, with this, he is able to create concepts about Yeshua that deludes people's faith.

Whoever can understand this, understand it.

PAUL AND THE SEFIROT

Briefly, in order to serve as proof of what I have been

talking about and how this is all strongly inserted within the new testament, I will propose a simple comment from Paul on this regard:

> *Which none of the princes of this world knew: for had they known it, they would not have hung the **Lord of glory**.*
>
> 1 Corinthians 2:8

It must be clear here that this "lord of glory" is Yeshua. Now let us see a comment from one of the greatest Kabbalistic sages:

> *The category of Mashiach Ben David is in the sefira HOD.*
>
> Gaon De Vilna

As seen earlier, the Sefirah HOD represents GLORY, is Paul sending a hidden message? Was this the only one?

Without Torah, without Binah and without Torah, without spiritual understanding and thus the bible is old only stories.

XXII - JEALOUS GOD

You adulterers and adulteresses, know you not that the friendship of the world is enmity with God? whoever therefore will be a friend of the world is the enemy of God. Do you think that the scripture said in vain, The spirit that dwells in us is a jealous spirit?

James 4:4-5

The new testament suffers so much with translations and revisions that I wasn't able to find two different English bible versions with the translation from those verses that looked more or less the same, it amazes me the differences among the bible's version. For this reason, I am using my own translation made from an Italian bible.

James, as a good Pharisee, a rabbi and a Torah-observing Jew, follows a line of thought wholly within that reality in which he was raised. Such a mentality is clearly proven in the way he exposes his teachings. The terms that he uses in his book show that a prior knowledge of certain themes concerning his reality becomes necessary.

ADULTERERS AND ADULTERESSES

A reading of these verses without a minimum prior knowledge about James' mentality may lead one to understand that the aim of his words is concerning the commandment against adultery, against extramarital affairs. I see some problems if that were the case, for adultery is a very serious behavioral failure, something that goes beyond just a sinful attitude towards Adonai, but a sin of a character flaw. The way James treats his audience, as adulterers and adulteresses, is not only a very serious accusation, but it gives the impression that there is in his midst a group of people with a very serious deviation of character. As I do not believe this is the case, we should look at "adulterers and adulterers" in another way, as another type of sin.

Oh that I had in the wilderness a lodging place of wayfaring men; that I might leave my people, and go from them! for they be all ***adulterers****, an assembly of treacherous men.*
Jeremiah 9:2

And they that escape of you shall remember me among the nations where they shall be carried captives, because I am broken with their ***adulterer*** *heart, which has departed from me, and with their eyes, which go a whoring after their idols: and they shall loathe themselves for the evils which they have committed in all their abominations.*
Ezekiel 6:9

The accusation James presents, does not actually refer to an extramarital relationship, but rather to idolatry itself, which is something much more intimate and hidden within the human being. Unlike adultery in the literal sense of the word, which is an act to be consummated, idolatry intertwines with one's faith in a way that it becomes unrecognizable, being confused with Adonai's own truth.

The proof of this is the connection that James makes between "adulterers" with "*friendship of the world*", this confirms that James does not address the act of cheating itself, but rather idolatry, for in the rabbinic language, it is represented by "the world".

And God said to Noach, the end of all flesh has come before me, illicit relations and ***idolatry*** *have brought the destruction of the* ***world,*** *for the earth is full of wickedness through*

them and behold, I will destroy them of the world.
Targum Yohanan, Genesis 6:13

In the Torah's Aramaic translation, we see that God resolves to destroy the world in order to destroy idolatry, since both ideas are associated. This is extremely delicate, for idolatry is not only about worshiping false gods made of wood and stone, but it is about everything connected with this earthly reality that ends up becoming more relevant than God and His will.

To make this simpler, let us imagine two realities, an earthly one, where man worries about work, family, money, power, fame, possessions, influence, cars, houses, luxury items and a second one, a spiritual reality , where we have faith, prayer, Torah, commandments, studies on God's things and the search and devotion to His will. If anything from the first reality carries more weight in the life of a man than the things attached to the second reality, that man is idolatrous.

If a person's work is more important than the Torah, if earning money comes before studying Torah, if the football match takes the time of prayer, if the concern for the family is greater than the concern with the commandments, if love to what is material is bigger than the love to the Word of God, then this person is an idolater and adulterer before God.

It is very convenient to define the "world" as something sinful, such as alcohol, cigarettes, pornography and so on. This makes everything easier for the Christian, it is enough for him to turn away from these things and one might think he will not be considered a friend of the world by God, but even though one does none of this things and if he is someone concerned with money, someone who likes to exert influence, someone who does not bother to study Torah, someone who believes in the abolition of the commandments and someone who worries too much about his and his family wellbeing, even if he does not smoke, does not drink, does not go to worldly parties and lives a life according to what the church defines as holiness, if he does not observe the above mentioned, he is no better than an idol worshiper and a friend of the world. Let no one deceive himself.

[These are] the analogues of Solomon, son of David, king of Israel [e.g., Torah is compared to a good woman; idolatry, to an adulteress.]

Mishlei 1:1

A idolater person acts if he had denied the whole Torah.

Mishneh Torah, WCN 2:5

He who denies the Torah admits idolatry.

Rashi, Deuteronomy 11:28

What James teaches here is, if the one who has anything in his life, whatever it is, more importance than God and His word, this one is constituted an enemy of God. This is a very tough thing, for imagine someone who needs to work hard to support his family and therefore, does not have time to study the Word of God; it can even be justified that God understands it, because he does it for his family, something that in the eyes of the world is a very correct thing to do. But biblically speaking, in addition to being idolatry, he lacks faith, for he believes that he is the one who sustains and supports his family and not God. This is something to always be taken into account inside each one.

God holds His superiority over the other gods and severely punishes His enemies, those who worship the idols of the world.

Rashi, Exodus 34:14

JEALOUS GOD

Entering the next verse, which deals with a certain "jealous spirit" becomes easier after the above. This spirit, to which James certainly refers, is definitely not the Holy Spirit, for such an idea is not biblical, but rather God Himself, who manifests Himself within each of His servants.

You should not bow down to them and serve them. For I am Adonai, your Elohim, a jealous God (EL KANAH)...

Exodus 20:5a

For you should not worship other gods, for I am Adonai, called the jealous God (EL KANAH).

Exodus 34:14

For Adonai, your Elohim, is a consuming fire, a jealous God (EL KANAH).

Deuteronomy 4:24

You shall not prostrate yourself or serve them. For I, Adonai, your Elohim, am a jealous God (EL KANAH).

Deuteronomy 5:9

For Adonai, your Elohim, is among you, a jealous God (EL KANAH)...

Deuteronomy 6:15a

The term "jealous God" appears six times throughout the Torah as EL KANAH (אל קנא). Although this translation gives the impression that being jealous is a God's characteristic, it is actually one of His Names, which for some reason turned out to be translated as "jealous God". Let take a look at this name through the Gematria:

KANAH (קנא)
1א + 50נ + 100ק
= **151** = **7**

KANAH, besides possessing the value of 7, which is the number associated with God's acts, it also has the value of 151, which proves that this term is one of God's names.

By Gematria Mispar Perati, where the square value of each of the corresponding numbers is calculated, reveals that the first name by which God presents Himself to Moses in the burning bush is also 151:

EHIE (אהיה)

א(1x1) + (5x5)ה + (10x10)י + (5x5)ה

= **151**

This name (KANAH), due to its value of 151, also reveals a very important characteristic that is associated with it. Such a characteristic is the way in which God deals with idolaters, not only those who prostrate themselves to idols, but also with the friends of the "world", as stated by James:

ELOHIM (אלהים)

40ם + 10י + 5ה + 30ל + 1א

= **86**

ADONAI (אדני)

10י + 50נ + 4ד + 1א

= **65**

65 + 86 = 151 (ADONAI ELOHIM)

Whenever God brings strict justice on a man, or on a nation, He is treated as ADONAI ELOHIM. This name can represent a judgment without mercy, without middle term, without soft talk. Every time God does in this way, it ends in destruction and death, as reported in the flood's story.

This teaches us that if the essence that the name EL KANAH represents is not well understood, the judgment that will be made by God will be totally strict and without any mercy. This is a very clear thing throughout the Tanakh, God never tolerated any kind of idolatry, because EL KANAH represents a God who is zealous for those who understand these things and a God without mercy with those who do not understand them.

By Gematria Mispar Siduri, where each of the 22 letters of the Hebrew alphabet is numbered directly from 1 to 22, we can see that this name is totally associated with the sin of idolatry.

EL KANAH (אל קנא)
1א + 14נ + 19ק + 12ל + 1א
= **47**

CHET (חטא) - Sin
1א + 9ט + 8ח
= **18**

AVODAH ZARAH (עבודה זרה) – Idol worship, idolatry
5ה + 20ר + 7ז + 5ה + 4ד + 6ו + 2ב + 16ע
= **65**

65 = 18 + 47

IDOLATRY (65) = SIN (18) against EL KANAH (47)

What James teaches in this passage is very simple, one that places greater importance on earthly things, such as work, money, family, professional success, consumption, dreams or personal plans, above the will of God, the Torah and the commandments, is an adulterer (idolater) and becomes an enemy of God, that is, EL KANAH becomes ADONAI ELOHIM and the punishment He will bring will be made by a judgment without mercy.

It is useless to live Christian puritanism if one do not understand these things. That's why so many things in the lives of countless people who serve God go wrong. This is the "heaviest" warning in the book of James.

EL KANAH - He is Kanah, because he brings the right judgment, exercising His right not to forgive idolatry. Kanah is the exact punishment of those deeds.

Rashi, Exodus 20:5

May we never forget that.

XXIII - TO RESIST

Submit yourselves therefore to God. Resist the devil, and he will flee from you.

James 4:7

Throughout many Christian commentaries and many church's literatures, there are many interpretations regarding this passage in the book of James. A lot of them normally state that the real Christian can and should resist the temptation. The Christian theology also claims that temptation is something exclusively connected to satan and when one is able to resist to his trap, he will flee.

But with a somewhat careful reading of biblical passages, we shall see that it is not good for any man to face temptation. Temptation is something that we must flee and not resist, for we will always fail if we try to outmatch it. Due to this fact, this Christian understanding about temptation sounds more like fishy to me, for there is no point in trying to resist temptations with the hope that satan will flee from us, for he will not. For this reason, we must do a research in order to find out what James meant in this verse.

The approach I will take to this passage does not intent to teach about satan and everything about him. I will address some stuff about him so we can come to a conclusion consistent with the Jewish mentality, so that this passage can be understood in the way it meant to be understood. Therefore, I will cover some topics about satan, the mystical vision about him and teachings found in the New Testament.

HAsATAN

The word satan is not actually his name, it is rather a term that was adopted into Hebrew from the Aramaic *suh'tan*. This words means "opposite side" or "other side". In Hebrew it is commonly understood as "opposer" or "accuser", for it has been given him the authority to supervise this realm.

The most confusing thing concerning satan is about his origin. Satan is by no means an enemy of God, a God's opponent, nor a fallen angel as many claim him to be. Satan, in fact, is an angel in the service of the Creator, who was placed on this earthly realm to supervise it, just as a policeman supervise a certain region, looking for wrong doings in people's behavior, so that he can accuse them and be able to apply the penalty on those people.

Another thing we must take into account is that satan and demons are different beings. Satan is a cherub created in a reality where there were the absence of the light of God when tzimtzum took place. The demons however, are mystical creations in the absence of this light take took place in the earthly reality, that is, demons' existence are entirely connected do this earth (this is discussed in another chapter).

For now we must understand that satan is a cherub under the service of the Creator of all things, he was begotten by Him with another essence, another raw material so to speak, when compared to the cherubim that serve God near the Throne. His role is to make sure that God's justice is carried out, and for this reason he keeps his eyes widely open seeking for reaons to accuse and to destroy men, for even though he is working for Adonai, he is a being that came from the absence of God's light, thus making him the opposite from all that are represented by the sefirot.

His work is quite simple actually, as he knows God's law upside down, he is able to offer to man what can get him out of the ways of Hashem. This is basically satan and his mission given by God.

The basic idea about satan is not Christian but rather Jewish, it is an understanding that came from the people of Israel and passed on to the world by the divine mercy, so everyone can be aware of him. In all Jewish literature, the figure of satan is extensively discussed, in the Tanakh, Talmud, Zohar, the commentaries and in the New Testament, which is a Jewish compendium.

For this reason, we will seek answers from these sources and we shall see how cabalistic is the new testament on this subject.

Reish Lakish says: satan, the yetzer hara and the angel of death are as one, that is, they are three separated beings formed from the same essence. Satan is the one who seduces people and accuses them. The yetzer hara are the evil impulses of the heart. And he also represents the angel of death, for clearly the life of Job during the trial depended on him, for Job was in the hands of satan.

Talmud of Babylon, Tractate Bava Batra 16a

At the moment of the creation of all things, Hashem removed His light, as if He were "contracting it" and thus generated an empty space within Himself so that His holiness would not destroy everything that was just about to be created. This contraction generated a great emptiness, some sort of a creative space, but without the direct presence of Hashem, and this space served as a "raw material" so that everything that we know, could be created. This act is known as tzimtzum.

This empty space that God created, a space without His light, without the presence of the Creator, served as primary energy for the creation of what is contrary to His light, it was from the essence of the absence of light that Satan was begotten, the angel of death, the yetzer hara (evil instinct) and all the impurities that are present in this earthly realm, whether they are physical or spiritual.

By this we can understand that everything created through the light has its counterpart in the absence of light. Cherubim and angels created in the light to serve the throne have their counterparts coming from the absence of the presence. The yetzer hara comes from this darkness in contrast to the yetzer hatov that comes from the light of Adonai. Sin comes from this emptiness and the Torah from the light and so on. This explains one of the interpretations of when God says "*let us make man*" at the moment He decided to create man; this statement is presented in the plural form, for as if He were talking with both the essences that man was made of, both the yetzer hara and the yetzer hatov, two intrinsic "beings" in every human being.

There is a very interesting information about these beings that Gematria can reveal. Since satan, the angel of death and the yetzer hara are beings from the "opposite side", I will use Gematria's numerical values in the opposite way, that is, with the inversion of values, ALEF (א) gets the value of TAV (ת), BET (ב) the value of SHIN (ש) and so on. So, the first letter receives the value of the last one and the last one the value of the first. Such a method is known in Hebrew as "AtBash".

sATAN (שטן)

9ן + 50ט + 2ש

= **61**

MAL'AKH HAMUT (מלאך המות) - angel of death

1ת + 80ו + 10מ + 90ה + 30ך + 400א+ 20ל + 10מ

= **641**

In the kabbalah, among some other things, the number 6 represents the 6 days of creation, a creation that concerns this realm and because satan exerts his influence on it, the number 6 is somehow connected to him and to the abscense of light. In 6 days all earthly things were created, everything connected to what was created in those days are somehow under satan's authority that was given to him by God, except for the Shabbat.

Now, since the number 1 represents God, if we look the satan's numerical value, 61, we can see that behind the 6 that represents satan's authority, there is the number 1 which shows us that he is under God's strict supervision. This also reveals to us that the authority over the world was given to satan by God; amazing fact is that God does not lose control for a second, for He is right behind satan, watching him. We can picture this as if God were taking satan for a walk on a leash, like a dog, this is why the 1 comes right after the 6.

Now, concerning the angel of death we have the value of 641 which; and as above, 641 is the number 61 with the number 4 in its center. The 4 in kabbalah is a number that represents death. So, 641 is the essence of satan (61) with death (4) in the middle. This proves that both are from the same "place", but the angel of death has a more specific mission.

Thus reveals to us how these "opposing" forces operate. They have authority over all things created in the first six days of creation, but everything they do, must be according to God's permission. We also see that the Shabbat, that is, what it represents, is not under the influence or authority of this darkness, of this absence of God, of this 61.

The aspect of the Shabbat is like a circle, for the circle is the aspect of the Throne of Glory. During the 6 days of the week, the divine presence manifests itself in flashes of light, but on Shabbat the FULL divine presence manifests. In the future when all evil is eliminated, it will be like a great Shabbat.

Likutei Moharan 59:3

The Shabbat, as a day to be observed, is merely a physical representation of something spiritual, it becomes necessary, for without these representations the human understanding would be totally earthly, thus losing all connection with the Creator. The Shabbat represents the presence of

Adonai, represents the opposite of that which comes from His absence, is the representation of the Light emanating from His Throne. The Torah is the only "tool" that can lead man to this spiritual Shabbat, when one enters this "reality", one establishes an intimate relationship with HaShem and becomes immune to Satan. That is why satan number is 61, for he has authority only over what is earthly, under the supervision of the Creator.

The Talmud has a commentary on this God's "supervision" over the agents on the "opposite side."

> *Rabbi Levi says: Both satan, who brought charges against Job, and Peninnah, who tormented Hannah, mother of the prophet Samuel, acted in the name of the heavens. Satan, when he saw that the Holy One, Blessed Be He, bowed down in favor of Job and praised him, he said: may God not allow him to forget the love of Avraham. Concerning Peninnah, it is written: and his rival wife provoked her pain, that she might suffer. Penninah bothered Hannah to motivate her to pray to Hashem.*
>
> Talmud of Babylon, Tractate Bava Batra 16a

Satan works for Hashem, all that he does, though contrary in appearance, is for the benefit and honor of the Name of the One who created him. Except when man sins, then he has a different authority, a punitive one.

Well, the topic here is not satan, but rather the temptation he poses before the human being to overthrow us. I believe that the best example we have on this regard is described in the forty days that Yeshua spent in the wilderness where he was tempted by satan for three times. Such a fact has been previously addressed, but within these events, there are a few more "sensitive" things that show us a deeper side of what was happening.

One thing is certain, Yeshua dealt with satan using ONLY the Torah and not through prayer. Another fact is that Yeshua did not expel him, but rather he "draws a line on the sand", a line that satan cannot cross. It is precisely this what we must understand, it is not to expel the satan, this is done with demons, we must know how to "draw a line" in order to be "free" from his influence, it is like a barrier between us and him that we must know how to create.

In order to do so, we just have to look at Yeshua's behavior towards satan. Yeshua exposed the Torah to him, he used it as a shield and for this, Yeshua quoted four passages from the Torah that address four very specific things: bread, to tempt, to pray and to worship.

...But man shall not live by ***bread*** *alone, but from all things found in the mouth of Adonai.*
Deuteronomy 8:3b

Do not ***tempt*** *Adonai, your Elohim, as you did in Massah.*
Deuteronomy 6:16

I will ***pray*** *to Hashem...*
Deuteronomy 9:26a

Only Adonai, your Elohim, you shall fear and only Him you WILL ***worship*** *and only in His name you shall swear.*
Deuteronomy 6:13

LECHEM (לחם) - BREAD

Bread represents something earthly, totally connected to the physical and to the things concerning this earthly life. Bread, besides representing what keeps the human being alive, also represents what kills him.

The word LECHEM (לחם) has as root the letters (ל-ח-מ), which is the same root as the word MILCHAMAH (מלחמה) which means "war". This teaches us that the very bread that brings life to man is the same bread that brings him death. They are two sides from the same "coin".

This concept is wholly linked to the idea of the yetzer hara (evil instinct) and the yetzer hatov (good instinct), for just as the yetzer hatov guarantees life in the world to come, yetzer hara brings eternal death, and both are within every being human, they are the two facets of each one of us.

He's the destroyer comrade. The only intention of the destroyer is ***<u>to steal</u>*** *the divine spark and to absorb it and thus avoiding the return of holiness in every human. This is the hidden meaning of "But man shall not live by bread alone, but all things found in the mouth of Adonai."*

Pri Etz Hadar 1:5

LECHEM (לחם)
40ם + 8ח + 30ל
78 = 7+8 = 15 = 1+5 = **6**

LENASOT (לנסות) – TO TRY, TO TEMPT

This term is in a passage that has several mystical teachings. But within our theme, in order for us to have the true understanding, we should not look at the meaning of LENASOT itself, but rather at its root and what word is associated with it. Among a few, the one that most fits here is the word NES (נס) - *miracle* - from the same root of LENASOT and therefore can be used in a mutable way.

When the angel comes ***<u>to kill</u>*** *and the man receives a miracle by being delivered, he should sing a psalm, for his life was kept through a miracle (NES).*

Or Neerav, part I,4

According to our sages, the deliverance of the angel of death is a miracle, it is a NES (נס). Interesting as they necessarily connect the miracle with the angel of death and not with the yetzer hara. This shows us that the yetzer hara is our responsibility and the angel of death is taken care by Hashem.

LENASOT (לנסות)
400ת + 6ו + 60ס + 50נ + 30ל
546 = 5+4+6 = 15 = **6**

LEHITPALEL (להתפלל) – TO PRAY

The third mention of Yeshua is prayer, not as a weapon of exorcism, but as an intimate fellowship with the Creator. Today it is very common for people to use prayer for various things, except for a relationship with God and so they wonder why things do not go the way they want to.

The prayer that keeps satan away, first, must be made to God, Adonai, the Creator and not to any other, whoever it may be. I repeat, only to GOD.

Prayer must be done with all the heart, trusting one's heart in the hands of the One who created all things, it should be an expression of the soul, through a recognition of who He really is.

*And everyone who goes to his bed at night and through his prayer recognizes the sovereignty of the Creator, will no longer be under the influence of satan. Immediately he will be freed from all disease, violence and evil eye, and these things will have no more power **to destroy**. By His great mercy I enter into His presence and I bow in fear before His holiness.*

Zohar HaKadosh 1:11a

LEHITPALEL (להתפלל)

30ל + 30ל + 80פ + 400ת + 5ה + 30ל

575 = 17 = 1+7 = **8**

With this, it becomes clear why Yeshua brings these three passages to light. He is not actually only teaching how to drive away only the satan, but rather the essence from which satan, the angel of death and the yetzer hara were created. Nothing is by chance in the Word of God, everything connects and the basis for everything is the Torah.

Another teaching of Yeshua that clarifies all of this is found in John 10:10:

*The thief comes only **to steal, to kill, and to destroy**; I have* *come that you may have life, and may have it abundantly.*

John 10:10

As seen in the comments above, "to steal" represents the yetzer hara, "to kill" represents the angel of death and "to destroy" represents satan himself. Three beings from the same essence, that is, Yeshua is not teaching about the works that satan does, but he teaches about his essence, where he is from. This "thief" he quotes is not the "opponent", but the darkness that was originated from the tzimtzum, this thief represents the absence of the presence of God and not an entity.

It is striking the connection that Yehsua had with Judaism, its teachings, its mysticism and above all, the Torah, for without it, Yeshua becomes a myth called jesus.

LA'AVOD (לעבוד) – TO WORSHIP

Finally we have the worship. Although the verb LA'AVOD is commonly translated as "to work", biblically it refers to "worship."

In order for someone to serve God in the right way, this one needs knowledge about Him. That is, knowledge of His manifestations, of His sefirot, through which He leads all things and of His oneness, then that one will be able to truly worship Him.

Or Neerav Part II 1:3

What this text teaches us is that a person cannot worship a God that he does not know and for this God to be known, one must know His sefirot, that is, how He acts, behaves, determines, desires, and manifests, and also the full recognition that He is ONE and not three, then, true worship is possible.

Yeshua is quite clear about this when he says, "ONLY HASHEM I WILL WORSHIP".

LA'AVOD (לעבוד)

4ד + 6ו + 2ב + 70ע + 30ל

112 = 1+1+2 = **4**

THE GEMATRIA BEHIND YESHUA'S WORDS

I am fascinated by Yeshua's teachings, he cites four simple passages based on four simple ideas and from all of this, it is revealed to us the true essence of satan, how he works, what are his associations and so on.

If we use Gematria on the four key themes used by Yeshua, "bread", "to tempt", "to pray" and "to worship" and put them all together, as Yeshua has presented them, all that we saw until here will be confirmed.

As already calculated above:

LECHEM (6) + LENASOT (6) + LEHITPALEL (8) + LA'AVOD (4) =

6 + 6 + 8 + 4 = 24 = 2 + 4

= **6**

The number 6, as already seen, represents the mundane things, which were created in 6 days. The 6 is also the value of the word SHEKER (שקר) which means "lie", teaching us that this reality is a lie, it is all illusion and the influence and authority that satan has it is only on illusory things and no more.

The number 6 does not encompass the Shabbat, for the Shabbat is not of this reality, but a representation of the spiritual one. The value of the word SHABBAT (שבת) is 9, the opposite of the worldly illusion represented by 6, as well as the truth EMET (אמת) which also has the value of 9 and is the opposite of lie.

TO RESIST

Now we can understand James, the only way to resist satan is to keep him out of our lives through the Torah, its commandments, its study and by the lifestyle proposed therein. Whoever understands this shall not become a victim anymore.

Rabbi Avin said: Anyone who underestimates his yetzer hara, will become a victim of it. Rabbi Papa says, if your yetzer comes to tempt you, send him away using the words of the Torah.
Bereshit Rabbah 22

The teaching of this midrash is exactly what Yeshua did, he sent away only using the words of Torah. Anyone who knows the will of the Creator, will know how to behave, how to pray and how to worship Him.

Take the k'dushah from Hashem by curling yourself in the Talit, with the name of Hashem upon you through the tefillim on the forehead and with the bow of the name of Hashem in your hand through the tefillim tied in the right hand and the sword of Hashem in your waist through the tzitzit. The demons fear of Hashem will be upon you.
Siddur Hashacharit

This Siddur passage is fantastic, it teaches us how to simply protect ourselves with the Torah and its commandments. Funny thing, those words from the Siddur reminds me of a person who certainly had this idea very well defined within his faith.

Put on the whole armor of God, that you may be able to stand against the wiles of the devil.
For we wrestle not against flesh and blood, but against principalities, against powers, against the rulers of the darkness of this world, against spiritual wickedness in high places.
Why take to you the whole armor of God, that you may be able to withstand in the evil day, and having done all, to stand.
Stand therefore, having your loins girt about with truth, and having on the breastplate of righteousness;
And your feet shod with the preparation of the gospel of peace;
Above all, taking the shield of faith, with which you shall be able to quench all the fiery darts of the wicked.
And take the helmet of salvation, and the sword

of the Spirit, which is the word of God.

Ephesians 6:11-17

Paul speaks exactly the same thing. He begins by stating how to get rid of the devil and then talks about the armor. Certainly, this text, for being under the influence of the church for so many years is not fully trustworthy, but Paul was certainly speaking of the same thing as the Siddur, for that was Paul's faith.

Unfortunately theology interprets mystical things without any knowledge and for this reason we have a bunch of incoherent teachings.

XXIV - TO MOURN AND TO WEEP

Be afflicted, and mourn, and weep: let your laughter be turned to mourning, and your joy to heaviness.

James 4:9

The weeping (BEKHI - בכי) and the mourning (MISPED - מספד), in the way James presented them in this verse is a very commonplace throughout the Tanakh. There are several passages that bring together both terms, for when they are presented altogether, it represents pain, regret and Tshuvah.

When the Torah relates BEKHI (בכי) and MISPED (מספד) they kinda sound like a poetic word pun within the Hebrew language and they are applied with the intention of emphasizing a teaching. It is very likely that James is following an ideological process of expressing an idea established by the Tanakh.

James' intention is for his hearers to repent of their ways and to return to the God of Israel by doing the real Tshuvah, just as Isaiah did when he warned his hearers. "Weeping" and "mourning" is the state that the human being must attain before returning to the ways of God, for they demonstrate true regret and a without it, it is not possible to make a true, heartfelt Tshuvah. They are signs of a change from past attitudes and preliminary proofs of a real intention to obtain a more intimate connection with the Creator of all things. Both terms are signs of true regret within the Jewish mentality.

Some examples in the Tanakh that uses those words in

the same way found in the book of James:

> *My Lord, Adonai of Hosts, calls on that day to weep (BEKHI - בכי) and to mourn (MISPED - מספד), to shave the heads and to cover oneself with sackcloth.*
>
> Isaiah 22:12

> *And now, says Adonai, come back to me with all your heart, with fasting, weeping (BEKHI - בכי) and mourning (MISPED - מספד).*
>
> Joel 2:12

We can observe in these passages the tone of repentance that they have. The most important thing to note is that "weeping" as well as "mourning" are not only proofs of true regret but they are in fact direct ordinances from God Himself, that is, in order to a return to Him to be truly valid, one needs those things. This teaches us that a repentance that does not come from within our souls, a regret that doens't bring weeping and mourning due to past attitudes, is not a true repentanc nor a way to Tshuvah. A prayer with a simple requests for forgiveness, from what we see here, may not be enough for it to ascend to the throne of Adonai. That's something we should always think about.

> *In all provinces in which the command and the decree of the king came, there was a great sadness among the Jews, with **fasting** (TZUM - צום), **weeping** (BEKHI - בכי), **mourning** (MISPAD - מספד) and all covered themselves with **sackcloth** (SHAK - שק) and **ashes** (EFER - אפר).*
>
> Esther 4:3

This passage from the book of Esther reveals us all the secrets about regret and a perfect Tshuvah. The difference between regret and Tshuvah is that the Tshuvah begins with a feeling called "regret" that comes from the understanding of the errors and the need to get rid of them; the Tshuvah, which in Hebrew means "answer", is the attitude to return to the ways of Hashem, besides giving up past habits, Tshuvah is the adoption of a righteous life before God. It all start with a feeling (regret) and the understanding about the sins and then comes the attitude, the change; those two are what form the true repentance.

With a more mystical analysis, we first have regret, which in Hebrew is D'AVON (דאבון); the way in which this regret is to be done is demonstrated by an understanding of past errors and thus leading the one to weep (BEKHI - בכי) and to mourn (MISPAD - מספד).

BEKHI (בכי) - WEEPING
10י + 20כ + 2ב
32 = 3+2 = **5**

MISPAD (מספד) - MOURNING
4ד + 80פ + 60ס + 40מ
184 = 1+8+4 = 13 = **4**

If we join them both as they are always presented throughout the Tanakh and by James, we shall have **5 + 4 = 9.**

D'AVON (דאבון) - REGRET
50ן + 6ו + 2ב + 1א + 4ד
63 = 6+3 = **9**

Regret, the initial feeling, is only true when it causes the soul to weep and to mourn due to the internal pain caused by the past behaviors, just as Adonai commands it to be.

Then comes the time of the return, the time of Tshuvah, and the way the Tanakh teaches us that it should be done is through fasting (TZUM - צום) and covering oneself with ashes (EFER - אפר) and with sackcloth (SHAK - שק).

SHAK (שק) - SACKCLOTH
100ק + 300ש

400 = **4**

EFER (אפר) - ASHES

200ר + 80פ + 1א

281 = 2+8+1 = 11 = 1+1 = **2**

TZUM (צום) - FASTING

40ם + 6ו + 90צ

136 = 1+3+6 =10 = **1**

And through these three we have THE true TSHUVAH, the true "answer" that must be given to God as proof of repentance, for **4 + 2 + 1 = 7**.

HATSHUVAH (התשובה) - THE real REPENTANCE

5ה + 2ב + 6ו + 300ש + 400ת + 5ה

718 = 7+1+8 = 16 = **7**

For these terms to become more palpable in our lives, let's define each one of them.

-**WEEPING** (בכי) = the pain caused when the one acknowledges, through the understanding of the Torah, the sins he commited and the tortuous ways of his life.

-**MOURNING** (מספד) = the feeling of an urgent need for a change, it's a recognition of all the made mistakes. This only comes by the understanding of what these mistakes represent before Adonai.

-**SACKCLOTH** (שק) = the humility in recognizing the mistakes.

-**FASTING** (צום) = the sacrifice required for these changes to be made, no matter what it costs, whoever does the true Tshuvah, must leave behind all that is not in conformity with Adonai.

-**ASHES** (אפר) = the recognition that only Adonai is God, only He forgives, only He saves.

When these five things enter the soul of a person, one makes the true Tshuvah that comes through true repentance and then, this person is ready to enter into the ways of the true God.

This is what James teaches here.

THE WEEPING, THE MOURNING AND YESHUA

I believe to be fair to look at these terms within the messianic reality of James and how these words are embedded within the life and reality of Yeshua.

Then was fulfilled what the prophet Yrmiahu said.
A voice is heard in Ramah, lamentations and bitter weeping, Rachel weeping for her son and so on.

Matthew 2:17-18

Thus said Adonai: a voice is heard in Ramah, mourning, bitter weeping, Rachel weeping for her children. She does not want to be comforted, for they are gone.

Jeremiah 31:15

Matthew quotes this prophecy shortly after the account of the massacre caused by Horodos, when, in search of Yeshua, he orders a slaughtering of all the male newborns. The fact that Jeremiah's prophecy deals with "weeping" and "death" of children, gives us a simple impression that Matthew's mention was made because of the act of this murderer.

But if we look closely at the prophecy, it does not make much sense with that simple fact, for what does the matriarch Rachel have to do with that slaughter, since she was not even present at that moment?

Well, Rachel was the wife of Yaakov, the mother of Yosef and Benjamin. The Torah tells us that when Yaakov's favorite son, Yosef, was taken into captivity, his brothers told his father that he was killed and for years Yaakov wept for the loss of his son. Many years later, his brothers found him alive in Egypt and as the story unfolds, Benjamin, for being the youngest, ended up serving as a rescue tool to rid Yaakov's family from hunger and death.

If we make a simple connection with what has been seen until now, the two tribes from the sons of Yosef belonged to the Kingdom of Israel, they are two of the ten Israel's scattered tribes in the world. In contrast, the tribe of Benjamin, as well as the tribe of Judah, were part of the Kingdom of South, the Kingdom of Yehudah, which was not dispersed and assimilated by the nations.

By this we can understand that, just as one day Yaakov wept for having lost Yosef, Rachel's weep has the same symbology, the loss of her son Yosef to the nations of the world. But Benjamin, who represents the Kingdom of Yehudah, from where Mashiach Ben Yosef comes, will serve as a ransom for Yosef and his brothers, the lost tribes of Israel.

This idea is confirmed by the prophet Jeremiah himself in the following two verses:

> *Thus said Adonai, restrain your voice from weeping, your eyes from shedding the tears, for there is a reward for your labor, Adonai says, for they shall return from the lands of the enemy. And there will be hope at the end. Says Adonai, for your children will return to their country.*
>
> Jeremiah 31:16-17

Jeremiah, by continuing his prophecy, says that Adonai will return the sons of Rachel from the lands of the enemy, that is, those who have been assimilated by the nations will return. Adonai says that they will return to their country, to the land of Israel. Another interesting point is the word Ramah, there is a city in the territory of Benjamin called Ramah, which was right on the border with the tribe of Manasseh, one of the sons of Yosef. This city, after the separation of Israel in two kingdoms, ended up being annexed to the territory of the north, thus becoming part of the tribe of Manasseh. This is the city that made the connection between the two tribes that represented the sons of Rachel, Manasseh (Yosef) and Benjamin, and that city was eventually lost along with the rest of the Kingdom of Israel. The use of this prophecy by Matthew goes far beyond the atrocity caused by Horodos at that time, it shows that Mashiach Ben Yosef, who will come from the Kingdom of the South, will bring back the lost son of Rachel, that is, he will serve as a rescue tool to the lost tribes lost, just as Benjamin once did.

* This theme about the tribes is dealt with in the book *TORAT YEHOSHUA, ACCORDING TO THE HEBREW GOSPEL OF MATTHEW.*

*** Both Mashiach Ben Yosef and Mashiach Ben David are from the tribe of Yehudah. Benjamin, in this case, is only a representation of the Kingdom of the South, not that Mashiach is from the tribe of Benjamin.*

THE WEEPING, THE MOURNING AND MASHIACH BEN YOSEF

Something very common within Christianity is the lack of understanding that many have about what it is to be Mashiach. Some define him as "the anointed one" or "the savior", but deep down they do not know the true essence of that word and the profound meaning of his mission.

The mission of Mashiach occurs in two fronts, in two moments, in a first he is recognized as Mashiach Ben Yosef and in the second, as Mashiach Ben David. Mashiach Ben Yosef was the one Yeshua claimed to be, of course Mashiach is one, but he was referring to the moment of his mission. One of these missions is precisely to gather the "lost sheep of the House of Israel," something already discussed at the beginning of this book.

With this in mind, a passage from the book of the prophet Jeremiah reveals very deep things:

I will bring them out of the land of the north, and gather them from the ends of the earth, the blind and the lame among them, those with child, and those in labor; A large congregation shall return here. ***They shall come with weeping and mourning****, and I will lead them to the streams of water, by a level road where they will not*

stumble, for I am a Father to Israel, and ***Ephraim*** *is My firstborn.*
Jeremiah 31:8-9

In these two verses we have many important information, the first thing we should pay attention to is the prophecy that comes from the mouth of God concerning the return of the tribes. He does not refer, in this case, to the return of the Babylonian exile, for to this exile only the Jews, the tribes of Yehudah and Benjamin, were taken. However, in this case, God presents Himself as a Father to Israel, and this shows who's this message for.

A second information is found at the end of verse nine, where God refers to His firstborn Ephraim. Ephraim, in fact, was the firstborn of Yosef, thus making a connection between "Ephraim, My firstborn" with Yosef, and by looking at Yosef, we have the information we need, for God refers precisely to Mashiach, in this case, presented as Ben Yosef. This is why He mentioned Ephraim.

According to the Gematria of the one represented by Ephraim:

MASHIACH BEN YOSEF (משיח בן יוסף)
80ף + 60ס + 6ו + 10י + 50ן + 2ב + 8ח + 10י + 300ש + 40מ
= **566**

This proves, once again, that this mission of "gathering the tribes" will be done by Mashiach Ben Yosef.

A third piece of information can be taken from the phrase "They shall come with weeping and mourning", for it is this how the lost tribes will be when they realize and understand who they really are.

According to the great sage, Gaon of Vilna, the "weeping" and "mourning" presented in this verse are linked to Mashiach Ben Yosef, as we can see below:

*"They shall come with weeping and mourning" - this phrase has the numerical value of (**566**), thus referring to Mashiach*

Ben Yosef, as when He said "Ephraim is My firstborn."

Gaon of Vilna

"With weeping" refers to the joy of returning to Israel, "with mourning" refers to the forgiveness of past sins. This will be done through the works of Mashiach Ben Yosef. If we look at the work of Yeshua, it makes perfect sense, besides what was discussed above, about the knowledge of God reaching the Gentile world, Yeshua speaks often about the forgiveness of sins through his death and the enjoyment they will have in him.

XXV -HUMBLE

Draw near to God, and he will draw near to you. Cleanse your hands, you sinners; and purify your hearts, you double minded. Be afflicted, and mourn, and weep: let your laughter be turned to mourning, and your joy to heaviness. Humble yourselves in the sight of the Lord, and he shall lift you up.

James 4:8-10

Humbling oneself and humility are things with deep secrets in the Torah. The problem is, in Western languages, these two words have meanings a little different from what we find in the Word of God.

In the Western mindset, the humble one is a person who posses no wealth, has little cultural knowledge and is not an arrogant person. The latter is a very valid definition and, in a way, helps the individual to have a better relationship with his neighbor and with society where he takes part of. But I do not particularly believe that James referred to arrogance and to anything financial in this case, because in verse 8 he speaks about sinners, that is, about sin, then in verse 9 he speaks about repentance and then he brings up the term "to humble oneself". In fact, he followed a pattern found in many rabbinic teachings.

The basic concept of this idea comes from a little-known verse about a Moses' personal characteristic:

והאיש משה **ענו** מאד מכל האדם אשר על פני האדמה

*Moses was a very **humble** man, more than any other man on the face of the earth.*

Numbers 12:3

Certainly, most of rabbinic Jewish idea of "to humble" was born precisely from this verse. In those words, there are mysteries that reveal to us how we can follow Moses as an example of life and, as argued by James, to be lifted up just as Moses was by humbling oneself.

There is a small detail in this verse (in Hebrew) almost imperceptible by many who read it in its original language. The term "to humble", the way it is presented in this verse, appears with a spelling error. Humble in Hebrew is ANAV (עניו), but the word found in this verse is ANAV (ענו) without the letter YUD (י) and this is what we should pay attention to.

Moses was the greatest leader the People of Israel ever had in their more than 3000 years of history, he was the man who saw God and God spoke to him face to face and without enigmas. Only by those facts it shows the high spiritual level Moses had. But despite all of his greatness, due to a slight error of Moses, God did not allow him to enter into the promised land. This flaw that Moses committed is reported in chapter 20 in that same book:

> *Moses and Aharon gathered the congregation together before the rock, and he said to them, "Listen you rebels, should we draw water from this rock?" And Moses lifted up his rod and struck the rock twice, and there came out pure water, and the whole community and their animals drank.*
>
> Numbers 20:10-11

"Water coming out of a rock" happens twice in the Torah. In the first time, God commanded Moses to strike the rock with his rod, and on the second one, God commanded him to command the water to come out of the rock. But what we see in this verse is that instead of commanding the water to come out, he strikes the rock with his rod and thus he does not act as God has determined.

But in fact, the real mistake made by Moses was not quite that as many believe, let's look at what he said before striking the rock:

המן הסלע הזה **נוציא** לכם מים
"Should we draw water from this rock?"

By his own words we see exactly where the real mistake, that prevented him from entering Israel, happened. What he really should have said would be this:

המן הסלע הזה **יוציא** לכם מים
"Does He should draw water from this rock?"

Instead of IOTZI (יוציא) - *He should draw* - Moses said NOTZI (נוציא) - *we should draw* - and he ends up taking the glory that should be given to God for himself. The difference is, instead of using the letter YUD (י), Moses uses the letter NUN (נ). Because of this, by omitting the letter YUD (י), the letter YUD (י) of the word ANAV (עניו) – *humble* (see above) - has also been removed and this teaches us that although Moses was the most humble person on the face of the earth, he was not a completely humble person, because he did not obey what God commanded him to do.

What we initially perceive with this is that we should always give honor and merit to God, but what we also have here is the need to obey what God tells us to do, exactly as He says.

One of the ways of dividing the commandments of the Torah is between the positive commandments, those that God commands us to do and the negative commandments, those that God commands us not to do.

This shows us that the true humble person before God is the one who carefully observes the positive commandments, those that God commands man to do. The proof of this is shown by the word ANAV (ענו) that appears in this verse without the letter YUD (י).

ANAV (ענו) - Humble - without the YUD (י)

= **248***

*Mispar Shemi

ANAV (ענו) - *humble* - without the YUD (י) has the value of 248, just as the Torah has exact 248 positive commandments. Coincidence?

A commentary made by Rabbi Ibn Ezra concerning Moses' humbleness shows a behavior only a few have:

Moses never wanted recognition or reward. He was an ANAV man.
Ibn Ezra, Numbers 12:3

Praying to God without asking for anything is a very difficult thing, not wanting recognition and not expecting rewards from God is something alien for the nature of the human. Yeshua, in a somewhat indirect way, talks about this:

If EL thinks of you, do not worry about what
you shall eat or what you shall drink.
All that the body needs, your Father knows.
He knows all the things you need.
Seek rather the kingdom of Elohim and be tzadikim
and all these things will be given to you.
Matthew 6:31-33

Yeshua's guidance is the same of what we have seen so far. Although he is not clear when he says not to worry about what to eat or what to drink, he says that we should not actually pray for things, for God already knows it, what we should do is to seek the Kingdom of Elohim through our prayers, by giving glory to Him, by exalting His name and so we become tzadikim, that is, a tzadik is one who observes the Torah and obeys God.

Yeshua addresses the two kind of "humbleness", the first is by following the positive commandments, which makes a man a tzadik and the second is not seeking God for personal gains and rewards.

As we read the three verses of James again, we will see that he first speaks of sin, that is, first of all one must let go of all that God commands NOT to do by observing the negative commandments.

Then he speaks of weeping and moutning, terms that deal with Tshuvah, which is the repentance followed by action, an action focused on how to walk in the ways of the Creator.

Finally, James speaks of humbleness in a different way from the western mindset, for to humble oneself, for a Jew as James, is the observance of the positive commandments, for they are what make a person really humble, the " Biblical humble". And then, whoever does it, will be lifted up by God.

They we all may understand the need to follow God's will in the way He wants us to follow it.

Rabbi Levitas said: Be exceedingly humble in spirit.

Pirkei Avot 4:4

XXVI - DEFAMATION

Speak not evil one of another, brothers. He that speaks evil of his brother, and judges his brother, speaks evil of the law, and judges the law: but if you judge the law, you are not a doer of the law, but a judge.

James 4:11

In chapter 4, James once again deals with the tongue, the evil it can cause and the need of his hearers to control it. The theme "tongue" and the symbology it has within the Jewish mentality has been discussed earlier in this book.

However, in verse 11, James takes a slightly different approach, which got my attention in regard to this new James' interpretation about the "tongue" and the harm that "evil speaking" can cause. In a totally rabbinical way, James makes his own midrash, that is, his own interpretation about the one who speaks evil and compares him with the one who judges the law. Such an interpretation and comparison is of personal nature from the author of the book of James, for I have never seen anything in this regard in all over the Jewish literature that I know.

It is commonplace to equate sinful attitudes before God, that is, throughout the Torah there are sins of different origins that have the same weight before the eyes of God. I can use as an example the sin of blasphemy with that of idolatry, or the sin of bearing false witness with the sin of murder, among many others. With this idea, pretty much as Paul does several times in his letters, James presents the sin of defamation and compares it with the sin of judging the law, this is what he is doing here.

For a better understanding of how the hearers of James understood this midrash, we must first look at both sins that he compares, the evil speaking and the sin of judging the law.

DIBAH (דבה)

To speak evil of the neighbor, in Hebrew, is called DIBAH (דבה), which can be translated as "defamation". Defamation goes a little further than a simple malicious gossip, for defamation is an evil attitude that changes the way the defamed person is seen within society. Also, in most of the cases, DIBAH is made in an unjust way, for such an attitude is normally the result of rancorous feelings on the one who slanders.

This term DIBAH (דבה) appears few times throughout the Tanakh and always associated with a very serious punishment. The first case happens in a well-known story, when Moses decides to send spies to the land of Canaan and when they returned, they spread fake reports that did not correspond with the truth, thus defaming the promised land:

The men whom Moses sent to recognize the land, among those who returned, caused the whole community to murmur against him by spreading defamation (DIBAH) upon the earth. Those who spread defamation (DIBAH) on the earth were killed by a plague (DEVER), by the will of Adonai.

Numbers 14:36-37

By the very consequence, we can see the difference that exists between defaming and raising false witness, the one who raises false witness, receives the punishment of being judged in the same measure that he judged, the one who slanders is punished by death and in this case, death by disease.

I have already met some people who did not know how to control their tongue, people who had the bad habit of speaking evil of others and who ended up having premature deaths by horrible diseases.

By doing a Kabbalistic analysis, we can understand that the term DIBAH (דבה) has the semantic structure as DABAR (דבר), which means "word", since defamation is something purely connected to what is said.

The word DABAR (דבר) is written in the same way as the word DEVER (דבר), which means "plague". This reveals to us the reason why people who have no control over their DABAR - *word* - end up paying the price through DEVER - *plague* - or some fatal disease.

The term DIBAH (דבה) has a very negative numerical value:

DIBAH (דבה)

5ה + 2ב + 4ד

= **11**

Biblically speaking, the number 11 symbolizes disorder, chaos and judgment. In the bible, the number 11 appears 24 times and the term "eleventh" can be found 19 times, totaling 43 times.

In Hebrew, there is a word called HAKIYCHA (הכיח) which is a type of catarrh that is generated due to lung infections caused by diseases that are contracted in the air. The numerical value of this word is also 43 and maybe this can show us what kind of plague, or disease, has affected these people. By the connection made, we see that these plague mainly affected the lungs, causing respiratory problems or diseases that are contracted by the air, such as SARS. Another association that the "air" can teach us is the speed that a defamation spreads, just as the air moves, so the defamation can move, fast. Rabbi Bahya makes a very coherent commentary with this idea:

When the snake was questioned: why when you only bite one

organ, all other organs are affected by the bite? The snake responds: why do you ask me this instead of asking why people who slander are able to kill without biting? Such people open their mouths here (in Palestine) and the lethal effect of their words are felt in Rome.

Rabbeinu Bahya, Bereshit 3:1

Just as no one holds the air, no one can contain the damage of a defamation after it is spoken.

But back to number 11, this is a number that comes after the number 10, which represents Law, completeness and self-mastery. The number 11 represents the opposite, represents the breaking of the law, irresponsibility and rebellion against God. If we read the chapter 11 of the book of Genesis, we shall see the first rebellious man in the bible, when nimrod builds a tower to overcome God.

Yoachim, one of the last kings of Yehudah and an idolatrous king, reigned for 11 years (609 CE to 598 CE). His successor King Yehoiachin reigned for less than three months and was soon overthrown by the Babylonians. King Zedekiah, chosen by Nabuchadnezzar to reign Yehudah, rebelled against him and had an 11-year reign, which culminated in the exile and destruction of the Temple and Jerusalem. It is also interesting that in the book of James, this teaching is found precisely in verse 11.

DIBAH, the defamation, brings destruction, exile, disease and death. Something very serious within the rabbinical mentality. But until then, we have seen only physical consequences, consequences related to this earthly life, let us look at what happens regarding the spiritual life and what damage it does before the eyes of Adonai.

Spies will have no place in the world to come, as it is written (Num. 14:37), "they died by the plague by the will of Adonai", that is, in this world by the plague and in the world to come by Adonai's will. He who slanders has no place in the world to come, as the generation of the wilderness did not have.

Ein Yaakov, Sanhedrin 11:111

The first mention we have alleges that the one who slanders, besides bringing death by plagues and diseases, will not enter the world to come, so defamation is something that, in simple words, sends the soul straight to hell.

*Adonai said to Moses, "Bring **me** together seventy elders of Israel....*
Numbers 11:16a

*Send men by **yourself** to recognize the land of Canaan....*
Numbers 13:2a

*What a slander can be compared to? To a rich man who owns a vineyard. When he saw that good wine was produced, he said to his servants, "Bring them to **me** in my house." But when he sees that the wine is not good, he tells his servants, "Take it for **yourself** and take it home." When the Holy One, Blessed Be He, saw that the seventy elders were worthy, He said, "Gather unto **Me**," but when He saw that the spies were unworthy, He said, "BY YOURSELF". This shows that those who slander have no share with the Holy One, Blessed Be He.*
Midrash Tanchumah, Sh'Lach 4:1

I believe for the level of understanding, we have enough. We must be careful with what we say concerning others.

TO JUDGE THE LAW

The idea of "judging the law", i.e. "judging the Torah", is comparable to the one who perverts the Law, distorting it by misinterpreting it. The prophet Jeremiah speaks in a very hard tone to those who do this, in an almost threatening tone:

... would you pervert the words of the Living God, the God of Hosts, our God ??????
Jeremiah 23:36b

Such an attitude is so serious that Yeshua also comments this:

Therefore I tell you that all sins and blasphemies will be forgiven the sons of man, but blasphemy to the spirit of Elohim will not be forgiven. Everyone who says a word against the Son of man shall be forgiven. And all things spoken against the deeds of Ruach Elohim (Holy Spirit) will not be forgiven, neither in this world nor in the world to come.

Matthew 12:31-32

In Christianity, the Holy Spirit represents the third person of the trinity, along with the father and the jesus. The Holy Spirit was sent to sanctify and to give life to the church. The Spirit also brings, through its manifestation, some things known as "moving of the Spirit", "baptism in the spirit", among others. The Holy Spirit, for being part of the trinity, is also a god, possessing the same characteristics of god father and god son, without distinction between the three.

Such a definition, over the years, has taken different forms, but always with the same pagan essence, an idolatrous mess that was made based on concepts created by human minds. We cannot deny that if the three really were one, they would have to be one in every sense, essence, power, will and manifestation. If that were the case, when the Holy Spirit made Miriam (mary) pregnant with Yeshua, he actually made her pregnant with himself. Since this is not the main point of this book and we could go on with this crazy line of thinking for hours, I will stop here.

That is why we should look at the Ruach Elohim in the form and place where he was conceptualized. The Ruach is a Jewish conception, for it was a revelation given to the People of Israel and clearly not to the fathers of the church.

According to the sages of the Jewish Kabbalah, by using a very mystical language, they say that before creating the world, Adonai had to "shrink" a little of his holiness to open a space and in this space He created all things. In order to the world not to be destroyed by His holiness and also in order to the world not to be left without it, Adonai then generates some particles of His essence that come into contact with our reality, that being the way He works, acts and speaks in the earthly realm.

These particles have no life per se, for they are not part of a Relative One, nor are they independent beings, but a spirit detached from God Himself used as a kind of "tool" so that the human beings can have contact with Him without being destroyed. The Holy Spirit is nothing but a "bridge" created by God so that we can, from a world full of impurities, connect ourselves with His holiness.

Never, in any part of the Bible, did anyone pray to the Holy Spirit, no biblical person had a dialogue with the Holy Spirit, and the Holy Spirit never received any veneration from anyone. Everything we see about the Spirit happens "through" the Spirit, God spoke through the Spirit, healed through the Spirit, manifested through the Spirit, that is, this "tool" is nothing more than the very connection between God and man and not an independent being.

This is demonstrated by the very words of Yeshua which affirms that heresies against him and against the Father will be forgiven, if the Holy Spirit were part of the trinity and if there were any differences between the three, as in the case of heresies, one would automatically be different and if one is different, there is a breakdown on the concept of unity, for it becomes relative and God is absolute.

The Ruach HaKodesh, in short, represents the manifestation of God on this earth, His will and His representation. If we look at the Spirit in this way, we will see that the heresy that has no forgiveness is not a heresy to the person of God, but rather to the way He works, manifests, decides, judges, promises, reveals, in other words, how God relates with this reality.

This makes things much more complicated, as it is not an offense to a being, but it is a matter of thinking that we have the "authority" to judge right or wrong whatever God does or decides. Let me give two more practical examples.

The Law, the Torah, is the very manifestation of the will of Adonai, as well as the manifestation of His Being, decisions and the way he operates in this world. When we judge the Torah, that is, by perverting the Torah, we act against what God Himself defines as right and wrong and therefore, according to Yeshua, we are committing a sin that has no forgiveness.

He who perverts is regarded as renouncing the whole Torah.
Maimonides

Here is another factor that we should be very careful about, judging the Law is to define it in an erroneous way, to say that it speaks something while it speaks something else, it is to abolish its commandments, it is to believe that the Law has lost its validity, it is to act purposely against what it determines. This is very complicated, as it is defamation.

James teaches that he who slanders his neighbor acts as if he were altering the Torah itself, by perverting it. This would lead us to what Yeshua taught in relation to the Holy Spirit, a sin without forgiveness.

So, by James' midrash, we learn that he who speaks evil of his neighbor is practically a sinner who will not receive forgiveness.

XXVII - HEVEL

Whereas you know not what shall be on the morrow.
For what is your life? It is like a vapor, that appears
for a little time, and then vanishes away.

James 4:14

This teaching from James caught my attention. The vapor that comes out of a hot pan when its cap is removed or the vapor that comes out from one's mouth on a cold day, is the best way to describe life on this earth, something as fast as a vapor, when whoever perceives it, the vapor is already gone.

This kind of comparison within a biblical context is very interesting for it has many "hidden" teaching throughout the Tanakh. This vapor, the same James refers to, in Hebrew is HEVEL (הבל).

The term HEVEL (הבל) is found almost almost sixty times throughout the Tanakh and never as a positive thing. This word is basically used in two different contexts, where both contexts passes the same message through different perspectives.Let's look at these two facets of this term so that we can have a deeper insight into what James is teaching.

CAIN'S HEVEL

Now the man knew his wife Eve, and she conceived and bore Cain,
saying, "I have gained a male child with the help of the LORD."
She then bore his brother HEVEL. HEVEL became a
keeper of sheep, and Cain became a tiller of the soil.

Genesis 4:1-2

The story of Cain and Abel, at the same time it is well known to most, few really understand the true message it teaches. The only way to understand who really Cain, Abel, and the essence behind both were, is by first removing some preconceived concepts about this story that many people have and therefore, a more critical and detailed analysis on certain facts that the Torah exposes about these two characters is necessary.

The great problem of this story lies precisely in the moment in which it is related by the Torah. It is presented soon after the account of creation and the first sin practiced by man and before the story of Noach and the Flood. Because both accounts, Adam in Eden and Noach's ark, deal with issues more concerning to our society and moral behavior, the account of Cain and Abel's life turns out to be slightly unnoticed. Leaving only the basic understanding of a simple story that, due to a feeling of envy, Cain kills his brother and the final conclusion lies around the weight of murdering.

The only way to understand the HEVEL of this story is by looking at the real "hero", CAIN! The first impression we have as we read this story, as it is taught to us, is that we have an Abel hero and a villain Cain, for after all, he committed the first murder reported in human history. This act committed by Cain has some relevance to human reality that goes beyond a simple sin. Let's take a look on how it took place:

> *Cain said to his brother HEVEL ... and when they were in the field, Cain set upon his brother HEVEL and killed him.*
>
> Genesis 4:8

This passage presents us some very strange things, first, it relates that the reason that led to Cain to set upon HEVEL was not due to the envy that he had because of the sacrifice, but rather by a discussion that they previously had. This passage reports that Cain said something to HEVEL, but we are not told what, and soon after it, Cain attacks his brother.

Certainly, envy for not having his sacrifice accepted as Abel's had generated a bad feeling inside Cain, for God Himself comes and warns him about it, but the trigger for the murder was a conversation that both had about something the Torah does not tell us.

Another thing that is told to us in this verse in an indirect way is Cain's intention. Based on other passages, we can see that Cain's intention was not to kill his brother. If we think coldly, if this was the first murder in history, how could Cain know that if he attacked HEVEL, he would have him killed? No one guarantees that he knew it or not. The proof is the way God punishes Cain a few verses later:

> *If you till the soil, it shall no longer yield its strength to you. You shall become a ceaseless wanderer on earth."*
>
> Genesis 4:12

What should be pointed out here is that this punishment from God was not a capital punishment, that is, God did not condemn Cain to death, on the contrary, He condemned him to exile, to a life without direction and without land. Intriguingly, for this is not how the Torah determines the condemnation of a murderer, as it is said in Numbers:

> *You may not accept a ransom for the life of a murderer who is guilty of a capital crime; he must be put to death.*
>
> Numbers 35:31

God does not go against his own word, if God did not apply the death penalty on Cain, it is because the act that he committed was not intentional and what proves this to us is another passage also in the book of Numbers:

> *These six cities shall serve the Israelites and the resident aliens among them for refuge, so that anyone who kills a person unintentionally may exile there.*
>
> Numbers 35:15

Cain's punishment reveals his intention, he accidentally killed his brother and that's why he was exiled rather than sentenced to death.

Cain, in comparison to HEVEL, is far superior in all aspects that the Torah addresses. In the first verse, which reports his birth, he is called ISH (איש) - *man* - and his brother HEVEL is called GAM HU (גם הוא) - *he too* - showing a secondary position of HEVEL in history of mankind. Cain was the first human being to bring a sacrifice to Adonai, the entire sacrificial structure practiced in the Temple, as in all ancient religions, began with Cain, he was the precursor of what became the basis of a relationship between man and the spiritual world, sacrifices that are still practiced up to the present day.

The whole problem, which culminates in the murder of HEVEL, begins precisely in this area. The Torah tells us that Cain took the fruits of the land and HEVEL took the first-born of his flock. Although we get a feeling that the sacrifice of HEVEL was accepted because he, unlike Cain, gave his best, this is not quite the reality. The Torah never informs us about the quality of the offerings brought by Cain, it is not because it reports that HEVEL's were supposedly "better", does not mean that Cain's were not good, for the sacrifices they provided were not a competition of who would bring the best sacrifice and that only one would be accepted. I believe that both brought the best they had, but Cain's was not accepted for other reasons that are not revealed to us explicitly.

By what is reported this far, we can see another side of the story, Cain is not the great villain, he just made a mistake with serious consequences, but that does not mean that he was a bad person. In all this story, he is the main figure, it is he who initiates the mystical relationship between man and God, it is he who teaches his brother to do the same, it is he who reaches a spiritual level far above that which is reported about HEVEL.

HEVEL, in all this story, is just a secondary “actor”, he

did not represent anything at all, The Torah does not tell us anything he has said nor the kind of person he used to be, he is a "nobody", a "nothingness" and that is why he is called HEVEL, for this word, in a direct translation, means "emptiness", "nothing", "vapor", an useless thing.

Now we can better understand what was Cain's mistake, which made his offering not reach God and HEVEL'S empty and without representation life:

HEVEL, "emptiness". HEVEL sought dominion over others, which is why he resolved to be a pastor. Cain, on the other hand, had greed for material possessions and because of his lack of fear of heavens, he did not care whether the earth was cursed or not.

Chachomim Chumash of Abarbanel, Bereshit 4

Cain's mistake was the lack of fear and HEVEL's was his need for power. Both in this whole story were wrong, each with their own Yetzer Harah.

JEREMIAH'S HEVEL

But they are both dull and foolish; [Their] doctrine is but delusions (HAVALIM, plural of HEVEL); It is a piece of wood.

Jeremiah 10:8

The term HEVEL, as used by the prophet Jeremiah, brings us another understanding, which also does not differ much from the one related to Abel, however, for Jeremiah it has a much deeper meaning, for his "illusions (HAVALIM)" means idolatry. The prophet uses this term to teach that idolatry, pagan idols and religious' doctrines are nothing more than illusions, they are empty, they represent nothing and they are like a vapor that exist today, but tomorrow they will be no more.

Rabbi Yitzhak told Rabbi Nahman that Rabbi Yohanan said: there is a transgression that causes the perverse to burn in the gehinam. What is this transgression? Idolatry. This can be proven here: "their doctrines are works of illusion (Hevel)" (Jr. 10:15).

Talmud of Babylon, Tractate Taanit 5a

In this case we can understand HEVEL in many ways, not just as idolatry itself, but as the whole teachings of men, religions, sects, theologies, theories, dogmas, things we find in all faiths. Even when religion is primarily monotheistic, if one puts his faith in theologies and believes that they are divine, he enters into idolatry, one falls into illusions and becomes HEVEL, empty and his existence will be only as a brief "vapor".

SOLOMON'S HEVEL

הבל הבלים אמר קהלת **הבל הבלים** הכל **הבל**

Utter futility!—said Koheleth— Utter futility! All is futile!

Ecclesiastes 1:2

The whole concept of the term HEVEL is the central theme of the book of Ecclesiastes. As already said, HEVEL is the vapor that comes out as a breath in cold days and soon disappears. Solomon, when wrote this book, relied on this definition to point out the need for an accurate perception of everything found in our earthly reality.

The vital point of all of Solomon's teaching addresses the reality that is absorbed through our perceptions and how ephemeral they are, just like a brief vapor. The deepest notion that "hevel" stands for is related to the understanding that uncertainty is the most inflexible feature of the human being.

In short, "hevel" represents the "attachment" that man develops only in things that he can understand, because his insecurity does not allow him to go beyond what the earthly, fallen, and weak human mind can define. Therefore, it is the nature of the human being to develop futilities, such as material goods, possessions, money, appearance and so on, things that last for a few seconds, as well as a vapor, and this causes a "void", making the person vain, futile and idolatrous , for he clung only to what he can understand within his earthly limitation.

That is why the true God and His Torah are for the few,

for they are not grasped by the human mind and placing one's security in God and in the Torah is something beyond what many human beings can accomplish. Based on this thought, Rabbi Yonah makes a very firm comment:

> *"futility of futilities" - shows us the futility of all goods and all honor one can receive, for as he himself states in Ecclesiastes 12:13, the summary of everything must be reverence for God and observance of His commandments, that's all that's left for the real man.*
>
> Rabbeinu Yonah on Pirkei Avot 3:12

The author of Ecclesiastes was the wisest man in all history, not only the wisest, but also the most materially possessing king among all kings. Solomon, a man who had everything he desired, who had power, fame, wisdom, servants, peace in his lands, influence, control and in the end, claims that everything is futile, all that he obtained, which no other man obtained so abundantly, did not mean anything at all, all the power, gold, silver, sovereignty, everything is empty, useless and gone, just as the life of the human being is gone.

The word HEVEL is a great representation for king of Solomon's reign, who reigned over Israel for 37 years (counting the 3 years of exile):

HEVEL (הבל)
ה5 + ב2 + ל30
= **37**

This teaches us that even if man possesses absolutely everything that this earth can offer, thus becoming the most famous and powerful man in history, he will be no more that a futile and empty man, no better than a vapor.

An attentive reading of this verse, in Hebrew, shows us that in the same passage, Solomon quoted the word HEVEL seven times.

- HEVEL (הבל) - futile (3x)
- HAVALIM (הבלים) - 2x HEVEL (2x2 = 4x)

Our sages teach that the use of this term for seven times refers to the seven days of creation. Solomon comes to the conclusion that everything created in these days is futile and mere vanity, for there is nothing on this earth that does not have an end. Interesting thing is the seventh Hevel, for it would represent the Shabbat, an eternal commandment of Adonai.

If we pay attention to the verse, there is a semantic break, Solomon states that all is futility of futilities and then, at the end, independently, he asserts that all is futile. This kind of use of words in the Hebrew language can be interpreted as the end justifying the means, that is, the last "futile" is the cause of the "futility of futilities" mentioned before.

Shabbat is not only a holy day, but also a term commonly used for the commandments of the Torah in a general way. Nowadays, one who is a Torah observant is called a "shomer shabbat" (Sabbath-keeper), though quoting one commandment, it encompasses all. Thus, we should look at the verse with which Solomon concludes his book:

The sum of the matter, when all is said and done: Revere God and observe His commandments! For this applies to all mankind.

Ecclesiastes 12:13

If the conclusion and solution given by Solomon in reference to futilities is the observance of the Laws of God, then the last futile quoted by him in chapter 1 verse 2 (above) is precisely the non-observance of the Shabbat, that is, of the Torah.

Through the seven quotations from the Hebrew term, the latter being the reason for the former and the latter representing the seventh day, the Shabbat, it would be as if Solomon said that those who "make Shabbat as a futile thing" are those who do not cling in the things of God, then these people are futile, empty, vain, bound to earthly vanities, idolatrous and all will vanish as the vapor disappears, for they are the results of futility. The only thing that "escapes" from this futile reality is the Word of God, the Torah and those who follow it with true heart and faith.

ZOHAR'S HEVEL

The way Zohar approaches Hevel is very deep and peculiar, I will put here only a short passage, translated by me, to enter a little deeper into the mystical side of this term.

I emphasize, the Zohar is a book that uses allegories, its stories should not be taken literally. Because it is a book written in Aramaic, I will not put the translation word by word, but rather a contextual translation.

We have as follows:

It happened on a Shabbat night when a man walking on crutches encountered two Torah scholars, whom he called "masters of the generations" and "masters of wisdom". He greeted them cordially and asked them where they were going. When the sages of the Torah, who were on horses, said where they were going, the man on crutches said that he was going to the same place and could arrange them accommodation in case they needed. Upon hearing this, the sages questioned him how this would be possible, for on horseback they would arrive long before a man without his legs. As they were saying this, the man on crutches moved at a speed of a lightning bolt. He caused the two sages to move so fast that the three arrived at the same time at their destination, at the entrance of a cave. The crippled man asked the wise men to enter with him into the cave, and the three entered. It was inside the cave that they encountered an orchard and the crippled man started to get rid of his physical body and assuming a totally new body. Then the old crippled

man shone like the sun and sat upon a royal throne
surrounded by three hundred disciples at his feet.
The disciples repeated incessantly the verse of Ecclesiastes:
"futility of futilities" and repeated this verse
as if there were no other verses.
The sages turned to the disciples and asked them
if there were no other verses to recite.
When he heard this, the man sitting on the throne
immediately stood up and took the hands of both men
and transported them through seven palaces.
In each of these palaces the phrase "futility of futility"
was imbedded.
When they arrived in the seventh palace, the entrance was
decorated with the symbol of an eagle and of a crown, and in
the crown was the inscription: "all those who do not have the
understanding of the seven futilities of Ecclesiastes will be
subject to what Numbers 1:51 reports," any strange that enters
will be executed" and then the two sages turned away and left.
Tikkunei HaZohar, Ki Tavo, 12

This is the mystical account of Solomon's words, the futility of futilities, which teaches that nothing connected to this world is better than that which is merely futile. This implies that everything in this world is based on the attribute of CHESSED (חסד) - *grace* - and for this reason Paul in his letters is so categorical about grace, not that it has replaced the Torah, but it is through God's mercy that the human being can receive the true understanding of the Torah, so that life is not a great futility. So, the grace solves world's futility in one's life.

The sages teach that the understanding of Torah based on the human intelligence is HEVEL and only the Torah taught by Mashiach will be based on the true understanding and wisdom known as BINAH (בינה) and CHOKHMAH (חכמה). They also claim that it was in these two sefirot, BINAH (בינה) and CHOKHMAH (חכמה), that Cain was created, but Abel (HEVEL), was originated in MALKHUT (מלכות), a sefirah more connected to the earthly reality and human understanding, this is why he was a "nothing."

The strength found in the sefirah of CHESSED (חסד) - *grace* - is equivalent to the force found in the word CHAMOR (חמור) - *donkey* - which is a kabbalistic term that represents all that is earthly and mundane.

Through this we can understand the mystical meaning of the passage from Genesis 22:3, where is relates Abraham saddling his donkey on the way to Isaac's sacrifice. In this passage, the word donkey, which is written as CHAMOR (חמור), appears in an erroneous way, appears as (חמר), without the presence of the letter VAV (ו). This reveals that the act of "saddling the donkey", spiritually, is to surpass everything related to the futilities of this world. The numerical value of Abraham's name (אברהם) is 248, the same value as the word CHAMOR (חמר) without the VAV (ו). This shows the reason for the change of his name from Abram to Abraham, because it represented the patriarch's disconnection from earthly things and consequently his intimate connection with the Creator.

The Zohar's account, as presented above, is a criticism of the people who are attached to the wisdom of this world. The crutch man represents the angel who rules this world, for this reason his disciples only knew the "futility of futilities". The sages represent people who, as much as wise they are, by knowing the Word, by studying it and learning it and with an above average knowledge, are no more than futile people. They were not able to enter the last palace, for they did not understand the essence of the "futility of futilities", for their wisdom was associated with earthly things, such as religion.

Now we can make some connections of Neo-Testament passages on this, beginning with Paul in his letter to the Romans:

For sin shall not have dominion over you: for you are not under the law, but under grace.

Romans 6:14

What shall we say then? Is the law sin? God forbid.
No, I had not known sin, but by the law.

Romans 7:7a

Two passages of a contradictory appearance, the first affirms that "*sin has no dominion, for we are not under the law*", and the other affirms that "*Is the Law sin? God forbid*". The understanding of this apparent contradiction is only possible through the understanding of "futility of futilities".

In Romans 6, the term law refers to *halachah* (Jewish laws), which are formed by human minds based on interpretations based on human wisdom, laws made by sages equal to that reported in the text above from the Zohar. Because they are human, bound to this land, such laws are futilities, things that have an end. On the other hand, the Law that reveals sin and is NOT sin, is the Torah itself and the spiritual understanding of it.

Now let's connect the dots, if the true understanding of the Law is spiritual, something not futile, then whoever truly understands it, understands sin and does not stay under it. But those who interpret it humanly, end up creating laws contrary to the true Law and end up under the yoke of earthly understanding, which is futile, and that puts the person under the sin. But those who receive wisdom from above and are cut off from the futile things of that world will be like Abraham when he was saddling his donkey, surpassing earthly things, and this, as explained above, is the true grace. True grace is the detachment of earthly things and a connection with the true God.

Paul affirms that whoever lives the Torah from above, surpasses the futile things of this earth and thus live the true grace and out of the sin. Those who attach themselves to human theologies, whether of Judaism or Christianity, are under sin and consequently become futile and end up as the two sages, without authority to enter the spiritual palace, being just another disciple of the angel who dominates this world.

Whoever is capable to, let him understand.

JAMES' HEVEL

Go to now, you that say, To day or to morrow we will go into such a city, and continue there a year, and buy and sell, and get gain: Whereas you know not what shall be on the morrow. For what is your life? It is even a vapor, that appears for a little time, and then vanishes away. For that you ought to say, If the Lord will, we shall live, and do this, or that.

James 4:13-15

The simple understanding of these passages is very valid, for the day of tomorrow belongs only to God. For as much as we plan, ultimately we will end up doing what the Creator determines.

But if we look at the context in which this teaching is embedded, we will see that James is dealing with people who do not have the divine understanding of the Torah, for some verses above, James calls them sinners. Therefore, just as Paul attests in the verses in Romans, these sinners are nothing more than people who live tied to worldly things, the "futility of futilities" and like all futility, it leads one to a boat without rowing and without sail, a life always adrift, because it will be empty, idolatrous, meaningless and full of illusions.

But the warning of James is not for us to conform with that, but it is for us to seek the true understanding of the Word of God and through it, unlike the sinners, we will know what our tomorrow will be, for those who understands it and who lives it, know that tomorrow will be as follows:

Now, if you obey the LORD your God, to observe faithfully all His commandments which I enjoin upon you this day, the LORD your God will set you high above all the nations of the earth.

All these blessings shall come upon you and take effect, if
you will but heed the word of the LORD your God:
Blessed shall you be in the city and blessed
shall you be in the country.
Blessed shall be the issue of your womb, the produce of
your soil, and the offspring of your cattle, the calving
of your herd and the lambing of your flock.
Blessed shall be your basket and your kneading bowl.
Blessed shall you be in your comings and
blessed shall you be in your goings.
The LORD will put to rout before you the enemies
who attack you; they will march out against you by a
single road, but flee from you by many roads.
The LORD will ordain blessings for you upon your barns
and upon all your undertakings: He will bless you in
the land that the LORD your God is giving you.
The LORD will establish you as His holy people, as
He swore to you, if you keep the commandments of
the LORD your God and walk in His ways.
And all the peoples of the earth shall see that the LORD's name
is proclaimed over you, and they shall stand in fear of you.
The LORD will give you abounding prosperity in the issue of your
womb, the offspring of your cattle, and the produce of your soil
in the land that the LORD swore to your fathers to assign to you.
The LORD will open for you His bounteous store, the heavens, to
provide rain for your land in season and to bless all your under-
takings. You will be creditor to many nations, but debtor to none.
The LORD will make you the head, not the tail; you will
always be at the top and never at the bottom—if only you
obey and faithfully observe the commandments of the
LORD your God that I enjoin upon you this day,
and do not deviate to the right or to the left from any
of the commandments that I enjoin upon you this
day and turn to the worship of other gods.

Deuteronomy 28:1-14

This is the teaching of James, so that we are not futile listeners who do not know of tomorrow. He wants to his hearers do know and do fear Adonai; however, not under human theologies, but under the divine will of the Creator, so that we may live everything from above that last for ever and ever.

XXVIII - THE RICH AND THE RICH

Go to now, you rich men, weep and howl for
your miseries that shall come on you.
Your riches are corrupted, and your garments are moth-eaten.
Your gold and silver is corroded; and the rust of them shall
be a witness against you, and shall eat your flesh as it were
fire. You have heaped treasure together for the last days.
Behold, the hire of the laborers who have reaped down your fields,
which is of you kept back by fraud, cries: and the cries of them
which have reaped are entered into the ears of the Lord of sabaoth.
You have lived in pleasure on the earth, and been wanton;
you have nourished your hearts, as in a day of slaughter.
James 5:1-5

Because the book of James is a compendium of teachings, like the Pirkei Avot, the author does not take his time to explain some basic concepts about what he writes. This is a common custom among rabbis, for as the author is directing his teachings to Jews, he automatically assumes that his hearers already have a prior "baggage" of basic knowledge about what his is teaching. Unfortunately, this same baggage is not standard among the Christians, those who ended up interpreting this book.

Due to this fact, several ideologies were born out of interpretations made by minds far from the Jewish rabbinical mentality, such as the idea that poverty is divine, and God is opposed to those who have money and material possessions, which is not quite the truth. Through these words from the book of James, as well as from some others found in the New Testament, the ancient church propagated the necessity of poverty to obtain a holy life, of course that such concepts were only applied to its adepts, since the church institution benefits itself from the riches obtained throughout its history up to this day.

So that we may understand a little better what kind of rich James refers to, we must look to the Torah and understand through it, what makes a man legally rich in God's eye.

And there you shall bring your burnt offering and other sacrifices, your tithes and contributions, your offerings (נדריכם) and offerings of good will (נדבתיכם), and the firstborn of your flocks.
Deuteronomy 12:6

But only in the place that Adonai will choose within its tribal territory. There you must sacrifice (תעלה) your burnt offering (עלתיך) and there you must observe everything that I command.
Deuteronomy 12:14

You must not eat in your settlements the tithes of your grain or the wine or oil or the firstborn of your flocks, or of any offering (נדריך) you have promised, or of your goodwill (נדבתיך), or your contributions.
Deuteronomy 12:17

These three verses are found in a parashah called EREH (ראה). This parashah, among other subjects, reinforces the commandments about the offerings that should be made when the people enter the land of Israel. The sages say that this is the parashah that must be studied in depth by those who want to make financial gains, because it addresses much about the spiritual side of this topic.

In these passages, which speak about sacrifices, we find a very interesting feature in common, every time a commandment upon offer is presented, this commandment comes with some term repeatedly, that is, words that refer to offerings always come in pairs (as highlighted above). Our sages teach that the reason for this is that everything that man gives is firstly given to him by God, in other words, God only gives financial blessings to a man so that he can give it as well, in case that man does not give, he breaks this cycle and God automaticall ceases to give to that man.

Today there are two forms of contribution, the first is the "tithe" that is usually taken to the community where the person makes part of and where he learns the Word of God, this is vital in order to his community to support itself. Tithing accounts for 10% of all that this person earns from his or her work. Sages teach that if a person does not have any form of income, he is exempt from tithing.

The second is called by Torah as TZEDAKAH (תצדקה), which can be poorly translated as "charity". Many believe that Tzedakah is defined as giving some change to beggars or buying food from someone who is hungry, but Tzedakah has a much deeper meaning than just "alms". Tzedakah is an offer that goes from at least 10% up to 20% of everything that the person owns.

Let us suppose that a person without a source of income receives financial help, since this help is not a source of income from work, he is exempt from tithing, but he is not exempt from doing Tzedakah, so he must draw a sum from that amount which was given to him and also do Tzedakah. If one receives food, one should also take a portion and give it to someone close to him who is also hungry. This kind of attitude holds true for everything, including abstract things, such as learning for example.

When one receives knowledge from God, he has an obligation to share at least 10% of that knowledge, this is also a Tzedakah. Of all the languages I know, the Hebrew language is the only one that both LILMOD (ללמוד) – *to learn* - and LELAMED (ללמד) – *to teach* - have the same root (ל-מ-ד), for just as the words in the verses seen above repeat themselves, "Learning" and "teaching" follow the same logic, as if they were repeated. Whoever learns from God and does not teach, ceases to learn.

We learn thus that even the poor, somehow must do Tzedakah on everything he receives or posses. This Tzedakah is not necessarily the tithing given in a temple, it may be in the form of a help to someone in need.

Another thing that generates financial income is the study of Torah. That was this time when I met a person who owned a business that was never the way he wanted it to be, he was always living in debt and his company couldn't not grow. One day he decided to change his life; every day from 7 a.m. to 12 p.m., he stopped working in order to only study Torah at that time, after his study, he used to go to the office and normally work there from 1 p.m. to 6 p.m. He also began to take 10% as tithe from his gross profit and 15% as Tzedakah from net profit, from this 15% he gives 10% to other people who also studied Torah or those who helped him with his Torah study and the other 5% he gives to people in need in his community. After a few months, this man's business became so big that with the money he is making now, his children, grandchildren and great-grandchildren would never have to work.

This teaches us that the Tzedakah made over our time in the name of the Torah study and the Tzedakah made to those who study it have a unique spiritual return, for this man, even working half the daily hours he used to, has quadrupled his income and became a millionaire.

But one thing is certain, the Tzedakah presents great difficulties in two cases, when the person is very poor and thus thinks that he does not have the obligation to do it or when the person is very rich, therefore depending on the amount of money that one possesses , the value to be given can be very high. Imagine someone who has a billion Euro, making a check for 100 million Euros is not easy.

The Zohar tells a very interesting story about a great sage who was walking with his students around the streets of Jerusalem soon after the destruction of the second Temple.

It is reported that at a certain moment, this sage saw a Jewish girl cleaning the stables of an Arab man, when he looked at her, he realized that he knew her, for she was the daughter of a man named Nicodemus Ben Gurion (the same Nicodemus who meets Yeshua), one of the three richest men in Jerusalem. His fortune was so great that he could alone sustain the whole city for ten years.

When the sage realized this, outraged, he ran towards the girl and questioned her about what was happening. When she told him that her father lost all his fortune, he asked how could it be possible, for Nicodemus used to make great Tzedakot, he helped the poor, the Torah schools, the Torah students, and so on. So his daughter explained that no matter how much her father helped, that help never came close to 10% of everything he owned and so, God took everything He had given him.

Gematria, in a very mystical way, explains how this works in the spiritual world. As we have seen previously, in order for God to create all things, he had to "create" an emptiness, an emptiness within which ALL things have been created. This "creation of the void" is known as Tzimtzum (צימצום), which represents a "shrinking" of the divine light so that "nothingness" is created and that "nothingness" served as the "raw material" for all creation.

TZIMTZUM (צימצום)
40ם + 6ו + 90צ + 40מ + 10י + 90צ
276 = 2+7+6
= **6**

HATZEDAKAH (הצדקה) – THE TZEDAKAH
5ה + 100ק + 4ד + 90צ + 5ה
204 = 2+0+4 =
= **6**

What does this reveal? That when man makes Tzedakah, being a financial aid to a needy or to a Torah's student, or time to learning about the things of God and etc., just as God once "created" a space that served as the foundation for everything to be created, this man also "creates" a space, a space that was occupied by money, work and secular things. Then, in that same space, God will "create" all things in this man's life. The whole gap that the donated money and the given away time leave, are the raw materials that God needs so that everything in the life of this man is given to him. This man will never beat God on this, because as much as he gives, he will never be able to give more than God will give to him. Tzedakah is one of the deepest spiritual secrets and we can see what it brings in the lives of those who observe it:

MAASER (מעשר) - OFFER
200ר + 300ש + 70ע + 40מ
= **7**

KESEF (כסף) - MONEY
80ף + 60ס + 20כ
= **7**

LELAMED (ללמד) - TO TEACH (Torah)
4ד + 40מ + 30ל + 30ל
= **5**

TEVUNAH VEBINAH (תבונה ובינה) - WISDOM AND KNOWLEDGE
5ה + 50נ + 10י + 2ב + 6ו + 5ה + 50נ + 6ו + 2ב + 400ת
= **5**

N'DAVAH (נדבה) - CHARITY (poor, orphans, widows)
5ה + 2ב + 4ד + 50נ
= **7**

SHALOM (שלום) - PEACE
40ם + 6ו + 30ל + 300ש
= **7**

TZEDAKAH (צדקה)
5ה + 100ק + 4ד + 90צ
= **1**

LEKABEL HAKOL (לקבל הכל) – TO RECEIVE EVERYTHING
300ל + 20כ + 5ה + 30ל + 2ב + 100ק + 30ל
= **1**

Whoever helps his neighbor, the student of Torah, the teacher of Torah, the community in which he is inserted with offers in money, he will open a space to receive more money.

Whoever teaches Torah opens space to receive more wisdom and knowledge of God.

Whoever does charity, by giving food, time, care and attention to the poor, widows, orphans and the elderly, will open space for a life full of peace.

Whoever does all these things, the true TZEDAKAH, opens space to RECEIVE EVERYTHING in this life, and when I say everything, it is EVERYTHING, from peace, to a blessed family, health, money and so on.

It is interesting that among of all the organs of the human body, the only one that never develops any type of cancer is the heart. It is an organ that distributes the blood through the body, all the blood that comes in, that it receives, it's passed forward, that is, everything that it receives, it donates.

Now, in order to understand what James refers to, we must look at other types of people, those who enrich themselves in other ways than doing the Tzedakah, such as through illicit behavior, corruption and theft. Others, as honest as they might be, end up devoting themselves entirely to work, putting all their focus and effort on the professional success, they enrich, but also become idolaters for reasons already seen. In both cases, some behavioral attitudes become apparent, such as arrogance, greed and a false sense of power, because they believe that everything they have, was generated by their own merit.

I believe that James refers to these types of rich people, who have become rich by their selfish and self-centered efforts. This way leads the human being to overvalue himself and to devalue his neighbor, because if his neighbour is not rich like him, he does not have the same "greatness" that he has. What we should look at in a rich man's life is not how much money he has, but how he got it and how that money affects his moral behavior.

Keep in mind, having money is not a sin, sin might be the way that money is obtained and used. to donate time by studying the Torah, to financially help those who study and teach it, to help the community where you belong with tithing, whether you are rich or poor, for the gap that this Tzedakah makes, will be where God will “create” EVERYTHING you need.

XXIX - RAINS

Be patient therefore, brothers, to the coming of the Lord. Behold, the farmer waits for the precious ***fruit of the earth****, and has* ***long patience*** *for it, until he receive the* ***early and latter rain****. Be you also* ***patient;*** *establish your hearts: for* ***the coming of the Lord draws near****.*

James 5:7-8

Some things caught my attention in these passages, the patience that is tied to the fruit of the earth, the two most common times of rain in the territory of Israel and the connection that all of this has with the coming of Mashiach.

With a little attention, we will see that both time periods, called by James as "early and latter rain", are precisely spring and autumn, for those are the periods that rain at most in Israel. Continuing his line of thought, James also mentions the expectation for the fruit the of the earth, which is a symbolic language for the harvest season. This helps to approximate the period of time in which the author refers to, since the most important harvest season in the Middle East takes place in the time of Omer, that is, in the 49 days between Pessach and Shavuot, which occurs between the months of April and May and a second harvest season around September and October, when we have both the Rosh Hashanah and the Yom Kippur celebrations.

Both times, the Omer, which is the period between Pessach and Shavuot, and the ten days between Rosh Hashanah and Yom Kippur, are two epochs that represent repair, introspection, correction, improvement, and repentance. Making associations of these times with the coming of Mashiach, or his return, within the Jewish mentality, makes full and complete sense, for we must all be prepared for when he comes in order to be worthy to enter his kingdom.

OMER

The 49 days of Omer represent the preparation of the Hebrew people to receive the Torah. A people who lived under the yoke of a pagan nation for 210 years, with a slave mentality and with strong impure habits, couldn't receive holy things without being purified and prepared beforehand. According to our sages, the Hebrew people during these 49 days have received the 7 corrections that a person must make in order to walk in the ways of God. Each of these corrections is represented by one of the seven weeks that make up the Omer and each one of them can be represented by the seven lower sefirot.

Through these seven corrections the human being can free himself from all negative spiritual influences by a behavioral change. Often the process can be painful, for it directly affects many customs and habits that one develops throughout his life and suddenly, he needs to change them. But the benefits of such attitudes are incalculable, for they the changes that prepare the man for the coming of Mashiach as it represented the preparation for the receiving of the Torah.

WEEK 1 – SEFIRAH CHESSED

Chessed represents God's mercy and kindness, it is the first step to be taken by those who begin to approach God and His Torah. For this reason that Paul, when dealing with countless people of pagan origin, that is, the Gentiles, speaks so much about grace, for it is the initial step they must take toward the necessary corrections.

The correction represented by chessed deals with "to love the neighbor", it is the awareness that one needs to have a life governed by ethics in relation to his neighbor, an ethic that is determined by the Torah, that is, the commandments contained therein about the relationship "man x man"; for example, do not kill, do not steal, do not cheat, do not practice sexual immorality, do not make profit from borrowed money, do not take revenge and so on. The chessed, because it represents the goodness and the mercy of God, in roder to be practiced, requires acts of kindness and mercy towards one's neighbor.

The first week represents a total change of character and attitude by which the human being relates to this reality, although it is a more earthly change, it is a human change and very hard to achieve for it encompasses intrisic behaviors.

WEEK 2 – GEVURAH

Gevurah is known as judgment. Gevurah is the opposite of chessed, where Gevurah grows a lot, chessed decreases, so it is vital to understand that in this repair a balance between both must be maintained.

Gevurah is necessary because it represents the firm pulse, it is at that moment that the human being, by the judgment made through his understanding, decides to follow Adonai's ways consciously and not emotionally. It is the moment when one makes a commitment to serve God knowing that this decision is for life.

This step is taken only by few people, for many believe only in grace and they stop at the first week. It is here that one must take responsibility before the Creator, to serve Him unconditionally and to take the yoke of his commandments. A decision that must be made with no stepping back, for there is no return.

WEEK 3 – TIFERET

Tiferet can only be attained through the mercy, kindness and knowledge of the Torah, for the compassion represented by the Tiferet is what gives the man a broken heart. It is a spiritual step taken where one begins to understand God and truly begins to fear Him.

The man who reaches the Tiferet is the man who makes the decisions in his life according to his fear of God, he gives up a life of sin and impurities, for he recognizes the power of the Creator and with that, he begins to abandon his old habits, just because they are not according to God's will.

This is the time when Torah practices become constant making the one who reaches this stage, a tzadik. This was the level that Job attained and by which he was recognized as righteous before Adonai.

WEEK 4 – NETZACH

Netzach represents victory, but in a more earthly way, it represents desires and dreams. This is the moment where the human being understands the greatness of God's will; in His name, one leaves aside his dreams and desires to live and do what Adonai desires and dreams, even at the cost of what constitutes one's "person" as a human being.

This repair is only achieved when the person obeys God without expectation of reward, when in his prayers, he leaves personal requests aside and only blesses Hashem with his words. This stage represents a total detachment from earthly things and a certainty that all that he needs will be given by Adonai, in other words, it is here that the true Emunah arises, something that surpasses what the Western world knows as "faith".

WEEK 5 – HOD

Hod represents the awareness that everything that is placed in the hands of man has a greater purpose. It is the humbleness and the understanding that nothing belongs to the human being and he only possesses what he has so that his possessions are used as tools by God. In this way man achieves the purpose for which he was created.

Whoever reaches this degree realizes that even his life is not deserved by him, he just breathe because God has a plan in his life, a plan that glorifies the name of the Creator.

According to Paul and Gaon of Vilna, as HOD represents Mashiach Ben David, this is the minimal level that one must attain to be worthy of the Messianic Era.

WEEK 6 – YESOD

Yesod is the total devotion to God, it is when man places everything connected in this earthly life as background, even what society defines as important. The awareness that the human being develops in this level is that everything that revolves around his life, such as work, money, profession, success, fame, family, wife or husband, children, are only there for him to accomplish the full will of God and not because he deserves them in some way or were created to do those things.

To attain the Yesod is to get rid of all forms of idolatry, it is when God becomes the only reason for existence and everything else becomes secondary. It is a very difficult level to achieve because of human mind's inability to understand spiritual matters.

WEEK 7 – MALCHUT

Although Malchut is the sefirah closest to the earthly reality, it is it that connects us to all the others, just as all the others are connected to us through Malchut. Like Keter's sefirah, it represents the junction of all others, the apex that man must attain, which is the love of God. However, not a sentimental love, but a love that comes through the wisdom given by God in order to man to be able understand Him and thus develop a love that is not in the heart, but in the mind, as determined by God in Deuteronomy 6:4-5 .

This should not be confused with a love for which one rejoices when receiving blessings from God or with the one one feels for his neighbor or family. This love is not the feeling of love, it is a state of existence, they are different things, a state known only to those who reach it.

These seven steps represent “the long patience" that James mentions in the above verse. "to have patience" is not a waiting, but a preparation, a repair and a walk that should be taken as a preparatory act for the coming of Mashiach, for it is the only way for man to become worthy to be accepted and to reign with him . Faith alone is not enough, just as works alone are not enough, it is a middle ground between the two. For this reason I believe that only a few will be worthy, this is the narrow path.

ROSH HASHANAH AND YOM KIPPUR

The Rosh Hashanah, also known as the "Jewish New Year", is the commemoration of the creation of all things, it was at that time that the first words reported by the Torah "BERESHIT BARA ELOHIM" - *In the beginning created Elohim* – took place. This "beginning" occurred exactly on the Rosh Hashanah. This is proven with an analysis of these terms, where we see the connection that both, the beginning and Rosh Hashanah, have:

BERESHIT BARA (בראשית ברא) – IN THE BEGINNING CREATED
1א + 200ר + 2ב + 400ת + 10י + 300ש + 1א + 200ר + 2ב
= **1116**

BEROSH HASHANAH NIBRAH (בראש השנה נברא) - IN ROSH HASHANAH THE WORLD WAS CREATED
50נ + 300ש + 5ה + 300ש + 1א + 200ר + 2ב
1א + 200ר + 2ב + 50נ + 5ה +
= **1116**

Ten days later we have Yom Kippur, the day of atonement, the day on which God gives His judgment upon men. These ten days between the two feasts are of utmost importance because they represent days of repentance, prayer, and devotion to the commandments of God. It is a time of preparation for it is a time where God will determine what will happen in the life of every human being until the next Rosh Hashanah.

In addition to all of this preparation, these ten days have a messianic connection with the 49 days of Omer because the preparation that takes place in those 7 weeks between Pessach and Shavuot will be "felt" in the ten days between Rosh Hashanah and Yom Kippur.

In order for us to understand this, let's look at a brief teaching of Yeshua, a teaching full of mysticism behind:

> *At that time, after those days, the sun will darken, the moon will not give forth its light, the stars will fall from the heavens and all hosts* ***(chail)*** *of the heavens will tremble. And then the sign of the son of man will appear in heaven and all the families of the earth will weep and will see the son of man among the clouds of heaven with a great host* ***(chail)*** *and with a dreadful appearance. And he will send his angels with a trumpet and with a loud voice to gather all his chosen ones from the four winds of the heavens, from one end of heaven unto the other.*
>
> Matthew 24:29-31

Yeshua quotes a prophecy from the prophet Isaiah that deals with a moment in the future to come. The mysticism that surrounds any prophecy found in the Tanakh makes its interpretation possible only when the prophesied fact occurs, for this reason, getting into that subject is very difficult, for it could be no more than speculation.

However, something caught my attention in Yeshua's mentioned prophecy, because these prophecy has a lot of mysticism behind it; it served as one of the bases for rabbinical Kabbalistic thought to prove the ancient idea about the existence and the influence of the zodiac. First of all, I would like to make it clear that I am not an astrologer, I am not interested in this subject and I do not know much about it, this little I know comes from the teachings and conceptions formed by the rabbis. Such ideas may differ a little, or a lot, from the modern Western astrology, those found on the Internet or in books that address this theme.

THE JEWISH ZODIAC

The sages say that the idea of the existence of a zodiac, which exerts influence on the behavioral character of the human being, was developed by the Jews through revelations of secrets from the book of Genesis. Such teachings are found in *Sefer Yetzirah* and although it has never been written, it is the fifth oldest "book" of the Jews.

Throughout the Tanakh we find descriptions of how God condense His force and divine will in our world through the celestial bodies, thus causing a strong influence on our behaviors. Such a concept within Judaism is not a way of knowing ourselves, as astrologers do, but a knowledge about an obstacle that we must overcome. For through the observance of the Torah we will be plugged with the supernatural, with the true divine will, which will make us to overcome the influences of the astrological forces, that is, the zodiac influence is something that must be overcame and not accepted.

Just as there are 12 signs defined by Judaism, there are 12 months in the year, 12 soul roots, 12 tribes of Israel and so on. The sign indicates a strength and characteristics hidden within each individual that must be overcome.

I will bring up the passage of Isaiah mentioned by Yeshua and we will see that it has a very bizarre term and its connection to what was said above.

כי כוכבי השמים ו**כסילים** לא יהלו אורם חשך
השמש בצאתו וירח לא יגיה אורו

*The stars and **constellations** of heaven Shall not give off their light; The sun shall be dark when it rises, And the moon shall diffuse no glow.*

Isaiah 13:10

Yeshua makes a quotation from the verse of Isaiah almost in its entirety, except for a term added by him, translated as hosts in verses 29 and 30 (see above). The word CHAIL (חיל) has some meanings, such as "strength", "hosts", "a force that holds something together", but its meaning in Aramaic is the collective noun for Astros, which in other words means "constellation" and this leads us to the understanding that, like Isaiah, Yeshua is also speaking about something hidden and connected to the stars.

In Isaiah's verse, the word translated as "constellations", in Hebrew, is KSILIM (כסילים), plural of KSIL (כסיל) and not CHAIL (חיל) as used by Yeshua.

KSIL does not actually mean "constellation", but rather it is the name of a specific star, located at the South Pole. This star is also known as "the sign that the camels will die" because it only becomes visible in the northern hemisphere in the middle of summer, a time when camels are exposed to extreme temperatures and they die due to the heat.

<u>KSIL</u>

It is a star in the heart of the constellation of Scorpio, equinoctial point of the South. For a long time the constellation of Libra was considered being part of the constellation of Scorpio, being its center. According to the great Kabbalistic rabbi Ibn Ezra, Ksil was the star of the heart of Scorpio, representing the center of this constellation, which now is the constellation of Libra.

LIBRA (month: TISHREI) - The Libra period is the most delicate, it is the time that has two important festivals, the Rosh Hashanah (new year) and ten days later, Yom Kippur (day of atonement). Our sages teach that these ten days between one feast and another is precisely the time when the heavens will be opened so that we may reflect upon our sins and ask for real forgiveness for them, when the day of Yom Kippur comes, God will give the sentence, for this reason the scale is the symbol of that sign.

Yom Kippur is the most important date in the Torah,

it is an ordinance represented by the sacrifices that were brought to the Temple. The star of Ksil has a symbology associated with Yom Kippur, for it is part of the constellation which is represented by a scale, thus making a reference to the day of God's judgment.

No one knows the day of the coming of Mashiach, only God does, but there is something we can learn from it. Yeshua quotes a prophecy that talks about KSIL, a star that is part of the constellation of Libra and then he claims that the angels will come blowing trumpets, blowing the shofar, and the shofar is blew precisely in the Rosh Hashanah and the period of ten days before the Yom Kippur. Perhaps this is a hint of the time of year that all of this will occur, for the end of times for Yeshua is nothing more than God's judgment day, so I particularly understand that the coming of Mashiach will be on Rosh Hashanah and the final judgment about those who is worthy to enter the Messianic Era will be held ten days later, in Yom Kippur.

The words of James are now clearer. When he quotes both rains he refers to these two seasons, the 49 days of Omer, and the ten days between Rosh Hashanah and Yom Kippur.

When he asks for patience for the coming of the Lord, the Mashiach, he connects the dots. The first "patience" refers to the preparation that all of us must accomplish in order that we may be accepted by Mashiach, the preparation represented by the spring rain or the early rain, the 49 days of omer.

Then he says, "Be patient" again and by quoting "patience" for the second time he refers to the judgment that will be made by Mashiach, which is represented by the fall rain or latter rain, the ten days before Yom Kippur, the day that will be given the result of judgment, the result of what we did, represented by the 7 weeks of omer.

In this passage James reveals the season of the year in which Mashiach will come and how to prepare to be accepted by him, simple.

XXX - IYOV

Behold, we count them happy which endure. You have heard of the patience of Job, and have seen the end of the Lord; that the Lord is very pitiful, and of tender mercy.

James 5:11

Bringing the example of Job in his book serves as further proof of the time period in which his teaching took place. The book of Job, written by Moses, is the oldest book of the bible and full of spiritual mysteries. There are a lot about the life of this man that goes far beyond what is "clearly " reported in his book, things known only by a few.

What is reported about Job's life in the book that carries his name, occurs precisely at the time of the plagues that struck Egypt, the people's departure from these lands, the 49 days before the Torah is given, and ends during the feast of Shavuot, at the moment when Moses descends from the Mount Sinai. For this reason, studies about Job is common at the time of year that those feasts are celebrated (Pessach, Omer, Shavuot), and many rabbis make a point of mentioning him as an example when dealing with spiritual matters that concern those celebrations. This fact reinforces my thesis of when this teaching from James was held.

An understanding about Job's life, which goes beyond what his book tells, greatly helps us to understand what this "Job's patience" actually is and what James uses as an example to his listeners, for James quotes "*you have heard*" before mentioning Job's patience, which shows that his listeners already had a more intimate understanding of this man's life.

THE MAN CALLED IYOV

Job is known for his spiritual devotion to God and his material possessions, but nothing else is told about him, neither his past, his origin, his profession, nor where his understanding of who the true God is came from, an understading only few possessed in his time.

According to the rabbinical literature, at the time the plagues hit Egypt, Pharaoh had three counselors in his palace. Men who exerted enormous influence on the decisions of the one who was considered the most powerful man in the world of his time. Each had an attribute that was useful to Pharaoh, the first had the gift of prophecy, the second knowledge about sacrifices, and the last one, a wisdom that exceeded that of many, this last one was the voice that exerted the greatest influence on the decisions made by the Pharaoh. Let's see who those three were:

Bil'am

He sent emissaries to Bil'am son of Beor, to Pesor...

Numbers 22:5

The first of Pharaoh's counselors was the famous prophet Bil'am who was called by the Amalekites to curse the people of Israel while they were in the wilderness. Bil'am, at first refutes the invitation, but after a certain insistence he ends up going to meet the Israelites with the intention of cursing them, but at the moment he opens his mouth, only blessings come out and the plan of Amalek goes the other way.

Bil'am was an extremely enigmatic figure, for he was a person who knew the true God, but at the same time he was involved with idolatrous nations and made the poor decision to curse the chosen people.

Bil'am answered them, spend the night here and I will give you the answer according to what Adonai, my God, tells me.

Numbers 22:8

What actually happened to Bil'am is the same thing we see now a days among many of those so called "men of god". There is an immensity of leaders all around the world, who know the word, know God, but because they have absorbed corrupt theologies and theories, they end up "mixing up" things and acting in a way pretty much like Bil'am.

This side of Bil'am is commented by the Zohar:

This evil man (Bil'am) became proud of knowing many things. By acting in this way, he seduces the people into error, making them to believe that he has a high spiritual level. He exaggerated in everything he did. But every time he spoke about the forces of impurity, he spoke the truth - in the literal sense - for anyone who heard him had the impression that he was the greatest prophet in the world.
Zohar HaKadosh 193b

The Gemara says: No creature was able to determine the moment when Adonai is angry, except for Bil'am, the wicked, on which is written: He who knew the knowledge of the Most High.
Talmud of Babylon, Tractate Brakhot 7a

Bil'am had a very unique knowledge about Adonai, and from what we can see, he used it for his personal gain, in this case, for the recognition from men. Now I wonder, how common are those things now a days? Men seeking fame, success, recognition, and riches at the expense of gifts they receive from God, leading many to believe that they are true men of God? This is the "spirit" of Bil'am that devastates Judaism and now the church, where leaders deprived of the true knowledge of God are found, leaders that use certain gifts to promote their own name. As Bil'am spoke the truth, those leaders gifts are also true, but they are used in a wrong way, for the teachings that come from these people distort the belief of those who follow them, as John warns in the book of Revelation:

But I have a few things against you, because you have

there those who follow the teaching of Balaam, who taught Balak to stumble before the children of Israel, to eat the sacrifices of idolatry, and to commit fornication.

Revelation 2:14

The name Balaam is interpreted as one who wore down the Jewish people [bila am]. He is the son of Beor, one who engaged in bestiality [be'ir].

Talmud of Babylon, Tractate Sanhedrin 105a

Bil'am knew Adonai, he had gifts from Adonai and to some extent, sought the will of Adonai, but by the lack of an intimacy with the Creator, by his arrogance, by his need of power and fame, ends up having condemnable and ludibrious teachings and attitudes.

When a man, a spiritual leader, knower of God and possessor of God's gifts, uses these gifts for some personal gain and instead of teaching the true word of God, teaches theologies of men, this leader is no different than Bil'am, for the gifts that this man possesses have the same origin of the gifts of Bil'am and the end is always tragic.

And Bil'am, the son of Beor, was put down by the sword.

Numbers 31:8

As seen before, where satan and the angel of death possess in their Gematria the number 61, for they both have control over the number 6, which represents the 6 days of creation, i.e. the earthly things, but under the supervision of God, represented by the number 1, we will see that the name of Bil'am shows something very interesting.

By calculating the Gematria Mispar Katan, where all the zeros are removed, we will have:

Bil'am (בלעם)

4ם + 7ע + 3ל + 2ב

= **16**

This teaches us that unlike satan, who everyone knows is evil and is controlled by God's "leash", the spirit of Bil'am acts in a contrary way, for first we have the number 1, which gives an appearance of something Godly, something holy, but behind the number 6 is found, showing its true face, a face linked to earthly things and to the essence of what comes from the absence of the presence of God.

Yitro

Yitro, priest of Midian, father-in-law of Moses ...
Exodus 18:1

Yitro was the man who welcomed Moises shortly after his scape from Egypt after killing a man. Moses, during his 40 years in seclusion, was a shepherd in the house of Yitro, who ends up becoming his father-in-law.

Little is related about the past of this man, but according to our sages, because he did not reveal the whereabouts of Moses to Pharaoh during all these years, he became worthy of doing Tshuvah and having a parashah with his own name (Exodus 18:1 - 20:23) and this is revealed to us by Gematria, for the value of his name has the same value as the word TIKUNIM (תיקונים), which means corrections, repairs, thus revealing to us that he has rectified his ways.

Iyov

Pharaoh's third and wisest counselor was Job, the man of the most influential ideas within the most powerful nation on earth, just as Joseph was before him. This raises much more doubts about him, for how could a man with such a position in a pagan nation possess so much knowledge about the living God? Was it for this the reason that God allowed him to be delivered into the hands of satan or was it because of a bet between God and the opposite side? Why does satan touches precisely three specific areas of Job's life, financially, family, and health? The story of Job has always been treated as one of the greatest mysteries of the Bible and little is known or taught about it in the Christian milieu.

Besides of what is related by the bible, there are several historical sources within the Jewish literature that address the life and the man who Job was, such as *Sefer HaYuval*, *Sefer HaYashar* and the mystical *Zohar HaKadosh*. But what I propose here is not a historical Job, but rather a more mystical Job, a more spiritual look at what has happened in this man's life, a life that had a change that was decided in only 6 verses and they are the base of all the teaching that this book passes on.

The LORD said to the Adversary, "Where have you been?" The Adversary answered the LORD, "I have been roaming all over the earth."
The LORD said to the Adversary, "Have you noticed My servant Job? There is no one like him on earth, a blameless and upright man who fears God and shuns evil!"
The Adversary answered the LORD, "Does Job not have good reason to fear God?
Why, it is You who have fenced him round, him and his household and all that he has. You have blessed his efforts so that his possessions spread out in the land.
But lay Your hand upon all that he has and he will surely blaspheme You to Your face."
The LORD replied to the Adversary, "See, all that he has is in your power; only do not lay a hand on him." The Adversary departed from the presence of the LORD.

Job 1:7-12

There is a popular saying that fits well with Job's life, "appearances deceive". The impression that comes to the reader concerning his life is that, Job, as a righteous man, ends up being tried, for apparently God wanted to prove something to satan. Despite all the hardness of his trials, Job, for being a righteous man, goes through it without blaspheming the name of God and for this reason, at the end, God restores all that he lost during this difficult time.

But we should look at some small nuances that are very subtle in the verses quoted above. Both God and satan make a common statement about Job, both say that he "fears" God and that term reveals Job's entire relationship with Adonai.

Know that serving the Creator, Blessed Be He, out of fear is not what makes a pious servant, but only an evil servant of the nations of the world, as He said to the wicked, "You shall fear Me" (Jer. 5:22) and concerning the Egyptians: "They feared the word of Adonai" (Exodus 9:20), for they did not obey Him out of love, but out of fear. But concerning the pious He says, "And you must love Adonai, your Elohim." (Deut. 6:5).

Sefer HaYashar 2:7

Job is reported as a man who feared God and not as a man who loved God, it changes a lot about him. Serving God out of fear has a very strong relationship with self-love, for the person who serves God, whether out of love or fear, is rewarded accordingly.

Job knew this, knew that everything he possessed, all his influence, his family, his possessions, lands, everything, came from Adonai. Job apparently had a very strong appreciation for these things and therefore served Adonai, for he was very much afraid of losing them. Proof of this is how Job related to God, he feared God's name Elohim, a name that represents God's justice and the use of that name in this verse is not by chance, for it teaches that it was actually the hand of God and an unfavorable judgment that Job feared.

This is the attitude of the one who serves God out of fear and not out of love; he is the one who fast for a reward, who prays for a reward and who makes a mitzvah for a reward.

Another point that says a lot about Job is what God allows satan to have control, things connected with this earthly reality, his money, his family and his health. Interesting that those three things are what make many people come to serve God, financial, family and health problems fill temples and denominations. It is also three things that subtly make one who serves God an idolater, for it is very easy to place any of these three things above God and His will.

But we must always have something in mind when it comes to the Tanakh, nothing is by chance and nothing happens for unexplained reasons. If satan touched on these three things in Job's life it is because a motive existed from behind.

Rabbi Hiyya Bar Abba says that Rabbi Simai says: three notable people were consulted by the pharaoh. In the consultation that Pharaoh did about what to do with the Jewish people, Bil'am, Yitro, and Iyov were present. Rabbi Hiyya Bar Abba teaches what happened to each one of them: Bil'am, who advised the Pharaoh to kill them, was punished by death. Yitro withdrew in protest, and this gave him merit and Iyov advised him to withdraw their possessions and put heavy burdens on them to tire their bodies, but not to kill them.

Talmud of Babylon, Tractate Sotah 11a

According to our sages, during one of Pharaoh's meetings with his counselors, the theme "Hebrew people" was brought up. Job, in all his wisdom, tries to bring about a "reasonable" solution, to withdraw their possessions so that they will always be dependent on Egypt and to put upon the people a great deal of work, so that it will affect the physical body and this would avoid any rising against the Pharaoh, at the same time he advised him not to kill them, as an act of mercy on Job's part.

This teaches us why satan attacked his possessions and his health, his physical body, for the same way he judged the Hebrew people, he was judged. Job was a victim of his tongue, something James has been dealing with since the beginning of his book.

Despite everything seen so far, there remain many doubts about Job's story and the connection it has with the book of James and the reasons about God's motives by bringing Job before satan, this is something very obscure, for why did God have to do that, since hitherto satan had not said anything about him?

The Zohar HaKadosh gives a brief account of the moment in which the dialogue between God and satan, as mentioned above, took place. It shows us some small details that are only perceptible through a deep analysis and knowledge about the Tanakh. This account is presented in the form of a dialogue between two rabbis who begin to discuss the crossing of the sea of reeds by the Hebrew people.

Rabbi Eleazar argued: to calm down satan? Well, God gave Job to calm him down. For when the nation of Israel came out of Egypt, satan planted agents among the people, they all came to prosecute Israel. Although satan had sent many agents, he decided to join them because something big was about to happen. So when Hashem saw all these agents infiltrating and going against the people of Israel, Hashem asked satan, where have you been? It is revealed to us that the reason for this question is to begin a conversation with satan, who replies that he was only wandering the land and taking a look, just as Hashem had commanded him to do at the beginning of all things. This teaches us that the earth was given into the hands of satan to observe and watch, except the land of Israel, for the eyes of Hashem have fallen upon the land of Israel.

But satan says, wait a minute, I was passing by and I've realized that you want to take these people out of Egypt, but why, since two days ago they were worshiping idols? Then satan tells Hashem that he was there to prosecute Israel. For how could He deliver these people who were worshiping false gods two days ago? This is not how the law should be applied.

Hashem thinks and hands over Job, for satan will be busy and will not disturb when He takes the people out of Egypt. Then Hashem gives him Job and says, "This one is yours". But before, satan asks Hashem, why are you giving me someone for free without you objecting it first? I see you did many good things for Job (there enters the conversation in the book of Job).

When Satan went after Job and was busy with him, the people crossed the sea and after that, Hashem goes to Job.

When Job was given to satan, satan immediately forgot the people.
Zohar HaKadosh, Parashat Bo, 33a

The Zohar is not an easy book, for its mystical language requires a lot of attention, otherwise it will be only a bunch of confusing biblical stories. A few chapters earlier, the Zohar tells us the motive that led satan to infiltrate his agents in the midst of the Hebrew people upon their departure from Egypt. It also tells us that just as Hashem and satan talked about Job, so they did about Abraham.

In this dialogue, as presented by Zohar, satan tells Hashem that Abraham only serves Him, because God never demanded a great sacrifice from Abraham and he (satan) was sure that, if Hashem asks for the greatest dream of Abraham, his son, Abraham would not obey God. Here begins the whole story about the sacrifice of Isaac as reported by the Torah. The Zohar also tells us that when satan saw Abraham rising in the morning to go and sacrifice his son, he became so desperate that he placed ten obstacles in Abraham's way so that he would not arrive at the altar.

It is also reported that because God prevented the sacrifice, satan said that "it was not valid", because as Abraham did not go all the way to the end, God was "in debt" with satan, owing him blood of Abraham, which would have been given through of the sacrifice of Isaac, for there were still a “bet” among them.

For this reason, satan, while he "watched the earth", begins to observe that something strange began to occur in

Egypt. A certain descendants of Abraham, long slaves, began to move massively in the opposite direction from what was their yoke. When satan realizes that Hashem decided to take the Hebrew people out of Egypt in order to serve Him, he rushes before God, pulls out the notebook from his pocket where he kept all his records and reminds God about the blood of Abraham that He owned him. Ironically, he also made a point of reminding God that the people he took from Egypt, coincidentally, was Abraham's blood and therefore, he resolved that he wanted to receive his debt at that moment by destroying the people. The answer given by Hashem at this moment is what we find in Job 1:8, "Have you noticed my servant Job?" And this answers all the questions.

*Some time later, they told **Abraham** that Milcah*
*had borne children **to his brother Nahor**.*
***Uz**, the firstborn and Buz his brother and Kemuel*
the father of Aram.

Genesis 22:20-21

*There was a man in the land of **Uz**, named Job. He was*
righteous and feared Elohim, and turned away from evil.

Job 1:1

God spoke about Job, not because satan wanted Job, but because satan was charging the blood of Abraham at one of the most critical time in Israel's history. Satan was so dirty that God made a point of treating him like a "fool".

Job was from the family of Abraham, a descendant of his brother Nahor, by his firstborn Uz. God solved three problems in a simple way. The first is in relation to the idolatry of the people, by which satan could kill them all. As we have seen before, Job, even though he was a righteous man, served God out of fear of His hand, fear of losing all that he possessed, which in a way made him an idolater. Thus satan could get “paid” for the idolatry practiced by those who came from Abraham.

The second is the "debt" satan had been charging in relation to Abraham's blood, as satan wanted the blood and not a specific person, anyone from the patriarch's house would be valid.

Lastly, since God was doing a great work and did not want to be bothered with the adversary, He kept him distracted with Job. It is like a watchdog , when someone needs to cross the area guarded by it, throws a bone that leaves him busy while this one does what needs to be done.

Among all the sacrifices that were made in the Temple, there is one established in the book of Leviticus which deals with one goat that must be let loose in the desert for satan, while another one is sacrificed within the Temple. I have seen much confusion about this commandment and teachings completely alienated from the spiritual reality that this sacrifice has.

And he shall place lots upon the two goats, one marked for the LORD and the other marked for Az''el (satan).
Aaron shall bring forward the goat designated by lot for the LORD, which he is to offer as a sin offering;
while the goat designated by lot for Az''el shall be left standing alive before the LORD, to make expiation with it and to send it off to the wilderness for Az''el.

Leviticus 16:8-10

This passage reveals a very deep spiritual secret. On the day of Yom Kippur, the most important day of the year, while one goat is sacrificed for the forgiveness of the people, another is given to satan so he will not disturb this important day for Adonai and His people. This goat set loose in the desert represents Job, for he acts as a distracting agent to "entretain" satan, preventing him from acting upon the people while crossing the see, so does the *az"el* goat, a goat that prevents satan to charge the people on Yom Kippur.

This is also shown by Gematria:

Hasatan (השטן) - the satan

50ן + 9ט + 300ש + 5ה

= **364**

364 represents every day of the year minus one, that is, satan exerts influence every day of the year, except on Yom Kippur, when he is distracted with his goat, as a watching dog is all entertained with a piece of bone.

These are the secrets behind Job's life. God gave him to satan so that satan would not get in the way while He was taking His people out of Egypt, so that he would be distracted while God worked the miracle among His people, deserving them or not, and That's the most important and fascinating thing.

Job was the victim of his own judgment, all that his decisions caused to Hebrew people, was what was caused to him by satan and all this happened because Job served Elohim out of fear and not Adonai out of love. As God does not make things with loose ends, all of this also happened because the mercy God had for Job's life, as he states at the end of his book:

I had heard You with my ears, But now I see You with my eyes;
Job 42:5

Job really served God, but he served a God about whom he was taught about, he had no experience with Him, and when you do not know someone, you cannot love that person, so all the feeling left to Job that motivated him to serve this God was only Fear.

God, knowing this and knowing his heart, does a work in his life, a very painful work, but with a spectacular end. The God that Job only heard about, the God that he feared, was now before his eyes and he learned how to love Him. A theoretical God became a practical God. Fear has become love and that was the real Job.

Now, the Job's "patience" that James quotes takes on a much deeper and mystical context.

Patience, in Hebrew, is SAV'LANUT (סבלנות), a term that has the root composed of the letters (ס-ב-ל). These same letters also form the root of two other words SEVEL (סבל) - *suffering.*

First James reveals that the one who *suffers* is blessed, then he quotes "Job's patience" and at the end, he mentions God's mercy. What the author does in reality is to reveal what "suffering" would that be and what "bless" would that be only by mentioning Job's patience, for James does not speak of patience *per se*, but he is talking to all who suffer as Job suffered and blessed they will be for they will no longer fear God, rather love Him.

The suffering of the bless is nothing more than a school itself, where our superficial relationship with a God we always heard about becomes a deep relationship with a God that we see each day in our lives. In spite of being a hard thing to go through, the word "suffering" should not be used in this case, but rather "treatment", or perhaps "re-education", because its end is very fabulous to share the same sentence with the word "suffering".

XXXI - TO SWEAR

But above all things, my brothers, swear not, neither by heaven, neither by the earth, neither by any other oath: but let your yes be yes; and your no, no; lest you fall into condemnation.

James 5:12

And you have heard what was spoken by the ancients:
"Do not swear falsely in my name, for you must answer before Adonai your promises.
And I say unto you, Swear not in vain for anything, nor by the heavens which is the throne of Elohim.
And not by the earth which is the footstool of His feet, nor by the city of the heavens (Yerushalayim), for it is the city of Elohim.
And not by your head because you cannot make your hair white or black.
But let your words be yes, yes and no, no. Anything added to this is bad.

Matthew 5:33-37

There is no way not to make an association between the words of James and the words of Yeshua, his brother. I find very interesting how they use similar terms and similar Torah interpretations to pass on their message. This proves how Yeshua's teachings were really focused on the Torah and on how it should be observed.

Both James and Yeshua brought up the theme "oath" due to some motive that is not revealed to us by the books. The "oath" theme is approached by both Torah and Tanakh, but in a somewhat different way from what we see in the words of Yeshua and James.

Looking at the book of Matthew, the most sensitive point we have is the famous "hear what was said, but I tell you...", giving a false impression that Yeshua was replacing the Torah by the famous Christian jargon "law of christ".

Certainly, if we look at the way he speaks, we can have this understanding, an understanding that, at least, I call erroneous, because in order for Yeshua to be worthy of the title of Mashiach, which he himself claimed to be, he had to teach only and exclusively the Torah. Before going a little deeper, let's take a look at what the One-God vision is about this theme:

And Adonai, your God, you shall fear, only Him you shall serve, and by His name you shall swear.

Deuteronomy 6:13

And King Solomon swore by Adonai...

1 Kings 2:23a

And David swore again...

1 Samuel 2:3a

And it shall come to pass, if they shall learn the ways of my people, and swear by my LIVING NAME, as they taught my people to swear by the name of Baal, they shall be built in the midst of MY PEOPLE.

Jeremiah 12:16

The depth of these passages impresses me. First, if we look closely at the passage in Deuteronomy, to swear is not only a permission, but actually a commandment. It is an ordinance that the oath must be made in the name of God. This is so profound that in Jeremiah the prophet tells the Gentiles that if they learn the ways of His people (Torah) and swear by His Living Name, they will be grafted onto the People of Israel. Two other figures of extreme weight before Adonai, David and his son Solomon, also swore in the name of Adonai.

So how could Yeshua forsake such a commandment? He who believes that Yeshua abolished the Torah, the work of the

One who he called "my father", thus making him a rebellious and an undisciplined son and not worthy to be called Mashiach, it is time to revise his own concepts. And this is not all, if Yeshua had abolished the commandment of "swearing" he would be nullifying Jeremiah's prophecy about the adoption ofthe Gentiles, which would be inconceivable.

Anyone who believes in a jesus who has done so, believes in a mythological figure created by the church, who despite having some similarities with the true Yeshua, they are not the same. We must pay attention to the words of Yeshua, he at no time forbids the oath or cancels the commandment concerning the oath, what he actually says is DO NOT SWEAR FALSELY. And he quotes this passage:

Neither swear falsely by my name, for ye shall profane the name of your God, I am Adonai.

Leviticus 19:12

Yeshua did not abolish the oath, he did not deny the Torah, but rather he sets two commandments in parallel to each other, stating that if one is to swear falsely, it is better not to swear at all. The problems that existed in his day, as they still exist, were some interpretations of certain Pharisaic schools concerning this verse.

Some Pharisees used this passage to justify their habit to swear falsely since it was not in the name of Adonai. They swore in the name of the Temple, of Yerushalaim, by the heavens, by the earth, and so forth. If it were not by the name of Adonai, they were not obliged to fulfill what they swore.

To swear by his name and not on behalf of other gods. In other words, you should not swear by the names of other gods, but in the name of Adonai. But if it is not in the name of other gods, an oath may be taken to affirm a testimony or enter into a contract, even if it is not in His Name.

Ibn Ezra, Deuteronomy 6:13

One of the great sages and commentators of the Torah, Ibn Ezra, claims that one can by no means swear by false gods, but he also states that if the oath is not in the name of false gods, the person is free to swear on behalf of anything. Unfortunately many did not understand that the prohibition of Leviticus was not to swear falsely only in the name of Adonai, it was simply to not swear falsely.

Yeshua was exhorting some Pharisees that if they swear by anything, they should fulfill it. It is not because they did not specifically swear in the name of Adonai that they were exempt from doing as said, if one knows that won't be able to, then it is better not to swear by absolutely nothing. Other rabbis fully agree with the teaching of Yeshua, as well as many other Pharisaic schools:

> *If you have all the characteristics mentioned here, if you worship His name and if you serve Him then you have the right to take an oath in His name. But be very careful with any oath, otherwise, it is better not to swear by anything.*
>
> Rashi, Deuteronomy 6:13

The great sage Rashi fully agrees with the words of Yeshua, be very careful about oaths, otherwise it is better not to swear by anything. To conclude his exhortation, Yeshua cites "anything added to it is bad", though many have the understanding that this "bad" refers to swearing or refers to adding something to what Yeshua actually said, such a quote is a typical Orthodox/Pharisaic jargon concerning something very serious in the Torah, thus bringing another passage from the Torah:

> *Thou shalt not add anything to the Torah which I command you, neither shall ye diminish from it, that ye may keep the commandments of Adonai your God which I command you.*
>
> Deuteronomy 4:2

He is reaffirming a basic Torah principle, probably to

silence anyone who might be thinking that he is adding or removing something from the Law. What he talks about the oath is in accordance with the book of Leviticus when it teaches about the FALSE oath.

So in the end, by using a rabbinic language, Yeshua says that teaching other things that are not in the Torah as being God's laws is the real "bad" because it would be as adding things to it. He clarifies to his Talmidim that adding or removing anything from the Torah is what is bad.

What happened here was a ban on an apparent custom of some rabbinical schools to swear falsely from the moment it is not by the name of Adonai. Yeshua then uses the verse in Leviticus 19:12, which should serve as a basis for them to make such oaths, and on top of that, he reveals that the false oath is not to be done under any hypothesis. At the end he says that nothing should be added to the Torah, showing that the rabbinic laws that add anything to God's Law are bad and that he was, under no hypothesis, removing anything from the Torah.

When James presents this teaching to his hearers, I imagine him reminiscing all these words of his master. All the teachings of Torah as taught by Yeshua serve to prove him as Mashiach. So the repetition of words used by him, associates Yeshua more and more with the Torah and this was a common practice among his followers, just as it happens within any Jewish community, where its students pass the teachings of their masters to prove their connection with the Word of God.

THE OATH AND THE YOM KIPPUR

On the most holy day of all, Yom Kippur, also known as the day of atonement, or the day of the forgiveness of sins, there is a custom among all Jewish communities that, before the beginning of the service in asynagogue, a prayer called KOL NIDREI is recited. This prayer, when translated from Aramaic means ALL OATHS, is a prayer for forgiveness of all unfulfilled promises and oaths made during that year, showing the deep importance given to such acts.

The Gemarah in Niddah 30b says that before a body receives a soul, that soul takes an oath before Adonai, where it promises to become a righteous person and not a bad person. This idea is based on the two most common forms that the word "soul" appears in the book of Psalms, such as NAFSHI (נפשי) and NAFSHO (נפשו). Our sages teach that this variation appears as a representation of the spiritual ascension that the human soul promises to Adonai before incarnating.

NAFSHI (נפשי) is translated as "My soul of Adonai" and NAFSHO (נפשו) is translated as "Adonai's soul of man". NAFSHO represents the person in their lower and most basic levels of knowledge, when one begins to become a Tzadik person, his soul ceases to be NAFSHO (נפשו) and becomes NAFSHI (נפשי), a soul more connected to Adonai and the spiritual world.

In a more practical way, what our sages want to teach with this is that when a man takes an oath and does not perform it, he takes his own soul out of the hands and care of Adonai. As this soul has sworn to Adonai to become righteous, when the person who owns this soul breaks an oath, it causes its soul to lose the divine essence, for it was by an oath that this soul entered into this reality. That is why the prayer about the broken promises is very important on the day of Yom Kippur.

XXXII - PRAYER AND WORSHIP

Is any among you afflicted? let him pray. Is any merry? let him sing psalms.

James 5:13

Prayer in affliction, praises in joy. Although such attitudes have a Christian New Testament appearance, such attitudes are part of the foundations of the faith of the Jews and they are an essential part of the behavior from those who follow Torah. This recommendation of James happens innumerable times throughout the Tanakh, where reports about prophets praying for the sick and kings praising God are found.

But there is a difference, the way Christianity understands and practices prayer and praise is different from the way it happens in Judaism and in the Tanakh. On the Christian side, it is very common to pray for requests, such as the healing of someone, the resolution of some problem or even a prayer for exorcism; the praises and worships are basically defined as music and songs. On the other hand, within the Jewish faith, prayer does not deal with requests, but rather to magnify the name of Hashem, within the Jewish prayer there is also the custom of repeating some words from the Torah, which, for those who hear without understanding it, are mere words, but the mystical sense that each of these words have behind, make them powerful beyond what is imaginable. The praise and worship within Judaism are not limited to just songs, but it actually means changes of attitudes towards the will of the Creator through a deep studying and understanding of His word.

In order to have a better understanding of James' teaching, it is vital to look at such terms according to the faith he possessed, the Jewish faith. A good example given by him that symbolizes both prayer and praise is the book of Psalms. The usage of this book's words in prayer and in praise brings tremendous spiritual benefits, such as comfort to the afflicted and blessings to those who rejoice themselves in God.

Simply reciting the book of Psalms, though very valid, does not possess all the greatness of the one who recites it with the understanding about the true meaning behind each term that appears there. This book and its contents, among all the books in Tanakh, is the most mystical and the most difficult to obtain a complete understanding, for this reason there are innumerable mystical books that approach these songs. All the psalms found in this book, without exception, possess great hidden secrets not seen in a common reading which, when discovered, studied, understood, practiced, and recited, those secrets elevate the individual to a plateau that his prays will have such a power to reach the throne of God in the way one never imagined before.

In order for all of this to become clearer, I will present a mystical analysis of a simple psalm. This will be done for didactic purposes, so that it can serve as an example of how deep those "songs" are. In this case I will use one of the best known Psalm, Psalm 23.

PSALM 23

This may be the best-known King David's psalm, it is both a prayer of deliverance and recognition of the power of Adonai, as well as an exaltation of His name. Right at the beginning we have the famous phrase "*You are my shepherd and I lack nothing*", which is widely recited throughout the world. But, with a somewhat more critical analysis of it, we will see that if the Lord is our shepherd, that makes us like sheeps.

Being a sheep is by no means a good thing, for like the animal, the term sheep describes the kind of person who follows others blindly regardless of the consequences. This already teaches us that this psalm is more than meet eyes and more than the common understanding achieves.

Psalm 23 has in its entirety exactly 57 words (in Hebrew), the number 57 is the same numerical value of the word ZAN (זן) - *nourishment*- for it is a psalm used to nourish the faith and the soul of those who understand it. It also has a total of 227 letters within these 57 words, the number 227 is the numerical value of the word BRACHAH (ברכה) - *blessing* - and in this case, the word blessing is in the singular form, this teaches us that this psalm carries a very specific kind of blessing , a blessing that affects a very specific area in the life of the one who understands it. Let's look at every term in every verse of this psalm so we can understand this blessing behind it:

VERSE 1)

מִזְמ֥וֹר לְדָוִ֑ד יְהֹוָ֥ה רֹ֝עִ֗י לֹ֣א אֶחְסָֽר

A Psalm of David. Adonai is my shepherd, I lack nothing.

'S Shepherd - ROYI (רעי) = ROAH SHEL (רועה של)

ר200 + ו6 + ע70 + ה5 + ש300 + ל30

= **611**

611 is the same numerical value of the word TORAH (תורה) - *Torah* - The word Torah is not just a book, for its direct translation means "target". What David claims here is that Adonai is his target, his goal and by the secretly use of the word Torah, we understand that he real intention is to reach this "target" through obedience.

I lack nothing - LO ECHSAR (לא אחסר)

ל30 + א1 + א1 + ח8 + ס60 + ר200

= **300**

300 is the total value of the word RUACH ELOHIM (רוח אלהים) - *Holy Spirit* - which is a "thing" totally connected to Torah, for through the Spirit is the way the Torah is meant to be "used" in order to reach God. Both hidden claims of David in this verse make perfect sense and are confirmed by the prophet Ezekiel:

and I will put My spirit into you. Thus I will cause you to follow My laws and faithfully to observe My commandments.

Ezekiel 36:27

Finally, David reveals the result of having the Torah through the Holy Spirit and this can be found in the last letters of each word that makes up this verse:

ר200 + ד4 + ה5 + י10 + א1 + ר200

= **420**

420 is the numerical value of the word HAK'DUSHAH (הקדושה) – *the holiness* – and such a thing can only be obtained through a devotion to the Word of God. So, this verse can also be read as follows:

A Psalm of David. Adonai is my target, my goal, for He is my shepherd and it is Him that I will follow blindly. His Holy Spirit will not fail me and through it, Adonai will manifest Himself in my life and He will write His Law in my heart so that I can naturally follow it and become holy before His eyes, just as He is Holy and only then, I shall lack nothing.

VERSE 2)

בִּנְאֹ֣ות דֶּ֭שֶׁא יַרְבִּיצֵ֑נִי עַל־מֵ֖י מְנֻח֣וֹת יְנַהֲלֵֽנִי

He makes me lie down in green pastures; He leads me to water in places of repose.

Green pastures - BIN'OT DESSE (בנאות דשא)

ב2 + נ5 + א1 + ו6 + ת4 + ד4 + ש3 + א1

= **26**

*Mispar Katan

26 is the value of the Name above all names, the tetragram (יהוה). This name is associated with the sefirah TIFERET, which is the manifestation of the Creator's compassion in the life of His servant.

To water in places of repose - AL MEY
MENUCHOT (על מי מנחות)
ע7 + ל3 + מ4 + י1 + מ4 + נ5 + ח8 + ו6 + ת4

= **42**

*Mispar Katan

42 is the value of the divine name ELOAH (אלוה), or TOV'EL (טוב אל), which represents the total goodness of the Creator.

Interesting, because this verse is a result of the previous verse. The man who seeks Adonai, who has His Law written in his heart by the Holy Spirit and thus follows it and tries to evolve holiness in his own life, according to this Psalm, will not be a man who dependents solely on mercy, for he will be at a stage far above, a stage where he shall receive the compassion and the goodness of God, things much more deeper than mercy.

Evolving from the need for God's mercy to God's goodness and compassion is essential in the life of every human being, for this can be used as some sort of scale to define the degree of holiness in one's life. Mercy is for sinners, what we all are, but as less mercy as one gets, as less sins there will be found in one's life and this brings more goodness and compassion from God.

Adonai (יהוה) makes me lie down in the green pastures
of His compassion, Eloah guides me to water

in places of repose by His goodness.

VERSE 3)

נַפְשִׁי יְשׁוֹבֵב יַנְחֵנִי בְמַעְגְּלֵי־צֶדֶק לְמַעַן שְׁמוֹ

He renews my life; He guides me in right paths as befits His name.

The numerical value of the sum of all the letters of verse 3 is equivalent to 1773. Throughout the Torah, there is another verse that has the the exactly same sum equal to 1773 and, although apparently disconnected, it will reveal the message behind these words of David.

On the eighth day, the flesh of the foreskin
must be circumcised. = 1773

Leviticus 12:3

At first, this verse has no connection with that of Psalm, but there is a term in this passage that must be understood in two ways, the circumcision. The first meaning of this term is the famous biblical circumcision of the flesh and the second is something that deals with the heart, a spiritual circumcision.

Circumcise, therefore, the thickening about your
hearts and stiffen your necks no more.

Deuteronomy 10:16

But he is a Jew, which is one inwardly; and circumcision
is that of the heart, in the spirit, and not in the letter;
whose praise is not of men, but of God.

Romans 2:29

We see that the connection that Psalm 23:3 has with Leviticus 12:3 is about the circumcision of the heart, that means the covenant that man makes with God must be in his heart, it is to follow the Torah out of love and not out of obligation, it is to observe the commandments as if they were part of one's faith and not through religiosity. This idea walks hand in hand with the seen above verse found from Ezekiel, where the spirit will put the Laws in one's heart so that the commandments are lived in a natural way.

This reveals the renewal to which David refers, it is a renewal of the heart, a heart that develops a greater love and seeks a new relationship with the Living God.

To do so, David says that God guides him in the right path, in Hebrew is "path tzedek (במעגלי-**צדק**)". This word is from the same root of the word TZADIK (צדיק) – *the one who follows the Torah* - and this confirms once more the Ezekiel's saying in the previous verses, for this passage shows that the renewal is actually taking place in the heart, which is the Law being written in it by the Holy Spirit.

In the end we are told that all this is for the benefit of Hashem's name, but what would that benefit be?

As befits His name- LEMA'AN SHMO (למען שמו)

6ו + 5מ + 3ש + 5ן + 7ע + 4מ + 3ל

= **32**

*Mispar Katan

32 is the same value as the word KAVOD - *honor* - and this teaches us that the greatest honor one can give to the God of Israel is the submission to His will thus honoring Him.

He renews my life by giving me a new circumcised heart,
His spirit in this new heart will guide me to become
a Tzadik and to live His will in a natural way and in
order to befit His Name, I will honor Adonai.

VERSE 4)

גַּם כִּֽי־אֵלֵךְ בְּגֵיא צַלְמָוֶת לֹא־אִירָא רָע כִּֽי־אַתָּה
עִמָּדִי שִׁבְטְךָ וּמִשְׁעַנְתֶּךָ הֵמָּה יְנַחֲמֻנִי

Though I walk through a valley of deepest darkness, I fear no evil, for You are with me; Your rod and Your staff—they comfort me.

Valley of deepest darkness - GUI TZALMAVET (גיא צלמות)
400ת + 6ו + 40מ + 30ל + 90צ + 1א + 10י + 3ג
= **580**

Now we have something very complex, for 580 is also the numerical value of the word ASHIR (עשיר) - *rich* - and in order not to fall into erroneous interpretations, it is necessary a spiritual definition of "rich" according to the Torah. The most amazing thing is the strange and mystical way that the Torah defines this term. It is as follows:

Eye for eye, tooth for tooth, hand for hand, foot for foot.
Exodus 21:24

This Torah's commandment comes in an unusual way, for it quotes body parts such as eye, tooth, hand and foot. If we go a little further and leave the idea that this verse only talks about revenge, we can draw from it a very profound and spiritual teaching.

The eye, the tooth, the hand and the foot are representatives of the true wealth, for the eye symbolizes the window to understanding, it is mainly through the sight that man receives almost all the knowledge he absorbs. The tooth represents the power of speech as well as the tongue, for without them the words uttered by someone would be incomprehensible. The hand represents the human being's creative power and capacity, and the feet symbolize the ability to move.

It may sound kinda crazy, but it's precisely these four things that represent the Torah in one's life. The Eye to learn the Torah, the teeth to be able to speak in order to teach the Torah, the hand to follow its commandments and the feet to carry it to all men. This is the true wealth of the human being, for to achieve this is to attain the true purpose of creation, it is the maxim that God seeks from a person.

To prove this let's look at these four terms in Hebrew:

EYE - AYIN (עין)
TOOTH - SHIN (שין)
HAND - YAD (יד)
FOOT - REGEL (רגל)

When we get the first letters of each word (remembering that the Hebrew is read from right to left), we will have the word ASHIR (עשיר), which means RICH. The lesson we can draw from it is that he who is truly rich is not the one who has money, neither possessions nor fame, but the real wealthy person is the one who has the ability to study and learn the Torah, to go wherever one has to in order to teach it and to fulfill its commandments , this is the real richness and the lesson we can draw from it.

For you are with me - KI ATAH IMADI (כי אתה עמדי)
10י + 4ד + 40מ + 70ע + 5ה + 400ת + 1א + 10י + 20כ
= **560**

560 is the value of DA'AT ELOHIM (דעת אלהים), this is how deep one can know and understand God and thus relate more intimately with Him, this kind of knowledge is not attainable by any man, but is something given to men by God Himself.

And how to receive this understanding that brings the knowledge about the real God? Well, another verse with the same numerical value of 560 answers this question.

Adonai SPOKE to me. = 560
Deuteronomy 2:17

That is, the understanding about the Creator is possible only through what He speaks to us via His own Word. Hence it is said that His people suffer for lack of knowledge, this lack of knowledge that causes suffering is the lack of knowledge about what He speaks, in other words, is the lack of knowledge about the bible, this is the only way to get to know him in order for Him to be with us.

I fear no evil - LO EIRE RA (לא אריא רע)
70ע + 200ר + 1א + 10י + 200ר + 1א + 1א + 30ל
= **513**

513 is the same value of the word BESSORAH (בשורה) - *good news* - also known as gospel, this concept of good news, bessorah, though widely used in Christianity, was born within Judaism. It is a term used for when God brings a new revelation to His people. To carry this revelation is to take the Bessorah, the good news.

The Hebrew term translated as "staff" is SHEVET (שבט), this is not a word that appears much in the Torah, but there is one case that it appears in a very mystical way, as found in Numbers 24:17

אֶרְאֶנּוּ֙ וְלֹ֣א עַתָּ֔ה אֲשׁוּרֶ֖נּוּ וְלֹ֣א קָר֑וֹב דָּרַ֨ךְ כּוֹכָ֜ב מִֽיַּעֲקֹ֗ב וְקָ֥ם
שֵׁ֙בֶט֙ מִיִּשְׂרָאֵ֔ל וּמָחַץ֙ פַּאֲתֵ֣י מוֹאָ֔ב וְקַרְקַ֖ר כָּל־בְּנֵי־שֵׁתי
What I see for them is not yet, What I behold will not be soon: A star rises from Jacob, A ***staff (SHEVET)*** *comes forth from Israel; It smashes the brow of Moab, The foundation of all children of Seth.*
Numbers 24:16

In this passage the Torah relates the SHEVET MEISRAEL (שבט מישראל) - *staff from Israel* – as being someone and not a thing. Also, the way this “staff” is described, we are given the impression that this “staff” is something that comes from the People of Israel. By Gematria in the way it appears in Numbers, we have:

SHEVET MEISRAEL (שבט מישראל) – STAFF FROM ISRAEL
30ל + 1א + 200ר + 300ש + 10י + 40מ + 9ט + 2ב + 300ש
= **10**

The number 1 represents one of the facets of Mashiach, his mission as Ben David:

MASHIACH BEN DAVID (משיח בן דוד)
4ד + 6ו + 4ד + 50ן + 2ב + 8ח + 10י + 300ש + 40מ
892 = 8+9+2 = 19 = 1+9
= **10**

The other term presented by Psalm 23 is MISH'ENET (משענת) - *rod* - and although there are many confusions between rod and staff, both have very distinct spiritual meanings. The staff represents authority, represents Moses, who ruled the people and Mashiach Ben David who will rule the people. However the rod, it doesn't have a connection with Moses, but with Aharon, the first high priest and therefore, the "rod" represents priesthood, spiritual authority.

The rod appears in several passages throughout the Tanakh, but there is one that fits well with this Psalm:

וְהָיָה הָאִישׁ אֲשֶׁר אֶבְחַר־בּוֹ מַטֵּהוּ יִפְרָח
The rod of the man whom I choose shall sprout...
Numbers 17:20

This is a passage that tells how the choice of Aharon, Moses' brother, as the high priest took place. Just as it is a story full of mysteries, so too the verse that relates it is full of mysteries. Although it is a text that talks about Aharon, he also talks about Mashiach, because it is a verse that deals with leadership.

If we look at the terms MATERHU IPHRAKH (מטהו יפרח) - *his rod shall sprout* - and we will do the Gematria, we will have the following:

MATERHU IPHRAKH (מטהו יפרח)
8ח + 200ר + 80פ + 10י + 6ו + 5ה + 9ט + 40מ
= **358**

MASHIACH (משיח)
8ח + 10י + 300ש + 40מ
= **358**

The rod that will sprout is Mashiach himself, but which Mashiach, Ben David or Ben Yosef? Let us look at the first letters of this Hebrew term, out of order:

בו **מ**טהו **י**פרח
(מ) MASHIACH - (ב) BEN - (י) YOSEF

This reveals to us the ultimate authority of Mashiach Ben David as king and the priestly authority of Mashiach Ben Yosef, even though he is not from the tribe of Levi. This is why Yeshua was called priest even though he wasn't a Levite. I deal more on this subject in the book *Torat Yehoshua: According to the Original Book of Matthew*.

Finally David states: "they comfort me", which in Hebrew is HEIMAH INACHAMUNI (המה ינחמני):

They comfort me - HEIMAH INACHAMUNI (המה ינחמני)
1י + 5נ + 4מ + 8ח + 5נ + 1י + 5ה + 4מ + 5ה
= **38**

*Mispar Katan

38 is the same numerical value of GULAH (גלה), which is something like "To be revealed" in English. With this we can understand Psalm 23:4 as follows:

Though I walk in the valley of deepest darkness, I fear no evil, for I will live and teach His word. And the good news that will come through the wisdom of Elohim will reveal to me the royal authority of Mashiach Ben David and the priestly authority of Mashiach Ben Yosef and in that, I shall have comfort.

VERSE 5)

תַּעֲרֹךְ לְפָנַי | שֻׁלְחָן נֶגֶד צֹרְרָי דִּשַּׁנְתָּ בַשֶּׁמֶן רֹאשִׁי כּוֹסִי רְוָיָה

You spread a table for me in full view of my enemies;
You anoint my head with oil; my cup is abundant.

Right at the beginning we have a very interesting expression that is only understood within the rabbinical milieu. This idea of "*spreading a table*" remotes from something called SHULCHAN ARUKH (שלחן ערוך). Even though this is a name from a modern Jewish book, this term also deals with ethical, moral, and Torah observance within the Jewish mentality. Although *Shulchan Arukh* is a somewhat radical book on what it addresses, that name has been given to it, for the concept of a "spread table" is a concept related to the care about the observance of God's Law.

Another interesting thing to note is the way David calls his "enemies"; he calls them TZOR'RA'I (צררי); this is a word with the same root as the verb LITZROR (לצרור), which means "to bind".

Perhaps David does not deal with enemies in this passage, but rather he deals with things that binds his life and for this reason that he says that by his table being spread by God, that is, by his Torah and its knowledge given to him by God, everything that binds his life will no longer have power over him; he claims to be delivered from everything that binds him by the power of obedience.

Another consequence of this obedience is what we see next, the head that will be anointed with oil. The anointing with oil has many meanings and objectives, knowing what is behind of it makes a lot of difference:

My head with oil - BASHEMEN ROSHI (בשמן ראשי)

1י + 3ש + 1א + 2ר + 5ן + 4מ + 3ש + 2ב

= **21**

*Mispar Katan

The 21 is the value of God's name EHYE (אהיה), name by which God first introduced Himself to Moses in the burning bush. The 21 is also the value of the word BINA (בנה), without the YUD (י). This anointing that David receives on his head is an anointing of understanding on EHYE (אהיה), an understanding that no human mind can conceive concerning God, raising him to a spiritual level far above of a common human being.

To conclude, we have the "abundant cup" of David. The "cup" represents the 4 redemptions that Mashiach will bring, this is also represented by the four wine glasses in the Seder of Pessach. These four cups, representing the four redemptions, are conformed in the book of Psalms itself, the first is found in Psalm 16, the second in Psalm 23 and twice in Psalm 116, always with a representation of redemption.

You spread a table for me before my enemies, that is, by obedience to Your Word no spiritual binding will be upon my life; You anoint my head with oil and by this anointing, I will be given the understanding on EHYE and my cup is abundant, for I will receive Mashiach's redemption.

VERSE 6)

אַ֤ךְ ׀ט֤וֹב וָחֶ֣סֶד יִ֭רְדְּפוּנִי כָּל־יְמֵ֣י חַיָּ֑י וְשַׁבְתִּ֥י בְּבֵית־יְ֝הוָ֗ה לְאֹ֣רֶךְ יָמִֽים
Only goodness and steadfast love shall pursue me all the days of my life, and I shall dwell in the house of the LORD for many long years.

The numerical value of this entire verse is 2123, there are in the Torah two other verses with this same numerical value:

*And the Amalekites and the Canaanites who dwelt in that hill country came down and dealt them a shattering blow at **mount Hormah**.*

Numbers 14:45

*At **Mount Hor**, on the boundary of the land of*

Edom, the LORD said to Moses and Aaron.

Numbers 20:23

In spite of two distinct texts, both mention a common term, the word HAR (הר) - *mount* - in the first we have the mount Hormah and in the second, Mount Hor and each one has an enigmatic association with two well know names of God in the Torah:

HAR HORMAH (הר חרמה)
ה5 + ר2 + ח8 + ר2 + מ4 + ה5
= **26**

*Mispar Katan

26 is the value of the name of God that is above all names, the tetragrammaton (יהוה).

HAR HOR (הר הר)
ה5 + ר2 + ה5 + ר2
= **14**

*Mispar Katan

14 is the value of the name Elohim(אלהים).

The interesting thing is that the most common name of God in all the Torah is ADONAI ELOHIM (יהוה אלהים). This name represents the righteousness of God, His goodness, compassion and mercy all together. The association of this verse with ADONAI ELOHIM teaches us that David went through the judgment of God, he was approved and therefore he can now dwell in the House of Adonai, that is, he was approved to enter the messianic age.

It is made known that the messianic age of this verse is mentioned in the form of "house of Adonai" which refers to the BEIT HAMIKDASH (בית המקדש) - *Holy Temple* - The expression of dwelling in the Temple is a terminology used by the rabbis for over 2000 years . To dwell in the Temple represents the merit of being able to enter into the messianic era, that is, to be saved.

Yeshua comments on this:

In my Father' house are many dwellings: if it were not so,
I would have told you. I go to prepare a place for you.

John 14:2

This passage is used by the church to assert that the Christian will live in heaven, which cannot be more erroneous. The house to which Yeshua refers is the Temple to be rebuilt on his Ben David mission, these many dwellings refer to the restored Jerusalem, for it is the place where Mashiach will reign from.

The confirmation of this is in the Psalm itself, when David says it will be for many long years:

For many long years - L'OREKH YAMIM (לְאֹ֣רֶךְ יָמִֽים)

= **995**

* Mispar Shemi

995 + the 5 nekodot found in those words (small dots below the hebrew words)

= **1000**

Now, 1000 years is the time that the reign of Mashiach Ben David will last and for this reason, David claims that he will dwell in the Temple, in the restored Jerusalem, for exactly 1000 years.

To conclude, the goodness and steadfast love that shall pursue David are God Himself, as follows:

Kindness and steadfast love - TOV VECHESSED (טוב וחסד)

4ד + 6ס + 8ח + 6ו + 2ב + 6ו + 9ט

= **41**

*Mispar Katan

41 is the number of the name ELI (אלי) - *my God* - and it is the name that represents a more loving relationship with the Creator, it is precisely this side of God that shall pursue those

who serve Him; just as God went after Abraham and just as He went after of the Hebrew people to deliver them out of Egypt, He also will come after those who understand these things. This is an amazing and wonderful thing.

MY GOD will come after my life due to His goodness and His steadfast love and thus I will receive salvation and I will be able to dwell in the messianic age for 1000 years.

As in every Psalm, Psalm 23 has two forms of reading and understanding, the first is perceived through what is literally read, the second is as presented above. In Psalm 23, by the first way of understanding it, there are 23 explicit blessings and in the second way there are 23 hidden blessings, totaling 46 blessings only in Psalm 23.

The number 46, when both characters are added together, has the value of 10. That same number, the number 10, is one of the values for the word HAHAYYM (החיים) meaning THE LIFE.

By this we learn that Psalm 23 is a Psalm for life, the specific blessing that it passes on is precisely concerning the life on this earth, and a long one. The spiritual understanding also brings life into the world to come, for it teaches how it should be the behavior of he who seeks the God of Israel.

When James quotes prayer for the sick and praise for joy, I believe that this Psalm fits perfectly, for just as it represents life in this world, which is an analogy to healing, it also represents joy, joy for the Mashiach's redemption.

All the Psalms have endless hidden messages behind their words. According to the Cabbalists sages, this is the most mystical book of all human history and seeking wisdom to understand all the secrets it reveals, is something that transforms the life of every man. This was just an example of what the wisdom of God can reveal to each one who seeks it.

ELDERS OF THE CHURCH

Is any sick among you? let him call for the elders of the church; and let them pray over him, anointing him with oil in the name of the Lord:

James 5:14

In my view, we have a clear manipulation of the church here. Many believe and claim that the letter of James was written in Greek, but I have my doubts about that, for I do not see why a Jew within the land of Israel, whos addressed other Jews and not Gentiles, would write a letter in a foreign language.

I do not claim that it was written in Hebrew, I do only say that I have my doubts about the Greek, for just as the church claims that this letter was written in Greek, it also states that the Gospels were also; until couple years ago the church itself published the original gospels and they were not in Greek but in Hebrew.

At any rate, the terms church, elder, and the like are terms and ideas wholly outside the reality of James, and for this reason there is no way he might have used them in his book. We must be aware so we don't fall into what the church wants us to believe, for it may set one apart from God's will.

XXXIII - FORGIVEN SINS

And the prayer of faith shall save the sick, and the Lord shall raise him up; and if he have committed sins, they shall be forgiven him.
James 5:15

Sins and forgiveness have somewhat different definitions when Christian teachings are compared with Jewish teachings. In Christianity, sin is basically defined as the breaking of some "commandment" from the Pauline letters, attitudes contrary to Christian puritanism or immoral behavior. Forgiveness is something automatically conceived through a prayer made by the one who acknowledges the error and feels remorse for his actions.

In Judaism, sin is defined by the breaking of a negative commandment of the Torah, that is, when a person does something that God commands NOT to do. Forgiveness within the Jewish mentality is somewhat diverse, it is a process that begins with the feeling of repentance and culminates in something known as TSHUVAH (תשובה), which in a direct translation means "answer". Just as the act of "giving an answer" is an external action and not an internal feeling, so also should repentance and forgiveness be. This kind of repentance, Tshuvah, is something that every Christian should heed, for throughout the gospel of Matthew, in its original Hebrew version, Yeshua uses this term several times in his teachings on this subject.

For a more in-depth approach, I will raise a somewhat

unknown side about the first sin and its origin. Adam's story is widely known even to those who know little about the bible, but at the same time that many know it, very few really understand it. Unfortunately, the human being has the terrible habit of holding fast to what he sees with his eyes and believing in what is most commonly taught by the communities.

Throughout the account of the creation and the story of the first man, there are several emblematic terms that are used by the Torah in a cyclical way. In many cases, these terms are synonyms when used in a secular context, but by divine wisdom, the Torah use them to reveal the spiritual degree of those who are "connected" to these terms.

In Adam's case, the first living soul, there are three words that show how God idealized man and what would be the relationship of His greatest creation with the reality that the Creator had just formed. These words are BRIAH (בריאה), YETZIRA (יצירה) and ASSIAH (עשיה), which mean "creation", "formation", and "making or deed". Throughout the account of creation, the Torah circulates between these terms depending on the theme addressed and the message to be passed on.

*And **created** Elohim the man in His own image...*
Genesis 1:27

*And Elohim **formed** the man from the dust of the earth...*
Genesis 2:7a

***Let us make** man in our image and likeness...*
Genesis 1:26a

BRIAH (בריאה)

In the three passages that refer to the creation of man, each uses one of the terms quoted above. The first to appear in the Torah and the most common one, is the term BRIAH (בריאה), from the verb LIBROH (לברוא) – *to create*. This verb appears in the first and in the second chapter of Genesis during its account of the creation of all things, God created the heavens and the earth, God created the sea monsters, God created man, and finally God created "what He had made to do" (Gen 2:3).

Every time BRIAH (בריאה) appears, it represents something that was created by God in its fullness, that is, the creation linked to the term BRIAH (בריאה) was made, formed and finalized in the exactly way God has idealized it, according to all His perfection and will. BRIAH (בריאה) is the "level" that everyone, as God-created human beings, must attain.

YETZIRAH (יצירה)

When the Torah reports that God "formed" man, it does not refer to the physical man, but to man's soul. The soul that was given to man is what makes each living being a unique being, it is in it that wills, dreams, personality, goodness, evilness, etc. are found, as reported in the second chapter of Genesis:

וַיִּיצֶר יְהוָ֨ה אֱלֹהִ֜ים אֶת־הָֽאָדָ֗ם עָפָר֙ מִן־הָ֣אֲדָמָ֔ה וַיִּפַּ֥ח
בְּאַפָּ֖יו נִשְׁמַ֣ת חַיִּ֑ים וַֽיְהִ֥י הָֽאָדָ֖ם לְנֶ֥פֶשׁ חַיָּֽה

And Adonai Elohim ***formed*** *the man from the dust of the earth, and breathed into his nostrils the breath of life; and man became a living soul.*

Genesis 2:7

This is a passage that has generated a lot of rabbinic discussions because it has an apparent grammatical error, a writing error, but since nothing that is in the hands of God is by chance, what seems to be a mistake, is actually a message, it is something we must pay attention to.

The term "formed" in Hebrew is Yitzar (יצר) and is used when God formed the animals and the humanity on the sixth day, but in Adam's creation when the same term appears, its writing comes in a different and unique way in all Hebrew literature; In this case, we have the same word Yitzar (ייצר), but with an abnormal repetition of the initial letter YUD (י); This hidden fact reveals that Adam already knew very well what was good and what was bad.

This is because there is another word that is written in the exactly same way as the word Yitzar (יצר), which is the word Yetzer (יצר). This already changes everything, for Yetzer is the name of man's intrinsic inclination. Within each human being there are the Yetzer HaTov (good inclination) and the Yetzer HaRah (evil inclination), and everything one does and decides in life is influenced by one of these inclinations.

Rav Nahman bar Rav Hisda interprets: what does it mean what it is written: "then Adonai Elohim formed (vayyitzer) the man" with two Yud? These two Yud allude to the fact that the Holy One, blessed be He, has created two inclinations, one good and one bad.
Talmud of Babylon, Tractate Brakhot 61a

What we see here is God putting good and evil into His creation and through it, He might judge His creation. It is the man's soul that God seeks and it is to it that He reveals Himself, therefore the necessity of the negative side, because without it man would not understand the positive side of God. How to define goodness if there were no evilness?

The human being's ability to overcome his Yetzer HaRah, his evil inclination, is what will bring him to BRIAH (בריאה), a complete creation.

ASSIAH (עשיה)

This is a topic that creates enormous unbiblical and pagan conceptions. When God says "Let us make man", many depart from the assumption that the motive of this affirmation to be in the plural form, "let US", is because it is a dialogue between God and jesus and with that, both would be the creators of man. But such a statement is nothing more than human theology and such an idea can never be biblically proven, for Yeshua never said that he created anything. This theory is based only on the verbal conjugation that appears in this verse, where we have the verb LA'ASOT (לעשות) - *to make* - conjugated in the first person plural in the future, NA'ASEH (נעשה) – *Let us make.*

However, NA'ASEH (נעשה), exactly as it appears in this verse, is also the conjugated form of the first person singular in the present tense of the verb LEHI'ASOT (להיעשות) which means "to have been making". With that, we can understand this verse as follows:

I've been making man...

In the case of "our image" - B'TZALMENU (בצלמנו) - and "our likeness" - K'DMUTEINU (כדמותנו) - the last letter of each of these words is the letter VAV (ו). This letter may either have the "U" or "O" sound. If we read the above terms using the VAV as the letter "U", then we would have what is commonly translated, "our image and our likeness", but the great Rabbi Ibn Ezra takes into account the reading of these two terms with the VAV producing the "O" sound instead of the "U" sound.

If we read these two terms in this way, with VAV as the letter "O", their translations would be "in his form and in his likeness", the first person in plural becomes the third person in singular. Thus, we can re-read this God's statement once again:

I've been making man in his own image and in his own likeness.

According to Rabbi Ibn Ezra, what is happening here is that God had already conceived an "image" and a "likeness" that would be given to man. When God creates him, it is as if he materializes a concept he already had in mind.

There is something between the lines in this passage, and this "something" tells us why the verb "to make" was used. Mystically, the ASSIAH (עשיה) represents a work in progress, not finished, a work that had a beginning but did not reach its final form and this reveals a great truth about the human being, it reveals that the man "is still being made" by God. Man's completeness, that is, when man becomes BRIAH

(בריאה) it is actually the moment when he becomes the "image" and "likeness" which God has devised for him.

But there is still the question, what would this idealization and concept that Adonai have in relation to man that was reported as "image" and "likeness"? Well, an attentive reader certainly realizes that God's greatest will for man is that His creation follows His will so that he may be only His.

B'TZALMENU (בצלמנו) – our image
= **65** *Mispar Siduri
= **29** *Mispar Katan
= **2** *reduced

MITZVOT (מצוות) – Torah's commandments
= **65** *Mispar Siduri
= **29** *Mispar Katan
= **2** *reduced

K'DMUTEINU (כדמותנו) – our likeness
= **526**
= **4**

TEHYE LEKHA LEYHWH (תהיה לך ליהוה)
– you belong to Adonai
= **526**
= **4**

I think there is no doubt now. The man is still being "made", he stills in the production line, a working in progress. That is the reason for our existence, so that we can finish the work of Adonai, by finishing the ASSIAH (עשיה) in order to become BRIAH (בריאה). This is the main motive that God gave His Torah, so that through obedience to His will, man may become His alone and thus His greatest creation will become complete. Again a rereading of the same verse:

I've been making man that by the commandments he may be Mine.

A great sage, in his analysis of this verse, states the following:

The purpose of man's creation is for the benefit of the Torah, he must observe the negative and positive commandments that are in it. He must avoid transgressing the negative commandments. His mission on earth can be summed up when God uses the verb NA'ASSEH (we will do, I have been doing), because this verb alludes to when His people received the Torah and said: NA'ASSEH VeNISHMAH (we will do and we will listen).

Shenei Luchot HaBrit, Torah Ohr, Bereshit

THE SIN

And God blessed the seventh day and declared it holy, because on it God ceased from all the work that he created had to make".

Genesis 2:3

There are still two things to take into account, the first is why God placed Adam so close to the fruit that he should not eat. With a little more critical analysis, this may seem strange, because since God is omniscient, how would He not know the result?

The reason for this is because His creation was not ready and to continue His plans, Adam would have to disobey and sin, so that through sin, God could give man the mission of co-creator, that is, when Adam ate of the fruit, the ASSIAH (עשיה) was placed in the hands of man, this is why it was stated in the bible that man became "like one of us", so that in the same way God made man, man should also "make" himself, he should "finish" the divine creation by becoming a BRIAH (בריאה).

The second thing appears when the Torah states that "God finished what He had made to do created had to make" (Gen. 2:3). This affirmation occurs in the first Shabbat reported by the Torah. If we look at this strange phrase based on what we have seen above, we can read it as follow:

God finished creating (BRIAH) what He was making (ASSIAH).

The sages say that this seventh day reported in the Genesis creation's account is not a simple Shabbat, but rather the representation of the messianic age, i.e. the eternal life. As man's mission is to go from the state of ASSIAH (עשיה) to the state of BRIAH (בריאה) through the commandments, we understand that when man lives a sinless, obedient life and seeks to belong to Adonai, he will complete his own creation, he will become BRIAH (בריאה), thus being able to enter the messianic age and to have eternal life. This age, which is represented by the Shabbat, is when the Torah reports that what God was doing - ASSIAH (עשיה) - became "created" - BRIAH (בריאה).

The reality that we live today is still the sixth day of creation, the account that God rested on the Shabbat (Gen. 2:3) is not yet a consummate fact, but rather a future revelation of the messianic age and eternal life, only those that may complete their own creation going from ASSIAH (עשיה) to BRIAH (בריאה), just as God made all his ASSIAH (עשיה) into BRIAH (בריאה) on Shabbat, will be worthy on "resting" on God's Shabbat.

Rabbi Shmeon asks: what is the meaning of "making" if it is said that everything is complete? It is written that all that Elohim created in the six days of Bereshit still need to be completed and arranged, so it is written "created to make", for it is a creation to be finished.

Zohar HaKadosh, Parashat Bereshit 120

We now have enough information to understand why sin is so displeasing to the Creator. When man disobeys and falls into sin, he breaks this cycle established by God, he ceases to be the Creator's partner and interrupts Adonai's creation plans. Sin makes impossible for man to become a truly created creature, but rather a deformed being, a half made "thing".

James reports that God will raise up man and will forgive his sins, this term "to raise up" in Hebrew is ALIAH (עליה). This expression is much used by the Tanakh in reference to the person who "rises up" to go to Jerusalem, which is a symbolic language about the one who decides to make Tshuvah and to return to be God's partner in creation. Therefore, what James says is that he who repents must do Tshuvah by returning to the ways of the Torah, this is what to be raised up by God, it is when one is brought back to be His partner.

> *After Adam has sinned, the rehabilitation of the human being could only begin after the delivery of the Torah.*
>
> Shenei Luchot HaBrit, Torah Ohr, Bereshit

> *What shall we say then? Is the law sin? God forbid. No, I had not known sin, but by the law: for I had not known lust, except the law had said, You shall not covet.*
>
> Romans 7:7

By this we learn that the Torah is what teaches about sin, sin is nothing more than the disobedience of the Laws of God and this is what takes man away from the purpose of his creation, which is "to finish" the work begun by God, that is, when man ceases to be a "made" being in order to become a "created" being.

When God raises up man, it is when God makes him His partner again in creation, this occurs when there is true Tshuvah and a return to the absolute will of God. The result of all this is to "rest" on the Shabbat, to be worthy of the Messianic age and the eternal life, which is opened only to “created” beings and not to “made” beings.

This is the true result of sin and the reason it displeases the Creator so much.

XXXIV- ELIJAH, THE TZADIK

Confess your faults one to another, and pray one for another, that you may be healed. The effectual fervent prayer of a righteous man avails much.
Elias was a man subject to like passions as we are, and he prayed earnestly that it might not rain: and it rained not on the earth by the space of three years and six months.
And he prayed again, and the heaven gave rain, and the earth brought forth her fruit.

James 5:16-18

Elijah is the most important prophet within Judaism. He was the prophet who endure the most to prove the existence of the One God who rules over the whole world, as seen in the incident where he challenges the prophets of Baal on Mount Carmel. In this case, all of them offered sacrifices to their gods, but only upon the sacrifice of Elijah came a fire from the heavens, consuming it totally.

The figure of the prophet Elijah is found throughout several Jewish celebrations, as in the ceremony of circumcision and Pessach. But the most important Elijah's mission is his coming before Mashiach, announcing the beginning of the messianic age. For this reason, I believe to be vital two analyzes about Elijah, the first concerning James' words, which deal with the power of prayer of a Tzadik person and the second concerning the relationship between Elijah and Mashiach.

ELIJAH AND THE RAIN

Elijah the Tishbite, an inhabitant of Gilead, said to Ahab, "As the LORD lives, the God of Israel whom I serve, there will be no dew or rain except at my bidding".

I Kings 17:1

Elijah is the prophet who performed the deepest miracles. The Bible tells us that, like Enoch before him, Elijah did not experience death, at the end of his ministry God came to pick him up with a chariot of fire and took him to heaven.

For this reason, I believe that the two men who will come before the coming of Mashiach, as reported in the book of Revelation, will be Enoch and Elijah, for if any other person were to come who died and did not go through the resurrection, it would be an act of necromancy, something forbidden by God's Law.

And I will give power to my two witnesses, and they shall prophesy a thousand two hundred and three score days, clothed in sackcloth.

Revelation 11:3

James uses Elijah as an example to show the power of prayer. The author of James' book attempts to show this power through a known act of Elijah when he goes before Ahab, the king of the Northern Kingdom, and prophesies before him that, due to his acts of idolatry to the pagan god Baal, it wouldn't rain in his lands until he, Elijah, says otherwise.

However, unlike what is alleged by James, Elijah did not make a prayer to accomplish such a feat, he rather used the power of the word, that is, he declared that it would not rain again and it was so. Prayer is nothing more than words of honor and praise directed to Adonai, so we see that this "power" was actually concentrated in the mouth of the prophet and not in the simple act of prayer.

We must take into account a mention that James does, which reveals to us how this power was given to Elijah, he says: " *The effectual fervent prayer of a righteous man (tzadik) avails much*". I believe to be quite clear his statement, James is not talking about any prayer, but a prayer from someone who is a tzadik. The condition to be a tzadik, a term poorly translated as "righteous", is to be someone who observes the Torah with the heart and seeks to do good in all one's deeds. To become a tzadik is a very difficult matter to be achieved by human forces.

The verse from 1 Kings 17:1, where we find this feat of Elijah, has several mysteries "between the lines". By summing all the letters found in this entire verse, we shall have a numerical value of 4978. This value reveals some things, for there is in the Torah another verse that has the same value of 4978 and it is precisely in it that we will find the reasons that elevated Elijah to the status he had.

The Torah's verse that also has the numerical value of 4978 is as follows:

I will look with favor upon you, and make you fertile and multiply you; and I will maintain My covenant (BRITI) with you.

Leviticus 26:9

This is the verse that has the same numerical value as that found in 1 Kings 17:1. In it, we see two very important things, Adonai's look with favor and the covenant that will be maintained. When the bible speaks of "my covenant" - BRITI (בריתי) – as in this case, it ALWAYS refers to the Torah.

Now then, if you faithfully obey my covenant (BRITI) and keep My comandments, you shall be My treasured possession among all the peoples. Indeed, all the earth is Mine.

Exodus 19:5

Connecting James' words, the verse from the book of I Kings he mentions and the secret connected verse with this mentioned one, we have the revelation of what James says, the power of Elijah came precisely from his obedience to God's covenant, that is, the Torah and the commandments, things that made him a Tzadik and a man with favor before the eyes of Adonai. Many people, due to a poor knowledge of the Word of God, interpret this verse of James as he is talking about someone who believes in jesus and by that fact, that person has all of his prayers answered, or if he prays while believing too muchin something, he will be heeded.

Certainly, faith in prayer is essential, but the true secret for a prayer to be answered, as attested by James and the Torah, is the prayer of one who lives a life of devotion to the will and covenant of God. Unfortunately few have a faith unchained from dogmas and doctrines to see and understand this.

In the future the Tzadikim will be like Elijah and Elisha, who raised the dead.

Talmud of Babylon, Tractate Pesachim 68a

Now listen to this wonderful wisdom. Just as God is the Most High God and rules over man and all the worlds above and below, so can the man if he does the will of the Creator (Torah). As in the case of Elijah, of blessed memory, who declared that it would not rain again, that brought fire from the heavens, that killed the prophets of Baal and that raised the dead.

Orchot Tzadikim 28:28

ELIJAH AND MASHIACH

In every Pessach celebration, during the reading of the *Haggadah*, it is customary to leave a glass of wine on the table for Elijah. This represents the faith and a constant desire for him to come and celebrate it with us, for we would know that Mashiach Ben David is at the door.

The relation they both have is one of the 13 principles of the Jewish faith, for to believe in Mashiach is to believe also in Elijah and his coming. This relationship is mentioned by the Tanakh, by the prophets, by Yeshua and is something that has several mystical allegories behind it. The best-known verse about both, Elijah and Mashiach, is found in the book of the prophet Malachi, which reveals the coming of Elijah in a clear and direct way:

> *Lo, I will send the prophet Elijah to you before the coming of the awesome, fearful day of the LORD.*
>
> Malachi 3:23

The relation this two has is very little studied, especially by those who believes that Yeshua is Mashiach, because it is already settled in the minds of many that Yohanan, the immerser, is Elijah and no more studies are necessary. The problem is that this mindset leaves a great emptiness concerning the mysteries that this relation teaches us. Mashiach and Elijah walk together hand in hand and it is for this fact that Yeshua had to approach this idea, otherwise his proclamation of Mashiach would be inconsistent with the Tanakh.

> *It is written upon him that is written for my good: Behold! I am commanding my angel to open the way before me.*
>
> Matthew 11:10

The Torah, in a very hidden way, assembles this whole scenario of Mashiach, Elijah, the land of Israel, salvation and so on. It is fascinating how one of these approaches fits with Yeshua and the Mashiach he declared to be. Let's see an example.

After Moses' death and before the invasion of Canaan by the People of Israel, Joshua, the current leader, sends two spies to spy the first city to be invaded, Jericho. The first one was called Caleb, from the tribe of Judah, and the second one was Pinchas, member of the priestly tribe of Levi. In this infiltration, some people listened to these two men, heard what was about to happen and for having believed in them, they were saved.

Then Joshua appears in scene, a leader from the tribe

of Ephraim, who invades and fights the inhabitants of those lands, settles down his people and implements the Laws of God throughout the land of Israel.

Now, in order to compare this with Yeshua it is vital to understand who were those two spies, Caleb and Pinchas, and the angel that was behind them. A great Kabbalist sage shares this understanding with us through Gematria, he shows us a startling revelation.

When you combine the name of Eliyahu Hanavi (Elijah, the prophet) with the names of Adonai (72 names), we will have 45 plus 72. When we add an angel, which has a value of 91, the total value will be 208, which is the same value as the name of Pinchas.
Shenei Luchot Habrit, Torah Ohr

Mystically, this statement declares that the angel who was on Pinchas was the same one who was on the prophet Elijah, for the life and mission of this spy can be seen within the missions of Elijah, which in this case, is to announce something that is about to happen and to prepare the people who listen to him. Rahab was one example, which was alerted by Pinchas about the imminent invasion and the coming of the people led by Joshua.

Joshua, by leading the people, becomes the most important man in the tribe of Ephraim, the firstborn of Joseph, the son of Yaakov. His genealogy is extremely important, because it is through it that we can fit Yeshua in this story, both his work and his mission. It is upon this idea that the author of the book of Matthew uses some prophecies to prove what he writes. Let's take a look at this before gathering all information to a final conclusion.

In order to fulfill what was spoken by Isaiah,
Behold my servant whom I have selected, my chosen one
with whom my soul is pleased, I will put my spirit upon
him, and he will declare justice to the nations.
He will not fear nor will he run nor shall one hear him in the street.

A crushed reed he will not break and a dim wick he will
not quench until he establishes justice forever
And in his name, the gentile hope.

Matthew 12:17-21

Matthew uses prophecies from the Tanakh to prove Yeshua's messianism. The one we have above appears in Isaiah chapter 42 and this is a prophecy that generates a lot of discord between Christians and Jews, for there are points about these verses that Yeshua apparently did not fulfill. But Matthew's intention with these words of Isaiah, in this case, was not to prove the works of Yeshua, but rather to prove who he really was and his mission at that particular period of history.

In order to understand Matthew's intention, we must analyze this verse in Hebrew, only thus can we see what Matthew is talking about:

הן עבדי אתמך בו בחירי רצתה נפשי נתתי
רוחי עליו משפט לגוים יוציא

This is My servant, *whom I uphold, My chosen one,*
in whom I delight. I have put My spirit upon him,
He shall teach the true way to the nations.

Isaiah 42:1

If we take the first words that appear in this verse and look for its numerical value, we shall have:

הן עבדי אתמך

ה 5 + ן 50 + ע 70 + ב 2 + ד 4 + י 10 + א 1 + ת 400 + מ 40 + ך 20

602 = 6 + 0 + 2 = **8**

The number 8 is a number that represents one of the Maschiach's facets, one part of his mission in this world:

Mashiach Ben Yosef (משיח בן יוסף)

מ40 + ש300 + י10 + ח8 + ב2 + ן50 + י10 + ו6 + ס60 + ף80

= **8**

What we see here is the author of Matthew using a prophecy not in order to prove the deeds of Yeshua but rather to reveal the person and which mission of Mashiach, Yeshua was accomplishing. This chapter of the book of Isaiah makes several allusions about Mashiach, in some verses as Mashiach Ben Yosef, in some others as Mashiach Ben David and since they are all interconnected, it serves as proof that they are both the same person.

A Midrash on this verse reveals the same understanding and shows the association that this verse has concerning the work referred to Mashiach Ben Yosef:

We should not be ashamed of the generation of Mashiach. The Holy One, Blessed Be He, said to them, "This is My servant, My chosen, the one who pleases my soul, and so on" (Isaiah 42:1). At that moment, the Holy One, Blessed Be He, will tell you, "Ephraim, Mashiach, My Tzadik, I conceived you before the six days of creation. Now, my sorrow is for what you will go through...

Midrash Psikta Rabbati 36:1

The midrash makes a direct connection between Ephraim and Mashiach, for Ephraim was the firstborn of Joseph. In several other midrashim, we see that their authors refer to Mashiach Ben Yosef through the name "Ephraim".

Ephraim became a second term in reference to this facet of Mashiach, so we can connect the tribe of Ephraim with this facet of Mashiach that Yeshua claimed to be, Mashiach Ben Yosef.

It is now possible to understand the spiritual representation that the sending of the spies had. Pinchas is sent to Canaan before Joshua entered, he warns a few who listened to him about what would happen and this brought salvation to these people, as in the case of Rahab. Also Yohanan, the immerser, came before Yeshua entered into scene. Yohanan, like

Pinchas, warned of an imminent judgment and anyone who would listen to him, would have a chance to be saved.

Pinchas possessed the angel of Elijah over him, and therefore this angel was also over Yohanan, the immerser, making him worthy to announce the coming of Mashiach and that is why Yeshua said that "an **angel** would come before him" rather than saying Elijah himself (Mt 11:10). Just as Pinchas announced Joshua Bin Nun Ben Ephraim Ben Yosef, Yohanan announced Mashiach Ben Yosef.

Also, both Joshua and Yeshua had the same name, YEHOSHUA, both were called Joshua in English and Joshua, for being from the tribe of Ephraim, reveals to us that this angel that was over Pinchas and over Yohanan, has the specific mission of announcing Mashiach Ben Yosef and not Ben David.

Finally we should observe Caleb, Pinchas' companion. Their joint missions represent the joint missions of this angel that was over Pinchas and Mashiach. Not coincidentally, Pinchas was from Levi, as were Yohanan and Caleb from Judah, as well as Yeshua.

This account in the Torah is an allegory of what would be the coming of Mashiach Ben Yosef, how this coming would be announced by someone who was represented by Pinchas and the angel that was above him. Those two spies mission was a prelude that God's Law would be "scattered" throughout the land of Israel after the conquest by Joshua, just as Yeshua's death "scattered" the word of God throughout the world.

Concerning Mashiach Ben David, it will be Elijah himself who will announce him and not his angel, as prophesied. If Yeshua came as Ben Yosef, when he returns as Ben David, Elijah himself will come from the heavens alongside with Enoch.

Now it is clear the verse 10 from the 11th chapter of Matthew, where Yeshua calls "the one who will open the way for me" (see above) as "angel", for Yohanan, the immerser, was not Elijah, but someone who had the same angel that was with Elijah and Pinchas, as mentioned in the passage quoted above from *Shenei Luchot Habrit, Torah Ohr*.

I believe that all of this had a huge weight on James belief and it is for this reason he uses Elijah as an example.

*** More information on Maschiach Ben Yosef and Yeshua are found in the book TORAT YEHOSHUA ACCORDING TO THE HEBREW BOOK OF MATHEWS, of the same author.*

XXXV - FAITH VS. WORKS

But when I saw that they walked not uprightly according to
the truth of the gospel, I said to Peter before them all, If you,
being a Jew, live after the manner of Gentiles, and not as do the
Jews, why compel you the Gentiles to live as do the Jews?
We who are Jews by nature, and not sinners of the Gentiles,
Knowing that a man is not justified by the works of the
law, but by the faith of Yeshua HaMashiach, even we have
believed in Yeshua HaMashiach, that we might be justified
by the faith of Mashiach, and not by the works of the law:
for by the works of the law shall no flesh be justified.
But if, while we seek to be justified by Mashiach,
we ourselves also are found sinners, is therefore
Mashiach the minister of sin? God forbid.
For if I build again the things which I destroyed,
I make myself a transgressor.

Galatians 2:14-18

Even so faith, if it has not works, is dead, being alone.
Yes, a man may say, You have faith, and I have works: show me
your faith without your works, and I will show you my faith by
my works.
For as the body without the spirit is dead, so
faith without works is dead also.

James 2:17-18 + 26

One of the greatest legacies that the fathers of the church left for humanity was the abolition of the real will of the Creator, the Torah. The need for these men to form a new religion quite distinct from the religion that Yeshua had, led them to abdicate what most represented the people of Israel.

The corrupt theology that these men have created, in one way or another, is rooted in all strands of Christianity. Whatever the strand is, however "pure" its theology may be, the influence of these men is and will always be present. These so-called fathers of the church are nothing more than men from pagan origins, none of them were a Jew, they were people who came from societies strongly influenced by the Greco-Roman pantheon and with strong tendencies to adapt the new religion with the old religion, being Christianity no more than the Roman religion adapted, especially Catholicism, a faith clearly idolatrous.

Understanding the teachings of these men is as fruitful as understanding the Torah, just as to know evilness is necessary to recognize goodness. For this reason, I will raise some teachings from the most prominent fathers of Christianity:

The Jews and their cursed customs of killing Christian children in their annual rituals. We must understand that the prophecies are intended for Christians and not for Jews.

Eusebius of Caesarea

Any Christian who uses a Jewish symbol or a Jewish name or celebrates any Jewish celebration is liable to death, for he becomes an accomplice to the murderers of christ.

Marcion of Sinope

The God of the Old Testament died along with His Law to give life to the god of the New Testament and the Law of christ.

Marcion of Sinope

The synagogues are places of prostitution, full of thieves and wild beasts. The Jews are to blame for the death of christ. There is no forgiveness of these people, God has always hated them, and every Christian who considers himself a Christian must also hate them, for they are murderers of christ and worshipers of satan.

John Crisostomo

If one, through weakness of mind, resolve to observe the ordinances in the manner in which they were delivered to Moses, for they expect some virtue, we must understand that this was due to the hardness of their hearts. No Christian should gather with people who observe the Shabbat or any other ceremony. I am of the opinion that we should not join them nor associate with them in no way.

Justyn Martyr

Every Jew conspires to kill the Christians.

Origins of Alexandria

The Jewish people are cursed by God for the perversity of their law.

Hilary de Potiers

To the Jews we give the choice of exile, death or conversion.

Cyril of Alexandria

The Jews were never able to understand the scriptures, for this is the church's duty and they must be persecuted severely until they are forced to convert to the true faith.

Jeronimvs of Strido Dalmatiae

The Jews and the nation of Israel are only witnesses to the truth of Christianity, they served only to leave the legacy of Christianity. Now they should be in constant humiliation as the church triumphs over the synagogue. There is no salvation for the Jews, they are already lost anyway. Judaism is a corruption and the Jews must be enslaved.

Augustine of Hippo

Christians should burn synagogues and the Jews.

They must take away their Torah and their Talmud,
for they contain lies and blasphemy.
Martin Luther

Every Christian branch, without exception, has something from the teachings of these corrupt and putrid minds. For who never heard that Israel was replaced by the church, or even that the Shabbat is only for the Jews, or that the Christian has the christ's freedom to eat bacon? All of this line of thought comes from paganism and goes straight into the mind of the Christian.

The new testament without the Tanakh is like a tree without its root, which falls with the faintest breeze. This is clearly seen in many of the Christian teachings about the bible, all superficial, almost all Puritan and unrelated to the truth. Because of this great gap, the founders of Christianity misused Paul's teachings to fill in the lack left by the abolition of God's will with relative concepts such as grace and faith alone.

This was already something that James was noticing when he received information about the synagogues in the diaspora, and I believe that was the reason why he brought up the faith and works theme.

James's letter is a letter full of mentions of commandments given by the Torah, themes about the tongue, the poor, charity and all others he has addressed, are, without exception at all, in the Law that the fathers of the church so much hated. This letter is nothing more than moral counsels based on the commandments of God's Law concerning man's relationship with his neighbor. James did not invent anything of what he taught, he only highlights what all his listeners knew very well, but apparently did not practice.

Contrary to what many believe, this term "work" that James uses is not "work in the church" as an elder, deacon, or evangelist, none of this, the Hebrew word "work" is MA'ASSEH, a term widely used in Talmudic language when the rabbis approach the commandments of the Torah and indeed, it was this language that James used, for he was a rabbi.

So when James states that faith does not save, he is saying that believing in God and in Yeshua does not guarantee salvation to anyone, but the Torah, along with faith in the Absolute Oneness of the Creator, and in the case of the Gentile, faith that this opportunity was given to him through Yeshua's death, then yes, one obtains salvation. The jargon "jesus saves" is unbiblical.

James also states that faith without works is dead, which is a great truth, for faith, if not represented by the Torah, is relative. As Solomon teaches, the fools also have faith.

Finally he claims that he will show his faith by the works and this is a fantastic claim. The faith he possessed was a living thing, for it was seen through his behavior, it was something palpable, for he followed the Torah and it was something visible in his walk and behavior, that is THE living faith.

I approach this theme deeper in another book, *The Torah to the Galatians*, where I discuss the differences between Paul's "grace" and James' "works".

Shammai used to say: make your [study of the]
Torah a fixed practice; speak little, but do much; and
receive all men with a pleasant countenance.

Pirkei Avot 1:15

The understanding and belief in these things will come only to those from the lost and dispersed descendants of the tribe of Israel, for whom Yeshua died and whom Adonai will gather under His wings before the coming of Mashiach Ben David.

That it might be in our days, Amen.

Printed in Great Britain
by Amazon

40383784R00181